Goethe's Elective Affinities: With An Introduction

Johann Wolfgang Von Goethe

GOETHE'S

ELECTIVE AFFINITIES:

WITH AN INTRODUCTION

BY

VICTORIA C. WOODHULL.

BOSTON:

D. W. NILES, No. 8 BROMFIELD STREET.

1872.

Entered according to Act of Congress, in the year 1871, by
D. W. NILES,
in the Office of the Librarian of Congress, at Washington.

INTRODUCTION.

AT the request of Mr. D. W. Niles, publisher, Boston, I have re-read, having read with pleasure and profit in my early life, the "Elective Affinities" of Goethe, an English translation of which Mr. Niles proposes to publish for the use of the American public; and he does me the honor to think that my views of the value of the book may contribute somewhat to its success among us at this time.

It is very true that ideas of social freedom and of inevitable law governing the action of human affections are rapidly spreading in the world, at this day, and that I may have done something to aid their growth. Perhaps my name may *not*, therefore, be inappropriately associated with this reproduction of the work of the greatest Genius of Germany, the first who

3

promulgated the thought that there is a chemistry
of the mind, and that "Elective Affinities" are as
powerful and legitimate in the realm of human sentiment as in the realm of matter.

If this fundamental thought of the man who has
proved to be the seer or prophet of Science in so
many other things, is also a scientific truth, the fact
cannot be appreciated by the world too soon, nor its
immense sweep of consequences be too clearly fore-
seen and provided for. It will affect the whole
scope of morals and social order, whether we accept
it in our theories or not, and the less hurtfully and
the more beneficently, in proportion as we thoroughly study and understand the subject.

Themes of freedom on all subjects form the staple
public sentiment of the world in this age. A doctrine like that of Goethe's is, therefore, eminently
calculated to make progress even unconciously in
this century. Indeed, I think that if there is any
objection whatever, which will be felt to the really
chaste and simple tale of this great writer, as it shall
be read by the American public of to-day, it will be,
that it is too mild and unpronounced, rather than on

account of its radicalism. It may not be sufficiently spiced or high-seasoned either with adventure, or with audacity of speculation to suit the already stimulated palates of our modern and progressive community. Indeed, it strikes me almost ludicrous, that the translator has shrunk from appending his name to the work, if he has done so from any idea that its dangerous views might tend to impair his reputation.

The tale is, in a word, of the simple construction and genial and moderate character of the " Vicar of Wakefield " rather than in the exciting style of Dickens' Christmas Carols; but, everywhere, the interest is skilfully kept up, and the subtle insinuation of a great revolutionary doctrine pervades the whole, and to the thoughtful reader makes the chief point of interest. Doctrines, however, which are here merely insinuated and illustrated by allusions to science, are now so openly expounded and advocated that a portion of the community will regard the great German as too conservative, while yet, doubtless, to the great mass of readers, the radical element may startle, and in some instances offend.

But in any event Genius has its prerogatives, and

the genius of Goethe is incontestable and uncontes-
ted. The American public is entitled to know
what this great leader of modern thought, one of the
founders of Comparative Anatomy, has thought on
the more recondite subject of the Chemistry of
Mind. The question is not, in the first instance,
whether his views were right or wrong, true or false;
but simply, What were they? and in none of his
works is that question so effectively answered as in
" Elective Affinities." Undoubtedly, he shocked
the age he lived in, both by his writings and by his life,
even in Germany, where the puritanical element has
always had less sway than it has had among us; but
now, if the book runs any risk of a failure to command the public interest, it will be as I have said,
for the opposite reason, that it may be thought not
radical and outspoken enough. But even this circumstance adds a new ground of interest in the fact
that it presents vividly the opportunity to compare
two or three successive generations in respect to the
growth of opinion upon a most important subject,
and the comparison prepares the mind for the still

more radical change which the next few years will inevitably produce.

It is well to learn not to be shocked or astounded by any of the events which the impending progress of humanity presents, and especially at this epoch; for all of the signs of the times concur to indicate that we are entering upon the most revolutionary period in human society, not it is to be hoped of the old style and blind sort, but revolution in respect to opinions and general institutions.

VICTORIA C. WOODHULL.

15 *East* 38th *St., New York,*
    November, 1871.

ELECTIVE AFFINITIES.

PART I.

----◆----

CHAPTER I.

EDWARD — so we shall call a wealthy nobleman in the prime of life — had been spending several hours of a fine April morning in his nursery-garden budding the stems of some young trees with cuttings which had been recently sent to him. He had finished what he was about, and having laid his tools together in their box, was complacently surveying his work, when the gardener came up and complimented his master on his industry.

"Have you seen my wife anywhere?" inquired Edward, as he moved to go away.

"My lady is alone yonder in the new grounds," said the man; "the summer-house which she has been making on the rock over against the castle is finished to-day, and really it is beautiful. It cannot fail to please your grace. The view from it is perfect :— the village at your feet; a little to your right the church with its tower, which you can just see over; and directly opposite you, the castle and the garden."

"Quite true," replied Edward; "I can see the people at work a few steps from where I am standing."

"And then, to the right of the church again," continued the gardener, "is the opening of the valley; and you look along over a range of wood and meadow far into the distance. The steps up the rock, too, are excellently arranged. My gracious lady understands these things; it is a pleasure to work under her."

"Go to her," said Edward, "and desire her to be so good as to wait for me there. Tell her I wish to see this new creation of hers, and enjoy it with her."

The gardener went rapidly off, and Edward soon followed. Descending the terrace, and stopping as he passed to look into the hot-houses and the forcing-pits, he came presently to the stream, and thence, over a narrow bridge, to a place where the walk leading to the summer-house branched off in two directions. One path led across the churchyard, immediately up the face of the rock. The other, into which he struck, wound away to the left, with a more gradual ascent, through a pretty shrubbery. Where the two paths joined again, a seat had been made, where he stopped a few moments to rest; and then, following the now single road, he found himself, after scrambling along among steps and slopes of all sorts and kinds, conducted at last through a narrow more or less steep outlet to the summer-house.

Charlotte was standing at the door to receive her husband. She made him sit down where, without moving, he could command a view of the different landscapes through the door and window — these serving as frames, in which they were set like pictures. Spring was coming on; a rich, beautiful life would soon everywhere be bursting; and Edward spoke of it with delight.

"There is only one thing which I should observe," he added, "the summer-house itself is rather small."

"It is large enough for you and me, at any rate," answered Charlotte.

"Certainly," said Edward; "there is room for a third, too, easily."

"Of course; and for a fourth also," replied Charlotte. "For larger parties we can contrive other places."

"Now that we are here by ourselves, with no one to disturb us, and in such a pleasant mood," said Edward, "it is a good opportunity for me to tell you that I have for some time had something on my mind, about which I have wished to speak to you, but have never been able to muster up my courage."

"I have observed that there has been something of the sort," said Charlotte.

"And even now," Edward went on, "if it were not for a letter which the post brought me this morning, and which obliges me to come to some resolution to-day, I should very likely have still kept it to myself."

"What is it, then?" asked Charlotte, turning affectionately towards him.

"It concerns our friend the Captain," answered Edward; "you know the unfortunate position in which he, like many others, is placed. It is through no fault of his own; but you may imagine how painful it must be for a person with his knowledge and talents and accomplishments, to find himself without employment. I—I will not hesitate any longer with what I am wishing for him. I should like to have him here with us for a time."

"We must think about that," replied Charlotte; "it should be considered on more sides than one."

"I am quite ready to tell you what I have in view," returned Edward. "Through his last letters there is a prevailing tone of despondency; not that he is really in any want. He knows thoroughly well how to limit his expenses; and I have taken care for everything absolutely necessary. It is no distress to him to accept obligations from me; all our lives we have been in the habit of borrowing from and lending to each other; and we could not tell, if we would, how our debtor and creditor account stands. It is being without occupation which is really fretting him. . The many accomplishments which he has cultivated in himself, it is his only pleasure — indeed, it is his passion — to be daily and hourly exercising for the benefit of others. And now, to sit still, with his arms folded; or to go on studying, acquiring, and acquiring, when he can make no use of what he already possesses; — my dear creature, it is a painful situation; and alone as he is, he feels it doubly and trebly."

"But I thought," said Charlotte, "that he had had offers from many different quarters. I myself wrote to numbers of my own friends, male and female, for him; and, as I have reason to believe, not without effect."

"It is true," replied Edward; but these very offers — these various proposals — have only caused him fresh embarrassment. Not one of them is at all suitable to such a person as he is. He would have nothing to do ; he would have to sacrifice himself, his time, his purposes, his whole method of life; and to that he cannot bring himself. The more I think of it all, the more I feel about it, and the more anxious I am to see him here with us."

"It is very beautiful and amiable in you," answered Charlotte, "to enter with so much sympathy into your friend's position; only you must allow me to ask you to think of yourself and of me, as well."

"I have done that," replied Edward. "For ourselves, we can have nothing to expect from his presence with us, except pleasure and advantage. I will say nothing of the expense. In any case, if he came to us, it would be but small; and you know he will be of no inconvenience to us at all. He can have his own rooms in the right wing of the castle, and everything else can be arranged as simply as possible. What shall we not be thus doing for him! and how agreeable and how profitable may not his society prove to us! I have long been wishing for a plan of the property and the grounds. He will see to it, and get it made. You intend yourself to take the management of the estate, as soon as our present steward's term is expired; and that, you know, is a serious thing. His various information will be of immense benefit to us; I feel only too acutely how much I require a person of this kind. The country people have knowledge enough, but their way of imparting it is confused, and not always honest. The students from the towns and universities are sufficiently clever and orderly, but they are deficient in personal experience. From my friend, I can promise myself both knowledge and method, and hundreds of other circumstances I can easily conceive arising, affecting you as well as me, and from which I can foresee innumerable advantages. Thank you for so patiently listening to me. Now, do you say what you think, and say it out freely and fully; I will not interrupt you."

"Very well," replied Charlotte; "I will begin at once with a general observation. Men think most of the immediate — the present; and rightly, their calling being to do and to work. Women, on the other hand, more of how things hang together in life; and that rightly too, because their destiny — the destiny of their families — is bound up in this interdependence, and it is exactly this which it is their mission to promote. So now let us cast a glance at our present and our past life; and you will acknowledge that the invitation of the Captain does not fall in so entirely with our purposes, our plans, and our arrangements. I will go back to those happy days of our earliest intercourse. We loved each other, young as we then were, with all our hearts. We were parted: you from me — your father, from an insatiable desire of wealth, choosing to marry you to an elderly and rich lady; I from you, having to give my hand, without any especial motive, to an excellent man, whom I respected, if I did not love. We became again free — you first, your poor mother at the same time leaving you in possession of your large fortune; I later, just at the time when you returned from abroad. So we met once more. We spoke of the past; we could enjoy and love the recollection of it; we might have been contented in each other's society, to leave things as they were. You were urgent for our marriage. I at first hesitated. We were about the same age; but I as a woman had grown older than you as a man. At last I could not refuse you what you seemed to think the one thing you cared for. All the discomfort which you had ever experienced, at court, in the army, or in travelling, you were to recover from at my side; you would settle down and enjoy life; but only with me for your companion. I settled my daughter at a school, where she could be more completely educated than would be possible in the retirement of the country; and I placed my niece Ottilie there with her as well, who, perhaps, would have grown up better at home with me, under my own care. This was done with your consent, merely that we might have our own lives to ourselves — merely that we might enjoy undisturbed our so-long-wished-for, so-long-delayed happiness. We came here

and settled ourselves. I undertook the domestic part of
the ménage, you the out-of-doors, and the general control. My own principle has been to meet your wishes in
everything, to live only for you. At least, let us give
ourselves a fair trial how far in this way we can be enough
for one another."

"Since the interdependence of things, as you call it, is
your especial element," replied Edward, "one should
either never listen to any of your trains of reasoning, or
make up one's mind to allow you to be in the right; and,
indeed, you have been in the right up to the present day.
The foundation which we have hitherto been laying
for ourselves, is of the true, sound sort; only, are we to
build nothing upon it? is nothing to be developed out of
it? All the work we have done — I in the garden, you
in the park — is it all only for a pair of hermits?"

"Well, well," replied Charlotte, "very well. What we
have to look to is, that we introduce no alien element,
nothing which shall cross or obstruct us. Remember, our
plans, even those which only concern our amusements,
depend mainly on our being together. You were to read
to me, in consecutive order, the journal which you made
when you were abroad. You were to take the opportunity of arranging it, putting all the loose matter connected
with it in its place; and with me to work with you
and help you, out of these invaluable but chaotic leaves
and sheets to put together a complete thing, which should
give pleasure to ourselves and to others. I promised to
assist you in transcribing; and we thought it would be so
pleasant, so delightful, so charming, to travel over in recollection the world which we were unable to see together.
The beginning is already made. Then, in the evenings,
you have taken up your flute again, accompanying me

on the piano, while of visits backwards and forwards among the neighborhood, there is abundance. For my part, I have been promising myself out of all this the first really happy summer I have ever thought to spend in my life."

"Only I cannot see," replied Edward, rubbing his forehead, "how, through every bit of this which you have been so sweetly and so sensibly laying before me, the Captain's presence can be any interruption; I should rather have thought it would give it all fresh zest and life. He was my companion during a part of my travels. He made many observations from a different point of view from mine. We can put it all together, and so make a charmingly complete work of it."

"Well, then, I will acknowledge openly," answered Charlotte, with some impatience, "my feeling is against this plan. I have an instinct which tells me no good will come of it."

"You women are invincible in this way," replied Edward. "You are so sensible, that there is no answering you, then so affectionate, that one is glad to give way to you; full of feelings, which one cannot wound, and full of forebodings, which terrify one."

"I am not superstitious," said Charlotte; "and I care nothing for these dim sensations, merely as such; but in general they are the result of unconscious recollections of happy or unhappy consequences, which we have experienced as following on our own or others' actions. Nothing is of greater moment, in any state of things, than the intervention of a third person. I have seen friends, brothers and sisters, lovers, husbands and wives, whose relation to each other, through the accidental or intentional introduction of a third person, has been altogether changed — whose whole moral condition has been inverted by it."

" That may very well be," replied Edward, " with people who live on without looking where they are going; but not, surely, with persons whom experience has taught to understand themselves."

" That understanding ourselves, my dearest husband," insisted Charlotte, " is no such certain weapon. It is very often a most dangerous one for the person who bears it. And out of all this, at least so much seems to arise, that we should not be in too great a hurry. Let me have a few days to think; don't decide."

" As the matter stands," returned Edward, " wait as many days as we will, we shall still be in too great a hurry. The arguments for and against are all before us; all we want is the conclusion, and as things are, I think the best thing we can do is to draw lots."

" I know," said Charlotte, " that in doubtful cases it is your way to leave them to chance. To me, in such a serious matter, this seems almost a crime."

" Then what am I to write to the Captain?" cried Edward; " for write I must at once."

" Write him a kind, sensible, sympathizing letter," answered Charlotte.

" That is as good as none at all," replied Edward.

" And there are many cases," answered she, " in which we are obliged, and in which it is the real kindness, rather to write nothing than not to write."

CHAPTER II.

EDWARD was alone in his room. The repetition of the incidents of his life from Charlotte's lips; the repesentation of their mutual situation, their mutual purposes; had worked him, sensitive as he was, into a very pleasant state of mind. While close to her — while in her presence — he had felt so happy, that he had thought out a warm, kind, but quiet and indefinite epistle which he would send to the Captain. When, however, he had settled himself at his writing-table, and taken up his friend's letter to read it over once more, the sad condition of this excellent man rose again vividly before him. The feelings which had been all day distressing him again awoke, and it appeared impossible to him to leave one whom he called his friend in such painful embarrassment.

Edward was unaccustomed to deny himself anything. The only child, and consequently the spoilt child, of wealthy parents, who had persuaded him into a singular, but highly advantageous marriage with a lady far older than himself; and again by her petted and indulged in every possible way, she seeking to reward his kindness to her by the utmost liberality; after her early death his own master, travelling independently of every one, equal to all contingencies and all changes, with desires never excessive, but multiple and various — free-hearted, generous, brave, at times even noble — what was there in the world to cross or thwart him?

Hitherto, everything had gone as he desired! Charlotte had become his; he had won her at last, with an obstinate, a romantic fidelity; and now he felt himself, for

the first time contradicted, crossed in his wishes, when
those wishes were to invite to his home the friend of his
youth — just as he was longing, as it were, to throw open
his whole heart to him. He felt annoyed, impatient; he
took up his pen again and again, and as often threw it
down again, because he could not make up his mind
what to write. Against his wife's wishes he would not
go; against her expressed desire he could not. Ill at ease
as he was, it would have been impossible for him, even if
he had wished, to write a quiet, easy letter. The most
natural thing to do, was to put it off. In a few words,
he begged his friend to forgive him for having left his
letter unanswered; that day he was unable to write
circumstantially; but shortly, he hoped to be able to tell
him what he felt at greater length.

The next day, as they were walking to the same spot,
Charlotte took the opportunity of bringing back the conversation to the subject, perhaps because she knew that there
is no surer way of rooting out any plan or purpose, than by
often talking it over.

It was what Edward was wishing. He expressed himself in his own way, kindly and sweetly. For although,
sensitive as he was, he flamed up readily — although the
vehemence with which he desired anything made him
pressing, and his obstinacy made him impatient — his
words were so softened by his wish to spare the feelings
of those to whom he was speaking, that it was impossible
not to be charmed, even when one most disagreed, with
him.

This morning, he first contrived to bring Charlotte
into the happiest humor, and then so disarmed her with
the graceful turn which he gave to the conversation, that
she cried out at last:

"You are determined that what I refused to the husband you will make me grant to the lover. At least, my dearest," she continued, "I will acknowledge that your wishes, and the warmth and sweetness with which you express them, have not left me untouched, have not left me unmoved. You drive me to make a confession; — till now, I too have had a concealment from you; I am in exactly the same position with you, and I have hitherto been putting the same restraint on my inclination which I have been exhorting you to put on yours."

"Glad am I to hear that," said Edward. "In the married state, a difference of opinion now and then, I see, is no bad thing; we learn something of one another by it."

"You are to learn at present, then," said Charlotte, "that it is with me about Ottilie as it is with you about the Captain. The dear child is most uncomfortable at the school, and I am thoroughly uneasy about her. Luciana, my daughter, born as she is for the world, is there training hourly for the world; languages, history, everything that is taught there, she acquires with so much ease that, as it were, she learns them off at sight. She has quick natural gifts, and an excellent memory; one may almost say that she forgets everything, and in a moment calls it all back again. She distinguishes herself above every one at the school with the freedom of her carriage, the grace of her movement, and the elegance of her address, and with the inborn royalty of nature makes herself the queen of the little circle there. The superior of the establishment regards her as a little divinity, who, under her hands, is shaping into excellence, and who will do her honor, gain her reputation, and bring her a large increase of pupils; the first pages of this good lady's let-

ters, and her monthly notices of progress, are for ever
hymns about the excellence of such a child, which I have
to translate into my own prose; while her concluding
sentences about Ottilie are nothing but excuse after excuse — attempts at explaining how it can be that a girl in
other respects growing up so lovely seems coming to
nothing, and shows neither capacity nor accomplishment.
This, and the little she has to say beside, is no riddle to
me, because I can see in this dear child the same character as that of her mother, who was my own dearest friend;
who grew up with myself, and whose daughter, I am certain, if I had the care of her education, would form into
an exquisite creature.

" This, however, has not fallen in with our plan, and as
one ought not to be picking and pulling, or for ever introducing new elements among the conditions of our life, I
think it better to bear, and to conquer as I can, even the
unpleasant impression that my daughter who knows very
well that poor Ottilie is entirely dependent upon us, does
not refrain from flourishing her own successes in her face,
and so, to a certain extent, destroys the little good which
we have done for her. Who are well trained enough
never to wound others by a parade of their own advantages? and who stands so high as not at times to suffer
under such a slight? In trials like these, Ottilie's character
is growing in strength, but since I have clearly known the
painfulness of her situation, I have been thinking over all
possible ways to make some other arrangement. Every
hour I am expecting an answer to my own last letter, and
then I do not mean to hesitate any more. So, my dear
Edward, it is with me. We have both, you see, the same
sorrows to bear, touching both our hearts in the same
point. Let us bear them together, since we neither of us
can press our own against the other."

"We are strange creatures," said Edward, smiling.
"If we can only put out of sight anything which troubles
us, we fancy at once we have got rid of it. We can give
up much in the large and general; but to make sacrifices
in little things is a demand to which we are rarely equal.
So it was with my mother — as long I lived with her,
while a boy and a young man, she could not bear to let
me be a moment out of her sight. If I was out later
than usual in my ride, some misfortune must have happened to me. If I got wet through in a shower, a fever
was inevitable. I travelled; I was absent from her altogether; and, at once, I scarcely seemed to belong to her.
If we look at it closer," he continued, "we are both acting very foolishly, very culpably. Two very noble natures,
both of which have the closest claims on our affection, we
are leaving exposed to pain and distress, merely to avoid
exposing ourselves to a chance of danger. If this is not
to be called selfish, what is? You take Ottilie. Let me
have the Captain; and, for a short period, at least, let the
trial be made."

"We might venture it," said Charlotte, thoughtfully,
"if the danger were only to ourselves. But do you think
it prudent to bring Ottilie and the Captain into a situation
where they must necessarily be so closely intimate; the
Captain, a man no older than yourself, of an age (I am
not saying this to flatter you) when a man becomes first
capable of love and first deserving of it, and a girl of
Ottilie's attractiveness?"

"I cannot conceive how you can raise Ottilie so high,"
replied Edward. "I can only explain it to myself by supposing her to have inherited your affection for her mother.
Pretty she is, no doubt. I remember the Captain observing it to me, when we came back last year, and met her

at your aunt's. Attractive she is, — she has particularly
pretty eyes; but I do not know that she made the slightest impression upon me."

" That was quite proper in you," said Charlotte, " seeing
that I was there; and, although she is much younger than
I, the presence of your old friend has so many charms for
you, that you overlooked the promise of the opening
beauty. It is one of your ways; and that is one reason
why it is so pleasant to live with you."

Charlotte, openly as she appeared to be speaking, was
keeping back something, nevertheless; which was that at
the time when Edward came first back from abroad, she
had purposely thrown Ottilie in his way, to secure, if possible, so desirable a match for her protégée. For of herself, at that time, in connection with Edward, she never
thought at all. The Captain, also, had a hint given to
him to draw Edward's attention to her; but the latter,
who was clinging determinately to his early affection for
Charlotte, looked neither right nor left, and was only
happy in the feeling that it was at last within his power to
obtain for himself the one happiness which he so earnestly
desired; and which a series of incidents had appeared to
have placed for ever beyond his reach.

They were on the point of descending the new grounds,
in order to return to the castle, when a servant came
hastily to meet them, and, with a laugh on his face, called
up from below, " Will your grace be pleased to come
quickly to the castle? The Herr Mittler has just galloped
into the court. He shouted to us, to go all of us in search
of you, and we were to ask whether there was need,
' whether there is need,' he cried after us, 'do you hear?
but be quick, be quick.'"

" The odd fellow," exclaimed Edward. " But has he

not come at the right time, Charlotte? Tell him, there is need — grievous need. He must alight. See his horse taken care of. Take him into the saloon, and let him have some luncheon. We shall be with him immediately."

"Let us take the nearest way," he said to his wife, and struck into the path across the churchyard, which he usually avoided. He was not a little surprised to find here, too, traces of Charlotte's delicate hand. Sparing, as far as possible, the old monuments, she had contrived to level it, and lay it carefully out, so as to make it appear a pleasant spot on which the eye and the imagination could equally repose with pleasure. The oldest stones had each their special honor assigned them. They were ranged according to their dates along the wall, either leaning against it, or let into it, or however it could be contrived; and the string-course of the church was thus variously ornamented.

Edward was singularly affected as he came in upon it through the little wicket; he pressed Charlotte's hand, and tears started into his eyes. But these were very soon put to flight, by the appearance of their singular visitor. This gentleman had declined sitting down in the castle; he had ridden straight through the village to the church-yard gate; and then, halting, he called out to his friends. "Are you not making a fool of me? Is there need, really? If there is, I can stay till mid-day. But don't keep me. I have a great deal to do before night."

"Since you have taken the trouble to come so far," cried Edward to him, in answer, "you had better come through the gate. We meet at a solemn spot. Come and see the variety which Charlotte has thrown over its sadness."

"Inside there," called out the rider, "come I neither

on horseback, nor in carriage, nor on foot. These here
rest in peace: with them I have nothing to do. One day
I shall be carried in feet foremost. I must bear that as I
can. — Is it serious, I want to know?"

"Indeed it is," cried Charlotte, "right serious. For the
first time in our married lives, we are in a strait and difficulty, from which we do not know how to extricate ourselves."

"You do not look as if it were so," answered he. "But
I will believe you. If you are deceiving me, for the future
you shall help yourselves. Follow me quickly, my horse
will be none the worse for a rest."

The three speedily found themselves in the saloon together. Luncheon was brought in, and Mittler told them
what that day he had done, and was going to do. This
eccentric person had in early life been a clergyman, and
had distinguished himself in his office by the never-resting
activity with which he contrived to make up and put an
end to quarrels; quarrels in families, and quarrels between neighbors; first among the individuals immediately
about him, and afterwards among whole congregations,
and among the country gentlemen round. While he was
in the ministry, no married couple were allowed to separate; and the district courts were untroubled with either
cause or process. A knowledge of the law, he was well
aware, was necessary to him. He gave himself with all
his might to the study of it, and very soon felt himself a
match for the best trained advocate. His circle of activity extended wonderfully, and people were on the point
of inducing him to move to the Residence, where he would
find opportunities of exercising in the higher circles what
he had begun in the lowest, when he won a considerable
sum of money in a lottery. With this, he bought himself

1*

a small property. He let the ground to a tenant, and made it the centre of his operations, with the fixed determination, or rather in accordance with his old customs and inclinations, never to enter a house where there was no dispute to make up, and no help to be given. People who were superstitious about names, and about what they imported, maintained that it was his being called Mittler which drove him to take upon himself this strange employment.

Luncheon was laid on the table, and the stranger then solemnly pressed his host not to wait any longer with the disclosure which he had to make. Immediately after refreshing himself he would be obliged to leave them.

Husband and wife made a circumstantial confession; but scarcely had he caught the substance of the matter, when he started angrily up from the table, rushed out of the saloon, and ordered his horse to be saddled instantly.

"Either you do not know me, you do not understand me," he cried, "or you are sorely mischievous. Do you call this a quarrel? Is there any want of help here? Do you suppose that I am in the world to give *advice?* Of all occupations which man can pursue, that is the most foolish. Every man must be his own counsellor, and do what he cannot let alone. If all go well, let him be happy, let him enjoy his wisdom and his fortune; if it go ill, I am at hand to do what I can for him. The man who desires to be rid of an evil knows what he wants; but the man who desires something better than he has got is stone blind. Yes, yes, laugh as you will, he is playing blindman's-buff; perhaps he gets hold of something, but the question is what he has got hold of. Do as you will, it is all one. Invite your friends to you, or let them be, it is all the same. The most prudent plans I have seen miscarry, and the most foolish succeed. Don't split your brains about it; and if, one way or the other, evil comes of what you settle, don't fret; send for me, and you shall be helped. Till which time, I am your humble servant."

So saying, he sprang on his horse, without waiting the arrival of the coffee.

"Here you see," said Charlotte, "the small service a third person can be, when things are off their balance between two persons closely connected; we are left, if possible, more confused and more uncertain than we were."

They would both, probably, have continued hesitating some time longer, had not a letter arrived from the Captain, in reply to Edward's last. He had made up his mind to accept one of the situations which had been offered him, although it was not in the least up to his mark. He was to share the ennui of certain wealthy persons of rank, who depended on his ability to dissipate it.

Edward's keen glance saw into the whole thing, and he pictured it out in just, sharp lines.

"Can we endure to think of our friend in such a position?" he cried; "you cannot be so cruel, Charlotte."

"That strange Mittler is right after all," replied Charlotte; "all such undertakings are ventures; what will come of them it is impossible to foresee. New elements introduced among us may be fruitful in fortune or in misfortune, without our having to take credit to ourselves for one or the other. I do not feel myself firm enough to oppose you further. Let us make the experiment; only one thing I will entreat of you — that it be only for a short time. You must allow me to exert myself more than ever, to use all my influence among all my connections, to find him some position which will satisfy him in his own way."

Edward poured out the warmest expressions of gratitude. He hastened, with a light, happy heart, to write
off his proposals to his friend. Charlotte, in a postscript,
was to signify her approbation with her own hand, and
unite her own kind entreaties with his. She wrote, with
a rapid pen, pleasantly and affectionately, but yet with a
sort of haste which was not usual with her; and, most
unlike herself, she disfigured the paper at last with a blot
of ink, which put her out of temper, and which she only
made worse with her attempts to wipe it away.

Edward laughed at her about it, and, as there was still
room, added a second postscript, that his friend was to see
from this symptom the impatience with which he was expected, and measure the speed at which he came to them
by the haste in which the letter was written.

The messenger was gone; and Edward thought he
could not give a more convincing evidence of his gratitude, than by insisting again and again that Charlotte
should at once send for Ottilie from the school. She said
she would think about it; and, for that evening, induced
Edward to join with her in the enjoyment of a little music. Charlotte played exceedingly well on the piano,
Edward not quite so well on the flute. He had taken a
great deal of pains with it at times; but he was without
the patience, without the perseverance, which are requi-
site for the completely successful cultivation of such a
talent; consequently, his part was done unequally, some
pieces well, only perhaps too quickly — while with others
he hesitated, not being quite familiar with them; so that,
for any one else, it would have been difficult to have gone
through a duet with him. But Charlotte knew how to
manage it. She held in, or let herself be run away with,
and fulfilled in this way the double part of a skilful con-

ductor and a prudent housewife, who are able always to keep right on the whole, although particular passages will now and then fall out of order.

CHAPTER III.

THE Captain came, having previously written a most sensible letter, which had entirely quieted Charlotte's apprehensions. So much clearness about himself, so just an understanding of his own position and the position of his friends, promised everything which was best and happiest.

The conversation of the first few hours, as is generally the case with friends who have not met for a long time, was eager, lively, almost exhausting. Towards evening, Charlotte proposed a walk to the new grounds. The Captain was delighted with the spot, and observed every beauty which had been first brought into sight and made enjoyable by the new walks. He had a practised eye, and at the same time one easily satisfied; and although he knew very well what was really valuable, he never, as so many persons do, made people who were showing him things of their own uncomfortable, by requiring more than the circumstances admitted of, or by mentioning anything more perfect, which he remembered having seen elsewhere.

When they arrived at the summer-house, they found it dressed out for a holiday, only, indeed, with artificial flowers and evergreens, but with some pretty bunches of natural corn-ears among them, and other field and garden fruit, so as to do credit to the taste which had arranged them.

" Although my husband does not like in general to have his birthday or christening-day kept," Charlotte said, " he will not object to-day to these few ornaments being expended on a treble festival."

" Treble ? " cried Edward.

" Yes, indeed," she replied.   " Our friend's arrival here we are bound to keep as a festival; and have you never thought, either of you, that this is the day on which you were both christened?   Are you not both named Otto?"

The two friends shook hands across the little table.

"You bring back to my mind," Edward said, "this little link of our boyish affection. As children, we were both called so, but when we came to be at school together, it was the cause of much confusion, and I readily made over to him all·my right to the pretty laconic name."

" Wherein you were not altogether so very high-minded," said the Captain; " for I well remember that the name of Edward had then begun to please you better, from its attractive sound when spoken by certain pretty lips."

They were now sitting all three round the same little table where Charlotte had spoken so vehemently against their guest's coming to them.   Edward, happy as he was, did not wish to remind his wife of that time; but he could not help saying,

" There is good room here for one more person."

At this moment the notes of a bugle were heard across from the castle. Full of happy thoughts and feelings as the friends all were together, the sound fell in among them with a strong force of answering harmony. They listened silently, each for the moment withdrawing into himself, and feeling doubly happy in the fair circle of which he formed a part. The pause was first broken by Edward, who started up and walked out in front of the summer-house.

"Our friend must not think," he said to Charlotte, "that this narrow little valley forms the whole of our domain and possessions. Let us take him up to the top of the hill, where he can see farther and breathe more freely."

"For this once, then," answered Charlotte, "we must climb up the old footpath, which is not too easy. By the next time I hope walks and steps will have been carried right up."

And so, among rocks, and shrubs, and bushes, they made their way to the summit, where they found themselves, not on a level flat, but on a sloping grassy terrace, running along the ridge of the hill. The village with the castle behind it, was out of sight. At the bottom of the valley, sheets of water were seen spreading out right and left, with wooded hills rising immediately from their opposite margin, and at the end of the upper water, a wall of sharp, precipitous rocks directly overhanging it, their huge forms reflected in its level surface. In the hollow of the ravine, where a considerable brook ran into the lake, lay a mill, half hidden among the trees, a sweetly retired spot, most beautifully surrounded; and through the entire semicircle over which the view extended, ran an endless variety of hills and valleys, copse and forest, the early green of which promised the near approach of a luxuriant clothing of foliage. In many places particular groups of trees caught the eye; and especially a cluster of planes and poplars directly at the spectator's feet, close

to the edge of the centre lake. They were at their full
growth, and they stood there, spreading out their boughs
all around them, in fresh and luxuriant strength.

To these Edward called his friend's attention.

"I myself planted them," he cried, "when I was a boy.
They were small trees which I rescued when my father
was laying out the new part of the great castle garden,
and in the middle of one summer had rooted them out.
This year you will no doubt see them show their gratitude in a fresh set of shoots."

They returned to the castle in high spirits, and mu
tually pleased with each other. To the guest was allotted
an agreeable and roomy set of apartments in the right
wing of the castle; and here he rapidly got his books and
papers and instruments in order, to go on with his usual
occupation. But Edward, for the first few days, gave him
no rest. He took him about everywhere, now on foot,
now on horseback, making him acquainted with the
country and with the estate; and he embraced the opportunity of imparting to him the wishes which he had been
long entertaining, of getting some better acquaintance
with it, and learning to manage it more profitably.

"The first thing we have to do," said the Captain, "is
to make a magnetic survey of the property. That is a
pleasant and easy matter; and if it does not admit of
entire exactness, it will be always useful, and will do, at
any rate, for an agreeable beginning. It can be made,
too, without any great staff of assistants, and one can be
sure of getting it completed. If by-and-by you come to
require anything more exact, it will be easy then to find
some plan to have it made."

The Captain was exceedingly skilful at work of this
kind. He had brought with him whatever instruments

he required, and commenced immediately. Edward provided him with a number of foresters and peasants, who, with his instruction, were able to render him all necessary assistance. The weather was favorable. The evenings and the early mornings were devoted to the designing and drawing, and in a short time it was all filled in and colored. Edward saw his possessions grow out like a new creation upon the paper; and it seemed as if now for the first time he knew what they were, as if they now first were properly his own.

Thus there came occasion to speak of the park, and of the ways of laying it out; a far better disposition of things being made possible after a survey of this kind, than could be arrived at by experimenting on nature, on partial and accidental impressions.

" We must make my wife understand this," said Edward.

" We must do nothing of the kind," replied the Captain, who did not like bringing his own notions in collision with those of others. He had learned by experience that the motives and purposes by which men are influenced, are far too various to be made to coalesce upon a single point, even on the most solid representations. " We must not do it," he cried; " she will be only confused. With her, as with all people who employ themselves on such matters merely as amateurs, the important thing is, rather that she shall do something, than that something shall be done. Such persons feel their way with nature. They have fancies for this plan or that; they do not venture on removing obstacles. They are not bold enough to make a sacrifice. They do not know beforehand in what their work is to result. They try an experiment — it succeeds — it fails; they alter it; they alter, perhaps, what they ought to leave alone, and leave what they ought to alter;

2

and so, at last, there always remains but a patchwork, which pleases and amuses, but never satisfies."

"Acknowledge candidly," said Edward, "that you do not like this new work of hers."

"The idea is excellent," he replied; "if the execution were equal to it, there would be no fault to find. But she has tormented herself to find her way up that rock; and she now torments every one, if you must have it, that she takes up after her. You cannot walk together — you cannot walk behind one another with any freedom. Every moment your step is interrupted one way or another. There is no end to the mistakes which she has made."

"Would it have been easy to have done it otherwise?" asked Edward.

"Perfectly," replied the Captain. "She had only to break away a corner of the rock, which is now but an unsightly object, made up as it is of little pieces, and she would at once have a sweep for her walk and stone in abundance for the rough masonry work, to widen it in the bad places, and make it smooth. But this I tell you in strictest confidence. Her it would only confuse and annoy. What is done must remain as it is. If any more money and labor is to be spent there, there is abundance to do above the summer-house on the hill, which we can settle our own way."

If the two friends found in their occupation abundance of present employment, there was no lack either of entertaining reminiscences of early times, in which Charlotte took her part as well. They determined, moreover, that as soon as their immediate labors were finished, they would go to work upon the journal, and in this way, too, reproduce the past.

For the rest, when Edward and Charlotte were alone,

there were fewer matters of private interest between them than formerly. This was especially the case since the fault-finding about the grounds, which Edward thought so just, and which he felt to the quick. He held his tongue about what the Captain had said for a long time ; but at last, when he saw his wife again preparing to go to work above the summer-house, with her paths and steps, he could not contain himself any longer, but, after a few circumlocutions, came out with his new views.

Charlotte was thoroughly disturbed. She was sensible enough to perceive at once that they were right, but there was the difficulty with what was already done, — and what was made was made. She had liked it : even what was wrong had become dear to her in its details. She fought against her convictions ; she defended her little creation ; she railed at men who were for ever going to the broad and the great. They could not let a pastime, they could not let an amusement alone, she said, but they must go and make a work out of it, never thinking of the expense which their larger plans involved. She was provoked, annoyed, and angry. Her old plans she conld not give up, the new she would not quite throw from her ; but, divided as she was, for the present she put a stop to the work, and gave herself time to think the thing over, and let it ripen by itself.

At the same time that she lost this source of active amusement, the others were more and more together over their own business. They took to occupying themselves, moreover, with the flower-garden and the hot-houses ; and as they filled up the intervals with the ordinary gentlemen's amusements, hunting, riding, buying, selling, breaking horses, and such matters, she was every day left more and more to herself. She devoted herself more assidu-

ously than ever to her correspondence on account of the
Captain; and yet she had many lonely hours; so that the
information which she now received from the school became of more agreeable interest.

To a long-drawn letter of the superior of the establishment, filled with the usual expressions of delight at her
daughter's progress, a brief postscript was attached, with
a second from the hand of a gentleman in employment
there as an assistant, both of which we here communicate.

POSTSCRIPT OF THE SUPERIOR.

" Of Ottilie, I can only repeat to your ladyship what I
have already stated in my former letters. I do not know
how to find fault with her, yet I cannot say that I am satisfied. She is always unassuming, always ready to oblige
others; but it is not pleasing to see her so timid, so
almost servile.

" Your ladyship lately sent her some money, with several little matters for her wardrobe. The money she has
never touched, the dresses lay unworn in their place. She
keeps her things very nice and very clean; but this is all
she seems to care about. Again, I cannot praise her excessive abstemiousness in eating and drinking. There is
no extravagance at our table, but there is nothing that I
like better than to see the children eat enough of good,
wholesome food. What is carefully provided and set before them ought to be taken; and to this I never can
succeed in bringing Ottilie. She is always making herself
some occupation or other, always finding something which
she must do, something which the servants have neglected,
to escape the second course or the dessert; and now it
has to be considered (which I cannot help connecting
with all this) that she frequently suffers, I have lately

learnt, from pain in the left side of her head. It is only at times, but it is distressing, and may be of importance. So much upon this otherwise sweet and lovely girl."

SECOND POSTSCRIPT, BY THE ASSISTANT.

" Our excellent superior commonly permits me to read the letters in which she communicates her observations upon her pupils to their parents and friends. Such of them as are addressed to your ladyship I ever read with twofold attention and pleasure. We have to congratulate you upon a daughter who unites in herself every brilliant quality with which people distinguish themselves in the world; and I at least think you no less fortunate in having had bestowed upon you, in your step-daughter, a child who has been born for the good and happiness of others, and assuredly also for her own. Ottilie is almost our only pupil about whom there is a difference of opinion between myself and our reverend superior. I do not complain of the very natural desire in that good lady to see outward and definite fruits arising from her labors. But there are also fruits which are not outward, which are of the true germinal sort, and which develop themselves sooner or later in a beautiful life. And this I am certain is the case with your protégée. So long as she has been under my care, I have watched her moving with an even step, slowly, steadily forward — never back. As with a child it is necessary to begin everything at the beginning, so it is with her. She can comprehend nothing which does not follow from what precedes it; let a thing be as simple and easy as possible, she can make nothing of it if it is not in a recognizable connection; but find the intermediate links, and make them clear to her, and then nothing is too difficult for her.

" Progressing with such slow steps, she remains behind
her companions, who, with capacities of quite a different
kind, hurry on and on, learn everything readily, connected
or unconnected, recollect it with ease, and apply it with
correctness. And again, some of the lessons here are
given by excellent, but somewhat hasty and impatient
teachers, who pass from result to result, cutting short the
process by which they are arrived at ; and these are not
of the slightest service to her; she learns nothing from
them. There is a complaint of her handwriting. They
say she will not, or cannot, understand how to form her
letters. I have examined closely into this. It is true
she writes slowly, stiffly, if you like ; but the hand is
neither timid nor without character. The French language is not my department, but I have taught her
something of it, in the step-by-step fashion ; and this she
understands easily. Indeed, it is singular that she knows
a great deal, and knows it well, too ; and yet when she
is asked a question, it seems as if she knew nothing.

" To conclude generally, I should say she learns nothing
like a person who is being educated, but she learns like
one who is to educate — not like a pupil, but like a
future teacher. Your ladyship may think it strange that
I, as an educator and a teacher, can find no higher praise
to give to any one than by a comparison with myself. I
may leave it to your own good sense, to your deep
knowledge of the world and of mankind, to make the
best of my most inadequate, but well-intended expressions. You may satisfy yourself that you have much
happiness to promise yourself from this child. I com-
mend myself to your ladyship, and I beseech you to permit me to write to you again as soon as I see reason to
believe that I have anything important or agreeable to
communicate."

This letter gave Charlotte great pleasure. The contents of it coincided very closely with the notions which she had herself conceived of Ottilie. At the same time, she could not help smiling at the excessive interest of the assistant, which seemed greater than the insight into a pupil's excellence usually calls forth. In her quiet, unprejudiced way of looking at things, this relation, among others, she was contented to permit to lie before her as a possibility; she could value the interest of so sensible a man in Ottilie, having learnt, among the lessons of her life, to see how highly true regard is to be prized, in a world where indifference or dislike are the common natural residents.

CHAPTER IV.

THE topographical chart of the property and its environs was completed. It was executed on a considerable scale; the character of the particular localities was made intelligible by various colors; and by means of a trigonometrical survey, the Captain had been able to arrive at a very fair exactness of measurement. He had been rapid in his work. There was scarcely ever any one who could do with less sleep than this most laborious man; and, as his day was always devoted to an immediate purpose, every evening something had been done.

"Let us now," he said to his friend, "go on to what remains for us, to the statistics of the estates. We shall have a good deal of work to get through at the beginning,. and afterwards we shall come to the farm estimates, and much else which will naturally arise out of them. Only

we must have one thing distinctly settled and adhered
to. Everything which is properly *business* we must keep
carefully separate from *life*. Business requires earnestness and method; life must have a freer handling.
Business demands the utmost stringency and sequence;
in life, inconsecutiveness is frequently necessary, indeed,
is charming and graceful. If you are firm in the first,
you can afford yourself more liberty in the second; while
if you mix them, you will find the free interfering with
and breaking in upon the fixed."

"In these sentiments Edward felt a slight reflection
upon himself. Though not naturally disorderly, he could
never bring himself to arrange his papers in their proper
places. What he had to do in connection with others,
was not kept separate from what only depended on himself. Business got mixed up with amusement, and
serious work with recreation. Now, however, it was easy
for him, with the help of a friend, who would take the
trouble upon himself; and a second " I " worked out the
separation, to which the single " I " was always unequal.

In the Captain's wing, they contrived a depository for
what concerned the present, and an archive for the past.
Here they brought all the documents, papers, and notes
from their various hiding-places, rooms, drawers, and
boxes, with the utmost speed. Harmony and order were
introduced into the wilderness, and the different packets
were marked and registered in their several pigeon-holes.
They found all they wanted in greater completeness even
than they had expected; and here an old clerk was found
of no slight service, who for the whole day and part of
the night never left his desk, and with whom, till then,
Edward had been always dissatisfied.

"I should not know him again," he said to his friend, "the man is so handy and useful."

"That," replied the Captain, "is because we give him nothing fresh to do till he has finished, at his convenience, what he has already; and so, as you perceive, he gets through a great deal. If you disturb him, he becomes useless at once."

Spending their days together in this way, in the evenings they never neglected their regular visits to Charlotte. If there was no party from the neighborhood, as was often the case, they read and talked, principally on subjects connected with the improvement of the condition and comfort of social life.

Charlotte, always accustomed to make the most of opportunities, not only saw her husband pleased, but found personal advantages for herself. Various domestic arrangements, which she had long wished to make, but which she did not know exactly how to set about, were managed for her through the contrivance of the Captain. Her domestic medicine chest, hitherto but poorly furnished, was enlarged and enriched, and Charlotte herself, with the help of good books and personal instruction, was put in the way of being able to exercise her disposition to be of practical assistance more frequently and more efficiently than before.

In providing against accidents, which, though common, yet only too often find us unprepared, they thought it especially necessary to have at hand whatever is required for the recovery of drowning men — accidents of this kind, from the number of canals, reservoirs, and waterworks in the neighborhood being of frequent occurrence. This department the Captain took expressly into his own hands; and the observation escaped Edward, that a case of this kind had made a very singular epoch in the life of his friend. The latter made no reply, but seemed to be trying to escape from a painful recollection. Edward immediately stopped; and Charlotte, who, as well as he, had a general knowledge of the story, took no notice of the expression.

"These preparations are all exceedingly valuable," said the Captain, one evening. "Now, however, we have not got the one thing which is most essential — a sensible man who understands how to manage it all. I know an army surgeon, whom I could exactly recommend for the place. You might get him at this moment on easy terms. He is highly distinguished in his profession, and has frequently done more for me, in the treatment even of violent inward disorders, than celebrated physicians. Help upon the spot, is the thing you often most want in the country."

He was written for at once; and Edward and Charlotte were rejoiced to have found so good and necessary an object, on which to expend so much of the money which they set apart for such accidental demands upon them.

Thus Charlotte, too, found means of making use, for her purposes, of the Captain's knowledge and practical skill; and she began to be quite reconciled to his presence, and to feel easy about any consequences which might ensue. She commonly prepared questions to ask him; among other things, it was one of her anxieties to provide against whatever was prejudicial to health and comfort, against poisons and such like. The lead-glazing on the china, the verdigris which formed about her copper and bronze vessels, &c., had long been a trouble to her. She got him to tell her about these, and, naturally, they often had to fall back on the first elements of medicine and chemistry.

An accidental, but welcome occasion for entertainment of this kind, was given by an inclination of Edward to read aloud. He had a particularly clear, deep voice, and earlier in life had earned himself a pleasant reputation for his feeling and lively recitations of works of poetry and oratory. At this time he was occupied with other subjects, and the books which, for some time past, he had been reading, were either chemical, or on some other branch of natural or technical science.

One of his especial peculiarities — which, by-the-by, he very likely shares with a number of his fellow-creatures — was, that he could not bear any one looking over him when he was reading. In early life, when he used to read poems, plays or stories, this had been the natural consequence of the desire which the reader feels, like the poet, or the actor, or the story-teller, to make surprises, to pause, to excite expectation; and this sort of effect was naturally defeated when a third person's eyes could run on before him, and see what was coming. On such occasions, therefore, he was accustomed to place himself in such a position that no one could get behind him. With a party of only three, this was unnecessary; and as with the present subject there was no opportunity for exciting feelings or giving the imagination a surprise, he did not take any particular pains to protect himself.

One evening he had placed himself carelessly, and Charlotte happened by accident to cast her eyes upon the page. His old impatience was aroused; he turned to her, and said, almost unkindly,

"I do wish, once for all, you would leave off doing a thing so out of taste and so disagreeable. When I read aloud to a person, is it not the same as if I was telling him something by word or mouth? The written, the printed word, is in the place of my own thoughts, of my own heart. If a window were broken into my brain or into my heart, and if the man to whom I am counting out my thoughts, or delivering my sentiments, one by one, knew already beforehand exactly what was to come out of me, should I take the trouble to put them into words? When anybody looks over my book, I always feel as if I were being torn in two."

Charlotte's tact, in whatever circle she might be, large or small, was remarkable, and she was able to set aside disagreeable or excited expressions without appearing to notice them. When a conversation grew tedious, she knew how to interrupt it; when it halted she could set it going. And this time her good gift did not forsake her.

"I am sure you will forgive me my fault," she said, "when I tell you what it was this moment which came over me. I heard you reading something about Affinities, and I thought directly of some relations of mine, two of whom are just now occupying me a great deal. Then my attention went back to the book. I found it was not about living things at all, and I looked over to get the thread of it right again."

"It was the comparison which led you wrong and confused you," said Edward. "The subject is nothing but earths and minerals. But man is a true Narcissus; he delights to see his own image everywhere; and he spreads himself underneath the universe, like the amalgam behind the glass."

"Quite true," continued the captain. "That is the way in which he treats everything external to himself. His wisdom and his folly, his will and his caprice, he attributes alike to the animal, the plant, the elements, and the gods."

"Would you," said Charlotte, "if it is not taking you away too much from the immediate subject, tell me briefly what is meant here by Affinities?"

"I shall be very glad indeed," replied the Captain, 'to whom Charlotte had addressed herself. "That is I will tell you as well as I can. My ideas on the subject date ten years back; whether the scientific world continues to think the same about it, I cannot tell."

"It is most disagreeable," cried Edward, "that one cannot now-a-days learn a thing once for all, and have done with it. Our forefathers could keep to what they were taught when they were young; but we have, every five years, to make revolutions with them, if we do not wish to drop altogether out of fashion."

"We women need not be so particular," said Charlotte; "and, to speak the truth, I only want to know the meaning of the word. There is nothing more ridiculous in society than to misuse a strange technical word; and I only wish you to tell me in what sense the expression is made use of in connection with these things. What its scientific application is, I am quite contented to leave to the learned; who, by-the-by, as far as I have been able to observe, do not find it easy to agree among themselves."

"Whereabouts shall we begin," said Edward, after a pause, to the Captain, "to come most quickly to the point?"

The latter after thinking a little while, replied shortly;

"You must let me make what will seem a wide sweep, we shall be on our subject almost immediately."

Charlotte settled her work at her side, promising the fullest attention.

The Captain began:

"In all natural objects with which we are acquainted,

we observe immediately that they have a certain relation to themselves. It may sound ridiculous to be asserting what is obvious to every one; but it is only by coming to a clear understanding together about what we know, that we can advance to what we do not know."

"I think," interrupted Edward, "we can make the thing more clear to her, and to ourselves, with examples; conceive water, or oil, or quicksilver; among these you will see a certain oneness, a certain connection of their parts; and this oneness is never lost, except through force or some other determining cause. Let the cause cease to operate, and at once the parts unite again."

"Unquestionably," said Charlotte, "that is plain; rain-drops readily unite and form streams; and when we were children, it was our delight to play with quicksilver, and wonder at the little globules splitting and parting and running into one other."

"And here," said the Captain, "let me just cursorily mention one remarkable thing, I mean, that the full, complete correlation of parts which the fluid state makes possible, shows itself distinctly and universally in the globular form. The falling water-drop is round; you yourself spoke of the globules of quicksilver; and a drop of melted lead let fall, if it has time to harden before it reaches the ground, is found at the bottom in the shape of a ball."

"Let me try and see," said Charlotte "whether I can understand where you are bringing me. As everything has a reference to itself, so it must have some relation to others."

"And that," interrupted Edward, "will be different according to the natural differences of the things them-selves. Sometimes they will meet like friends and old acquaintances; they will come rapidly together, and unite without either having to alter itself at all—as wine mixes with water. Others, again, will remain as strangers side by side, and no amount of mechanical mixing or forcing will succeed in combining them. Oil and water may be shaken up together, and the next moment they are separate again, each by itself."

"One can almost fancy," said Charlotte, "that in these simple forms one sees people that one is acquainted with; one has met with just such things in the societies amongst which one has lived; and the strangest likenesses of all with these soulless creatures, are in the masses in which men stand divided one against the other, in their classes and professions; the nobility and the third estate, for instance, or soldiers and civilians."

"Then again," replied Edward; "as these are united together under common laws and customs, so there are intermediate members in our chemical world, which will combine elements that are mutually repulsive."

"Oil, for instance," said the Captain, "we make combine with water with the help of alkalies——"

"Do not go on too fast with your lesson," said Charlotte. "Let me see that I keep step with you. Are we not here arrived among the affinities?"

"Exactly," replied the Captain; "we are on the point of apprehending them in all their power and distinctness; such natures as, when they come in contact, at once lay hold of each other, and mutually affect one another, we speak of as having an affinity one for the other. With the alkalies and acids, for instance, the affinities are strikingly marked. They are of opposite natures; very likely their being of opposite natures is the secret of their effect on one another—they seek one another eagerly

out, lay hold of each other, modify each other's character
and form in connection an entirely new substance.   There
is lime, you remember, which shows the strongest inclination for all sorts of acids—a distinct desire of combining
with them.   As soon as our chemical chest arrives, we
can show you a number of entertaining experiments,
which will give you a clearer idea than words, and
names, and technical expressions."

"It appears to me," said Charlotte, "that if you choose
to call these strange creatures of yours related, the relationship is not so much a relationship of blood, as of soul
or of spirit.   It is the way in which we see all really deep
friendships arise among men; opposite peculiarities of
disposition being what best makes internal union possible.
But I will wait to see what you can really show me of
these mysterious proceedings; and for the present," she
added, turning to Edward, "I will promise not to disturb
you any more in your reading.   You have taught me
enough of what it is about to enable me to attend to it."

"No, no," replied Edward, "now that you have once
stirred the thing, you shall not get off so easily.   It is just
the most complicated cases which are the most interesting.
In these you come first to see the degrees of the affinities,
to watch them as their power of attraction is weaker or
stronger, nearer or more remote.   Affinities only begin
really to interest when they bring about separations."

"What!" cried Charlotte, "is that miserable word,
which unhappily we hear so often now-a-days in the
world; is that to be found in nature's lessons too?"

"Most certainly," answered Edward; "the title with
which chemists were supposed to be most honorably distinguished was, artists of separation."

"It is not so any more," replied Charlotte; "and it is

well that it is not. It is a higher art, and it is a higher merit, to unite. An artist of union, is what we should welcome in every province of the universe. However, as we are on the subject again, give me an instance or two of what you mean."

"We had better keep," said the Captain, "to the same instances of which we have already been speaking. Thus, what we call limestone is a more or less pure calcareous earth in combination with a delicate acid, which is familiar to us in the form of a gas. Now, if we place a piece of this stone in diluted sulphuric acid, this will take possession of the lime, and appear with it in the form of gypsum, the gaseous acid at the same time going off in vapor. Here is a case of separation ; a combination arises, and we believe ourselves now justified in applying to it the words 'Elective Affinity;' it really looks as if one relation had been deliberately chosen in preference to another."

"Forgive me," said Charlotte, "as I forgive the natural philosopher. I cannot see any choice in this; I see a natural necessity rather, and scarcely that. After all, it is perhaps merely a case of opportunity. Opportunity makes relations as it makes thieves; and as long as the talk is only of natural substances, the choice to me appears to be altogether in the hands of the chemist who brings the creatures together. Once, however, let them be brought together, and then God have mercy on them. In the present case, I cannot help being sorry for the poor acid gas, which is driven out up and down infinity again."

"The acid's business," answered the Captain, "is now to get connected with water, and so serve as a mineral fountain for the refreshing of sound or disordered mankind."

"That is very well for the gypsum to say," said Charlotte. "The gypsum is all right, is a body, is provided for. The other poor, desolate creature may have trouble enough to go through before it can find a second home for itself."

"I am much mistaken," said Edward smiling, "if there be not some little *arriére pensée* behind this. Confess your wickedness! You mean me by your lime; the lime is laid hold of by the Captain, in the form of sulphuric acid, torn away from your agreeable society, and metamorphosed into a refractory gypsum."

"If your conscience prompts you to make such a reflection," replied Charlotte, "I certainly need not distress myself. These comparisons are pleasant and entertaining; and who is there that does not like playing with analogies? But man is raised very many steps above these elements; and if he has been somewhat liberal with such fine words as Election and Elective Affinities, he will do well to turn back again into himself, and take the opportunity of considering carefully the value and meaning of such expressions. Unhappily, we know cases enough where a connection apparently indissoluble between two persons, has, by the accidental introduction of a third, been utterly destroyed, and one or the other of the once happily united pair been driven out into the wilderness."

"Then you see how much more gallant the chemists are," said Edward. "They at once add a fourth, that neither may go away empty."

"Quite so," replied the Captain. "And those are the cases which are really most important and remarkable — cases where this attraction, this affinity, this separating and combining, can be exhibited, the two pairs severally crossing each other; where four creatures, connected previously, as two and two, are brought into contact, and at once forsake their first combination to form into a second. In this forsaking and embracing, this seeking and flying, we believe that we are indeed observing the effects of some higher determination; we attribute a sort of will and choice to such creatures, and feel really justified in using technical words, and speaking of 'Elective Affinities.'"

"Give me an instance of this," said Charlotte.

"One should not spoil such things with words," replied the Captain. "As I said before, as soon as I can show you the experiment, I can make it all intelligible and pleasant for you. For the present, I can give you nothing but horrible scientific expressions, which at the same time will give you no idea about the matter. You ought yourself to see these creatures, which seem so dead, and which are yet so full of inward energy and force, at work before your eyes. You should observe them with a real personal interest. Now they seek each other out, attract each other, seize, crush, devour, destroy each other, and then suddenly reappear again out of their combinations, and come forward in fresh, renovated, unexpected form; thus you will comprehend how we attribute to them a sort of immortality — how we speak of them as having sense and understanding; because we feel our own senses to be insufficient to observe them adequately, and our reason too weak to follow them."

"I quite agree," said Edward, "that the strange scientific nomenclature, to persons who have not been reconciled to it by a direct acquaintance with or understanding of its object, must seem unpleasant, even ridiculous; but we can easily, just for once, contrive with symbols to illustrate what we are speaking of."

"If you do not think it looks pedantic," answered the Captain, "I can put my meaning together with letters. Suppose an A connected so closely with a B, that all sorts of means, even violence, have been made use of to separate them, without effect. Then suppose a C in exactly the same position with respect to D. Bring the two pairs into contact; A will fling himself on D, C on B, without its being possible to say which had first left its first connection, or made the first move towards the second."

"Now then," interposed Edward, "till we see all this with our eyes, we will look upon the formula as an analogy, out of which we can devise a lesson for immediate use. You stand for A, Charlotte, and I am your B; really and truly I cling to you, I depend on you, and follow you, just as B does with A. C is obviously the Captain, who at present is in some degree withdrawing me from you. So now it is only just that if you are not to be left to solitude, a D should be found for you, and that is unquestionably the amiable little lady, Ottilie. You will not hesitate any longer to send and fetch her."

"Good," replied Charlotte; "although the example does not, in my opinion, exactly fit our case. However, we have been fortunate, at any rate, in to-day for once having met all together; and these natural or elective affinities have served to unite us more intimately. I will tell you, that since this afternoon I have made up my mind to send for Ottilie. My faithful housekeeper, on whom I have hitherto depended for everything, is going to leave me shortly, to be married. (It was done at my own suggestion, I believe, to please me.) What it is which has decided me about Ottilie, you shall read to me. I will not look over the pages again. Indeed, the contents of them are already known to me. Only read, read!"

With these words, she produced a letter, and handed it to Edward.

CHAPTER V.

LETTER OF THE LADY SUPERIOR.

"YOUR ladyship will forgive the brevity of my present letter. The public examinations are but just concluded, and I have to communicate to all the parents and guardians the progress which our pupils have made during the past year. To you I may well be brief, having to say much in few words. Your ladyship's daughter has proved herself first in every sense of the word. The testimonials which I inclose, and her own letter, in which she will detail to you the prizes which she has won, and the happiness which she feels in her success, will surely please, and I hope delight you. For myself, it is the less necessary that I should say much, because I see that there will soon be no more occasion to keep with us a young lady so far advanced. I send my respects to your ladyship, and in a short time I shall take the liberty of offering you my opinion as to what in future may be of most advantage to her.

"My good assistant will tell you about Ottilie."

LETTER OF THE ASSISTANT.

"Our reverend superior leaves it to me to write to you of Ottilie, partly because, with her ways of thinking about

it, it would be painful to her to say what has to be said;
partly, because she herself requires some excusing, which
she would rather have done for her by me.

"Knowing, as I did too well, how little able the good
Ottilie was to show out what lies in her, and what she is
capable of, I was all along afraid of this public examination. I was the more uneasy, as it was to be of a kind
which does not admit of any especial preparation; and
even if it had been conducted as usual, Ottilie never can
be prepared to make a display. The result has only too
entirely justified my anxiety. She has gained no prize;
she is not even amongst those whose names have been
mentioned with approbation. I need not go into details.
In writing, the letters of the other girls were not so well
formed, but their strokes were far more free. In Arith-
metic, they were all quicker than she; and in the more
difficult problems, which she does .the best, there was no
examination. In French, she was outshone and out-
talked by many; and in history she was not ready with
her names and dates. In geography, there was a want
of attention to the political divisions; and for what she
could do in music there was neither time nor quiet
enough for her few modest melodies to gain attention;
In drawing she certainly would have gained the prize;
her outlines were clear, and the execution most careful
and full of spirit; unhappily, she had chosen too large a
subject, and it was incomplete.

"After the pupils were dismissed, the examiners consulted together, and we teachers were partially admitted
into the council. I very soon observed that of Ottilie
either nothing would be said at all, or if her name was
mentioned, it would be with indifference, if not disapproval. I hoped to obtain some favor for her by a can-

did description of what she was, and I ventured it with
the greater earnestness, partly because I was only speaking my real convictions, and partly because I remembered in my own younger years finding myself in the same
unfortunate case. I was listened to with attention, but
as soon as I had ended, the presiding examiner said to
me very kindly but laconically, 'We presume capabilities: they are to be converted into accomplishments.
This is the aim of all education. It is what is distinctly
intended by all who have the care of children, and silently and indistinctly by the children themselves. This
also is the object of examinations, where teachers and
pupils are alike standing their trial. From what we
learn of you, we may entertain good hopes of the young
lady, and it is to your own credit also that you have paid
so much attention to your pupils capabilities. If in the
coming year you can develop these into accomplishments,
neither yourself nor your pupil shall fail to receive your
due praise.'

"I had made up my mind to what must follow upon
all this: but there was something worse that I had not
anticipated, which had soon to be added to it. Our
good superior, who like a trusty shepherdess could not
bear to have one of her flock lost, or, as was the case
here, to see it undistinguished, after the examiners were
gone could not contain her displeasure, and said to
Ottilie, who was standing quite quietly by the window,
while the others were exulting over their prizes, 'Tell
me, for heaven's sake, how can a person look so stupid if
she is not so?' Ottilie replied, quite calmly, 'Forgive
me, my dear mother, I have my headache again to-day,
and it is very painful.' Kind and sympathizing as she

generally is, the Superior this time answered, 'No one can believe that,' and turned angrily away.

"Now it is true, — no one can believe it, — for Ottilie never alters the expression of her countenance. I have never even seen her move her hand to her head when she has been asleep.

"Nor was this all. Your ladyship's daughter, who is at all times sufficiently lively and impetuous, after her triumph to-day was overflowing with the violence of her spirits. She ran from room to room with her prizes and testimonials, and shook them in Ottilie's face. ' You have come badly off this morning,' she cried. Ottilie replied in her calm, quiet way, 'This is not the last day of trial.' — 'But you will always remain the last,' cried the other, and ran away.

" No one except myself saw that Ottilie was disturbed. She has a way when she experiences any sharp unpleasant emotion which she wishes to resist, of showing it in the unequal color of her face; the left cheek becomes for a moment flushed, while the right turns pale. I perceived this symptom, and I could not prevent myself from saying something. I took our Superior aside, and spoke seriously to her about it. The excellent lady acknowledged that she had been wrong. We considered the whole affair; we talked it over at great length together, and not ·to weary your ladyship, I will tell you at once the desire with which we concluded, namely, that you will for a while have Ottilie with yourself. Our reasons you will yourself readily perceive. If you consent, I will say more to you on the manner in which I think she should be treated. The young lady your daughter we may expect will soon leave us, and we shall then with pleasure welcome Ottilie back to us.

" One thing more, which another time I might forget to mention : I have never seen Ottilie eager for anything, or at least ask pressingly for anything. But there have been occasions, however rare, when on the other hand she has wished to decline things which have been pressed upon her, and she does it with a gesture which to those who have caught its meaning is irresistible. She raises her hands, presses the palms together, and draws them against her breast, leaning her body a little forward at the same time, and turns such a look upon the person who is urging her, that he will be glad enough to cease to ask or wish for anything of her. If your ladyship ever sees this attitude, as with your treatment of her it is not likely that you will, think of me, and spare Ottilie."

Edward read these letters aloud, not without smiles and shakes of the head. Naturally, too, there were observations made on the persons and on the position of the affair.

" Enough!" Edward cried at last, " it is decided. She comes. You, my love, are provided for, and now we can get forward with our work. It is becoming highly necessary for me to move over to the right wing to the Captain ; evenings and mornings are the time for us best to work together, and then you, on your side, will have admirable room for yourself and Ottilie."

Charlotte made no objection, and Edward sketched out the method in which they should live. Among other things, he cried, " It is really very polite in this niece to be subject to a slight pain on the left side of her head. I have it frequently on the right. If we happen to be afflicted together, and sit opposite one another, — I leaning on my right elbow, and she on her left, and our

3

heads on the opposite sides, resting on our hands, — what a pretty pair of pictures we shall make."

The Captain thought that might be dangerous. "No, no!" cried out Edward. "Only do you, my dear friend, take care of the D, for what will become of B, if poor C is taken away from it?"

"That, I should have thought, would have been evident enough," replied Charlotte.

"And it is, indeed," cried Edward; "he would turn to his A, to his Alpha and Omega;" and he sprung up and taking Charlotte in his arms, pressed her to his breast.

CHAPTER VI.

THE carriage which brought Ottilie drove up to the door. Charlotte went out to receive her. The dear girl ran to meet her, threw herself at her feet, and embraced her knees.

"Why such humility?" said Charlotte, a little embarrassed, and endeavoring to raise her from the ground.

"It is not meant for humility," Ottilie answered, without moving from the position in which she had placed herself; "I am only thinking of the time when I could not reach higher than to your knees, and when I had just learnt to know how you loved me."

She stood up, and Charlotte embraced her warmly. She was introduced to the gentlemen, and was at once treated with especial courtesy as a visitor. Beauty is a welcome guest everywhere. She appeared attentive to the conversation, without taking a part in it.

The next morning Edward said to Charlotte, " What an agreeable, entertaining girl she is ! "

" Entertaining ! " answered Charlotte, with a smile; " why, she has not opened her lips yet ! "

" Indeed ! " said Edward, as he seemed to bethink himself; " that is very strange."

Charlotte had to give the new-comer but a very few hints on the management of the household. Ottilie saw rapidly all the arrangements, and what was more, she felt them. She comprehended easily what was to be provided for the whole party, and what for each particular member of it. Everything was done with the utmost punctuality; she knew how to direct, without appearing to be giving orders, and when any one had left anything undone, she at once set it right herself.

As soon as she had found how much time she would have to spare, she begged Charlotte to divide her hours for her, and to these she adhered exactly. She worked at what was set before her in the way which the Assistant had described to Charlotte. They let her alone. It was but seldom that Charlotte interfered. Sometimes she changed her pens for others which had been written with, to teach her to make bolder strokes in her handwriting, but these, she found, would be soon cut sharp and fine again.

The ladies had agreed with one another when they were alone to speak nothing but French, and Charlotte persisted in it the more, as she found Ottilie more ready to talk in a foreign language, when she was told it was her duty to exercise herself in it. In this way she often said more than she seemed to intend. Charlotte was particularly pleased with a description, most complete, but at the same time most charming and amiable, which she gave her one day, by accident, of the school. She soon felt her to be a delightful companion, and before long she hoped to find in her an attached friend.

At the same time she looked over again the more early accounts which had been sent her of Ottilie, to refresh her recollection with the opinion which the Superior and the Assistant had formed about her, and compare them with her in her own person. For Charlotte was of opinion that we cannot too quickly become acquainted with the character of those with whom we have to live, that we may know what to expect of them; where we may hope to do anything in the way of improvement with them, and what we must make up our minds, once for all, to tolerate and let alone.

This examination led her to nothing new, indeed; but much which she already knew become of greater meaning and importance. Ottilie's moderation in eating and drinking, for instance, became a real distress to her.

The next thing on which the ladies were employed was Ottilie's toilet. Charlotte wished her to appear in clothes of a richer and more *recherché* sort, and at once the clever active girl herself cut out the stuff which had been previously sent to her, and with a very little assistance from others was able, in a short time, to dress herself out most tastefully. The new fashionable dresses set off her figure. An agreeable person, it is true, will show through all disguises; but we always fancy it looks fresher and more graceful when its peculiarities appear under some new drapery. And thus, from the moment of her first appearance, she became more and more a delight to the eyes of all who beheld her. As the emerald refreshes the sight with its beautiful hues, and exerts it is said, a benificent influence on that noble sense, so does human beauty work with far larger potency on the outward and on the inward sense; whoever looks upon it is charmed against the breath of evil, and feels in harmony with himself and with the world.

In many ways, therefore, the party had gained by Ottilie's arrival. The Captain and Edward kept regularly to the hours, even to the minutes, for their general meeting together. They never kept the others waiting for them either for dinner or tea, or for their walks; and they were in less haste, especially in the evenings, to leave the table. This did not escape Charlotte's observation; she watched them both, to see whether one more than the other was not the occasion of it. But she could not perceive any difference. They had both become more companionable. In their conversation they seemed to consider what was best adapted to interest Ottilie; what was most on a level with her capacities and her general knowledge. If she left the room when they were reading or telling stories, they would wait till she returned. They had grown softer and altogether more united.

In return for this, Ottilie's anxiety to be of use increased every day; the more she came to understand the house, its inmates, and their circumstances, the more eagerly she entered into everything, caught every look and every motion; half a word, a sound, was enough for her. With her calm attentiveness, and her easy, unexcited activity, she was always the same. Sitting, rising up, going, coming, fetching, carrying, returning to her place again, it was all in the most perfect repose; a constant change, a constant agreeable movement; while, at the same time, she went about so lightly that her step was almost inaudible.

This cheerful obligingness in Ottilie gave Charlotte the

greatest pleasure. There was one thing, however, which
she did not exactly like, of which she had to speak to her.
" It is very polite in you," she said one day to her, " when
people let anything fall from their hand, to be so quick in
stooping and picking it up for them ; at the same time, it
is a sort of confession that they have a right to require
such attention, and in the world we are expected to be
careful to whom we pay it. Towards women, I will not
prescribe any rule as to how you should conduct yourself.
You are young. To those above you, and older than you,
services of this sort are a duty; towards your equals they
are polite; to those younger than yourself and your inferi-
ors you may show yourself kind and good-natured by
such things, — only it is not becoming in a young lady to
do them for men."

" I will try to forget the habit," replied Ottilie; " I think,
however, you will in the mean time forgive me for my
want of manners, when I tell you how I came by it. We
were taught history at school; I have not gained as much
out of it as I ought, for I never knew what use I was to
make of it; a few little things, however, made a deep impression upon me, among which was the following : —
When Charles the First of England was standing before
his so-called judges, the gold top came off the stick which
he had in his hand, and fell down. Accustomed as he
had been on such occasions to have everything done for
him, he seemed to look round and expect that this time
too some one would do him this little service. No one
stirred, and he stooped down for it himself. It struck me
as so piteous; that from that moment I have never been
able to see any one let a thing fall without myself picking it up. But, of course, as it is not always proper, and

as I cannot," she continued, smiling, "tell my story every time I do it, in future I will try and contain myself."

In the mean time the fine arrangements which the two friends had been led to make for themselves, went uninterruptedly forward. Every day they found something new to think about and undertake.

One day as they were walking together through the village, they had to remark with dissatisfaction how far behindhand it was in order and cleanliness, compared to villages where the inhabitants were compelled by the expense of building-ground to be careful about such things.

"You remember a wish we once expressed when we were travelling in Switzerland together," said the Captain, "that we might have the laying out some country park, and how beautiful we would make it by introducing into some village situated like this, not the Swiss style of building, but the Swiss order and neatness which so much improve it."

"And how well it would answer here! The hill on which the castle stands, slopes down to that projecting angle. The village, you see, is built in a semicircle, regularly enough, just opposite to it. The brook runs between. It is liable to floods; and do observe the way the people set about protecting themselves from them; one with stones, another with stakes; the next puts up a boarding, and a fourth tries beams and planks; no one, of course, doing any good to another with his arrangement, but only hurting himself and the rest too. And then there is the road going along just in the clumsiest way possible, — up hill and down, through the water, and over the stones. If the people would only lay their hands to the business together, it would cost them nothing, but a little labor to run a semicircular wall along here, take the road in behind

it, raising it to the level of the houses, and so give themselves a fair open space in front, making the whole place
clean, and getting rid, once for all, in one good general
work, of all their little trifling ineffectual makeshifts."

"Let us try it," said the Captain, as he ran his eyes
over the lay of the ground, and saw quickly what was to
be done.

"I can undertake nothing in company with peasants
and shopkeepers," replied Edward, "unless I may have
unrestricted authority over them."

"You are not so wrong in that," returned the Captain;
"I have experienced too much trouble myself in life in
matters of that kind. How difficult it is to prevail on a
man to venture boldly on making a sacrifice for an after-
advantage! How hard to get him to desire an end, and
not hesitate at the means! So many people confuse
means with ends; they keep hanging over the first, without having the other before their eyes. Every evil is to
be cured at the place where it comes to the surface, and
they will not trouble themselves to look for the cause
which produces it or the remote effect which results from
it. This is why it is so difficult to get advice listened to,
especially among the many: they can see clearly enough
from day to day, but their scope seldom reaches beyond the morrow; and if it comes to a point where with
some general arrangement one person will gain while
another will lose, there is no prevailing on them to strike
a balance. Works of public advantage can only be
carried through by an uncontrolled absolute authority."

"While they were standing and talking, a man came
up and begged of them. He looked more impudent than
really in want, and Edward, who was annoyed at being
interrupted, after two or three fruitless attempts to get

rid of him by a gentler refusal, spoke sharply to him. The fellow began to grumble and mutter abusively; he went off with short steps, talking about the right of beggars. It was all very well to refuse them an alms, but that was no reason why they should be insulted. A beggar, and everybody else too, was as much under God's protection as a lord. It put Edward out of all patience.

The Captain, to pacify him, said, " Let us make use of this as an occasion for extending our rural police arrangements to such cases. We are bound to give away money, but we do better in not giving it in person, especially at home. We should be moderate and uniform in everything, in our charities as in all else; too great liberality attracts beggars instead of helping them on their way. At the same time there is no harm when one is on a journey, or passing through a strange place, in appearing to a poor man in the street in the form of a chance deity of fortune, and making him some present which shall surprise him. The position of the village and of the castle makes it easy for us to put our charities here on a proper footing. I have thought about it before. The public-house is at one end of the village, a respectable old couple live at the other. At each of these places deposit a small sum of money, and let every beggar, not as he comes in, but as he goes out, receive something. Both houses lie on the road which lead to the castle, so that any one who goes there can be referred to one or the other.

" Come," said Edward, " we will settle that on the spot. The exact sum can be made up another time."

They went to the innkeeper, and to the old couple, and the thing was done.

" I know very well," Edward said, as they were walk-

3*

ing up the hill to the castle together, " that everything in
this world depends on distinctness of idea and firmness of
purpose. Your judgment of what my wife has been
doing in the park was entirely right; and you have
already given me a hint how it might be improved. I
will not deny that I told her of it.

" So I have been led to suspect," replied the Captain;
" and I could not approve of your having done so. You
have perplexed her. She has left off doing anything;
and on this one subject she is vexed with us. She avoids
speaking of it. She has never since invited us to go with
her to the summer-house, although at odd hours she goes
up there with Ottilie."

" We must not allow ourselves to be deterred by that,"
answered Edward. "If I am once convinced about anything good, which could and should be done, I can never
rest till I see it done. We are clever enough at other
times in introducing what we want, into the general conversation; suppose we have out some descriptions of
English parks, with copper-plates, for our evening's amusement. Then we can follow with your plan. We will
treat it first problematically, and as if we were only in
jest. There will be no difficulty in passing into earnest."

The scheme was concerted, and the books were opened.
In each group of designs they first saw a ground-plan of
the spot, with the general character of the landscape,
drawn in its rude, natural state. Then followed others,
showing the changes which had been produced by art, to
employ and set off the natural advantages of the locality.
From these to their own property and their own grounds,
the transition was easy.

Everybody was pleased. The chart which the Captain
had sketched was brought and spread out. The only

difficulty was, that they could not entirely free themselves of the plan in which Charlotte had begun. However, an easier way up the hill was found; a lodge was suggested to be built on the height at the edge of the cliff, which was to have an especial reference to the castle. It was to form a conspicuous object from the castle windows, and from it the spectator was to be able to overlook both the castle and the garden.

The Captain had thought it all carefully over, and taken his measurements; and now he brought up again the village road and the wall by the brook, and the ground which was to be raised behind it.

"Here you see," said he, "while I make this charming walk up the height, I gain exactly the quantity of stone which I require for that wall. Let one piece of work help the other, and both will be carried out most satisfactorily and most rapidly."

"But now," said Charlotte, "comes my side of the business. A certain definite outlay of money will have to be made. We ought to know how much will be wanted for such a purpose, and then we can apportion it out — so much work, and so much money, if not by weeks, at least by months. The cash-box is under my charge. I pay the bills, and I keep the accounts."

"You do not appear to have overmuch confidence in us," said Edward.

"I have not much in arbitrary matters," Charlotte answered. "Where it is a case of inclination, we women know better how to control ourselves than you."

It was settled; the dispositions were made, and the work was begun at once.

The Captain being always on the spot, Charlotte was almost daily a witness to the strength and clearness of his understanding. He, too, learnt to know her better; and it became easy for them both to work together, and thus bring something to completeness. It is with work as with dancing; persons who keep the same step must grow indispensable to one another. Out of this a mutual kindly feeling will necessarily arise; and that Charlotte had a real kind feeling towards the Captain, after she came to know him better, was sufficiently proved by her allowing him to destroy her pretty seat, which in her first plans she had taken such pains in ornamenting, because it was in the way of his own, without experiencing the slightest feeling about the matter.

CHAPTER VII.

NOW that Charlotte was occupied with the Captain, it was a natural consequence that Edward should attach himself more to Ottilie. Independently of this, indeed, for some time past he had begun to feel a silent kind of attraction towards her. Obliging and attentive she was to every one, but his self-love whispered that towards him she was particularly so. She had observed his little fancies about his food. She knew exactly what things he liked, and the way in which he liked them to be prepared; the quantity of sugar which he liked in his tea; and so on. Moreover, she was particularly careful to prevent draughts, about which he was excessively sensitive, and, indeed, about which, with his wife, who could never have air enough, he was often at variance. So, too, she had come to know about fruit-gardens, and flower-gardens; whatever he liked, it was her constant effort to procure for him, and to keep away whatever annoyed him; so that very soon she grew indispensable to him — she became like his guardian angel, and he felt it keenly whenever she was absent. Besides all this, too, she appeared to grow more open and conversable as soon as they were alone together.

Edward, as he had advanced in life, had retained something childish about himself, which corresponded singularly well with the youthfulness of Ottilie. They liked talking of early times, when they had first seen each other; and these reminiscences led them up to the first epoch of Edward's affection for Charlotte. Ottilie declared that she remembered them both as the handsomest pair about the court; and when Edward would question the possibility of this, when she must have been so exceedingly young, she insisted that she recollected one particular incident as clearly as possible. He had come into the room where her aunt was, and she had hid her face in Charlotte's lap — not from fear, but from a childish surprise. She might have added, because he had made so strong an impression upon her — because she had liked him so much.

While they were occupied in this way, much of the business which the two friends had undertaken together had come to a stand still; so that they found it necessary to inspect how things were going on — to work up a few designs and get letters written. For this purpose, they betook themselves to their office, where they found their old copyist at his desk. They set themselves to their work, and soon gave the old man enough to do, without

observing that they were laying many things on his
shoulders which at other times they had always done for
themselves. At the same time, the first design the Captain tried would not answer, and Edward was as unsuccessful with his first letter. They fretted for a while,
planning and erasing, till at last Edward, who was getting
on the worst, asked what o'clock it was. And then it
appeared that the Captain had forgotten, for the first
time for many years, to wind up his chronometer; and
they seemed, if not to feel, at least to have a dim perception, that time was beginning to be indifferent to them.

In the meanwhile, as the gentlemen were thus slacken-
ing in their energy, the activity of the ladies increased all
the more. The every-day life of a family, which is composed of given persons, and is shaped out of necessary
circumstances, may easily receive into itself an extraordinary affection, an incipient passion — may receive it into
itself as into a vessel; and a long time may elapse before
the new ingredient produces a visible effervescence, and
runs foaming over the edge.

With our friends, the feelings which were mutually
arising had the most agreeable effects. Their dispositions
opened out, and a general good will arose out of the
several individual affections. Every member of the party
was happy; and they each shared their happiness with
the rest.

Such a temper elevates the spirit, while it enlarges the
heart, and everything which, under the influence of it,
people do and undertake, has a tendency towards the
illimitable. The friends could not remain any more shut
up at home; their walks extended themselves further
and further. Edward would hurry on before with Ottilie,
to choose the path or pioneer the way; and the Captain

and Charlotte would follow quietly on the track of their more hasty precursors, talking on some grave subject, or delighting themselves with some spot they had newly discovered, or some unexpected natural beauty.

One day their walk led them down from the gate at the right wing of the castle, in the direction of the hotel, and thence over the bridge towards the ponds, along the sides of which they proceeded as far as it was generally thought possible to follow the water; thickly wooded hills sloping directly up from the edge, and beyond these a wall of steep rocks, making further progress difficult, if not impossible. But Edward, whose hunting experience had made him thoroughly familiar with the spot, pushed forward along an overgrown path with Ottilie, knowing well that the old mill could not be far off, which was somewhere in the middle of the rocks there. The path was so little frequented, that they soon lost it; and for a short time they were wandering among mossy stones and thickets; it was not long, however, the noise of the water-wheel speedily telling them that the place which they were looking for was close at hand. Stepping forward on a point of rock, they saw the strange old, dark wooden building in the hollow before them, quite shadowed over with precipitous crags and huge trees. They determined directly to climb down amidst the moss and the blocks of stone. Edward led the way; and when he looked back and saw Ottilie following, stepping lightly, without fear or nervousness, from stone to stone, so beautifully balancing herself, he fancied he was looking at some celestial creature floating above him; while if, as she often did, she caught the hand which in some difficult spot he would offer her, or if she supported herself on his shoulder, then he was left in no doubt that it was a very exquisite human creature who touched him. He almost wished that she might slip or stumble, that he might catch her in his arms and press her to his heart. This, however, he would under no circumstances have done, for more than one reason. He was afraid to wound her, and he was afraid to do her some bodily injury.

What the meaning of this could be, we shall immediately learn. When they had got down, and were seated opposite each other at a table under the trees, and when the miller's wife had gone for milk, and the miller, who had come out to them, was sent to meet Charlotte and the Captain, Edward, with a little embarrassment, began to speak:

"I have a request to make, dear Ottilie; you will forgive me for asking it, if you will not grant it. You make no secret (I am sure you need not make any,) that you wear a miniature under your dress against your breast. It is the picture of your noble father. You could hardly have known him; but in every sense he deserves a place by your heart. Only, forgive me, the picture is exceedingly large, and the metal frame and the glass, if you take up a child in your arms, if you are carrying anything, if the carriage swings violently, if we are pushing through bushes, or just now, as we were coming down these rocks, — cause me a thousand anxieties for you. Any unforseen blow, a fall, a touch, may be fatally injurious to you; and I am terrified at the possibility of it. For my sake do this: put away the picture, not out of your affections, not out of your room; let it have the brightest, the holiest place which you can give it; only do not wear upon your breast a thing, the presence of which seems to me, perhaps from an extravagant anxiety, so dangerous."

Ottilie said nothing, and while he was speaking she kept her eyes fixed straight before her; then, without hesitation and without haste, with a look turned more towards heaven than on · Edward, she unclasped the chain, drew out the picture, and pressed it against her forehead, and then reached it over to her friend, with the words:

"Do you keep it for me till we come home; I cannot give you a better proof how deeply I thank you for your affectionate care."

He did not venture to press the picture to his lips; but he caught her hand and raised it to his eyes. They were, perhaps, two of the most beautiful hands which had ever been clasped together. He felt as if a stone had fallen from his heart, as if a partition-wall had been thrown down between him and Ottilie.

Under the Miller's guidance, Charlotte and the Captain came down by an easier path, and now joined them. There was the meeting, and a happy talk, and then they took some refreshments. They would not return by the same way as they came; and Edward struck into a rocky path on the other side of the stream, from which the ponds were again to be seen. They made their way along it, with some effort, and then had to cross a variety of wood and copse — getting glimpses, on the land side, of a number of villages and manor-houses, with their green lawns and fruit gardens; while very near them, and sweetly situated on a rising ground, a farm lay in the middle of the wood. From a gentle ascent, they had a view, before and behind, which showed them the richness of the country to the greatest advantage; and then, entering a grove of trees, they found themselves, on again emerging from it, on the rock opposite the castle.

They came upon it rather unexpectedly, and were of course delighted. They had made the circuit of a little world; they were standing on the spot where the new building was to be erected, and were looking again at the windows of their own home.

They went down to the summer-house, and sat all four in it for the first time together; nothing was more natural than that with one voice it should be proposed to have the way they had been that day, and which, as it was, had taken them much time and trouble, properly laid out and gravelled, so that people might loiter along it at their leisure. They each said what they thought; and they reckoned up that the circuit, over which they had taken many hours, might be travelled easily with a good road all the way round to the castle, in a single one.

Already a plan was being suggested for making the distance shorter, and adding a fresh beauty to the landscape, by throwing a bridge across the stream, below the mill, where it ran into the lake; when Charlotte brought their inventive imagination somewhat to a stand-still, by putting them in mind of the expense which such an undertaking would involve.

"There are ways of meeting that too," replied Edward; " we have only to dispose of that farm ·in the forest which is so pleasantly situated, and which brings in so little in the way of rent: the sum which will be set free will more than cover what we shall require, and thus, having gained an invaluable walk, we shall receive the interest of well-expended capital in substantial enjoyment — instead of, as now, in the summing up at the ·end of the year, vexing and fretting ourselves over the pitiful little income which is returned for it."

Even Charlotte, with all her prudence, had little to

urge against this. There had been, indeed, a previous intention of selling the farm. The Captain was ready immediately with a plan for breaking up the ground into small portions among the peasantry of the forest. Edward, however, had a simpler and shorter way of managing it. His present steward had already proposed to take it off his hands — he was to pay for it by instalments — and so, gradually, as the money came in, they would get their work forward from point to point.

So reasonable and prudent a scheme was sure of universal approbation, and already, in prospect, they began to see their new walk winding along its way, and to imagine the many beautiful views and charming spots which they hoped to discover in its neighborhood.

To bring it all before themselves with greater fulness of detail, in the evening they produced the new chart. With the help of this they went over again the way that they had come, and found various places where the walk might take a rather different direction with advantage. Their other scheme was now once more talked through, and connected with the fresh design. The site for the new house in the park, opposite the castle, was a second time examined into and approved, and fixed upon for the termination of the intended circuit.

Ottilie had said nothing all this time. At length Edward pushed the chart, which had hitherto been lying before Charlotte, across to her, begging her to give her opinion; she still hesitated for a moment. Edward in his gentlest way again pressed her to let them know what she thought — nothing had as yet been settled — it was all as yet in embryo.

" I would have the house built here," she said, as she pointed with her finger to the highest point of the slope

on the hill. "It is true you cannot see the castle from
thence, for it is hidden by the wood; but for that very
reason you find yourself in another quite new world; you
lose village and houses and all at the same time. The
view of the ponds with the mill, and the hills and mountains in the distance, is singularly beautiful — I have
often observed it when I have been there."

"She is right," Edward cried; "how could we have
overlooked it. This is what you mean, Ottilie, is it not?"
He took a lead pencil, and drew a great black rectangular
figure on the summit of the hill.

It went through the Captain's soul to see his carefully
and clearly-drawn chart disfigured in such a way. He
collected himself, however, after a slight expression of
his disapproval, and went into the idea. "Ottilie is
right," he said; we are ready enough to walk any distance
to drink tea or eat fish, because they would not have
tasted as well at home — we require change of scene and
change of objects. Your ancestors showed their judgment in the spot which they chose for the castle; for it
is sheltered from the wind, with the conveniences of life
close at hand. A place, on the contrary, which is more
for pleasure parties than for a regular residence, may be
very well yonder there, and in the fair time of year the
most agreeable hours may be spent there."

The more they talked it over, the more conclusive was
their judgment in favor of Ottilie; and Edward could not
conceal his triumph that the thought had been hers. He
was as proud as if he had hit upon it himself.

CHAPTER VIII.

EARLY the following morning the Captain examined the spot : he first threw off a sketch of what should be done, and afterwards, when the thing had been more completely decided on, he made a complete design, with accurate calculations and measurements. It cost him a good deal of labor, and the business connected with the sale of the farm had to be gone into, so that both the gentlemen now found a fresh impulse to activity.

The Captain made Edward observe that it would be proper, indeed that it would be a kind of duty, to celebrate Charlotte's birthday with laying the foundation-stone. Not much was wanted to overcome Edward's disinclination for such festivities — for he quickly recollected that a little later Ottilie's birthday would follow, and that he could have a magnificent celebration for that.

Charlotte, to whom all this work and what it would involve was a subject for much serious and almost anxious thought, busied herself in carefully going through the time and outlay which it was calculated would be expended on it. During the day they rarely saw each other, so that the evening meeting was looked forward to with all the more anxiety.

Ottilie meantime was complete mistress of the household — and how could it be otherwise, with her quick methodical ways of working? Indeed, her whole mode of thought was suited better to home life than to the world, and to a more free existence. Edward soon observed that she only walked about with them out of a desire to please; that when she stayed out late with them in the evening it was

because she thought it a sort of social duty, and that she
would often find a pretext in some household matter for
going in again — consequently he soon managed so to
arrange the walks which they took together, that they
should be at home before sunset; and he began again,
what he had long left off, to read aloud poetry — particularly such as had for its subject the expression of a pure
but passionate love.

They ordinarily sat in the evening in the same places
round a small table — Charlotte on the sofa, Ottilie on a
chair opposite to her, and the gentlemen on each side.
Ottilie's place was on Edward's right, the side where he
put the candle when he was reading — at such times she
would draw her chair a little nearer to look over him, for
Ottilie also trusted her own eyes better than another person's lips, and Edward would then always make a move
towards her, that it might be as easy as possible for her —
indeed he would frequently make longer stops than necessary, that he might not turn over before she had got to
the bottom of the page.

Charlotte and the Captain observed this, and exchanged
many a quiet smile at it; but they were both taken by
surprise at another symptom, in which Otttlie's latent feeling accidentally displayed itself.

One evening, which had been partly spoilt for them by
a tedious visit, Edward proposed that they should not
separate so early — he felt inclined for music — he would
take his flute, which he had not done for many days past.
Charlotte looked for the sonatas which they generally
played together, and they were not to be found. Ottilie,
with some hesitation, said that they were in her room —
she had taken them there to copy them.

"And you can, you will, accompany me on the piano?"

cried Edward, his eyes sparkling with pleasure. " I think perhaps I can," Ottilie answered. She brought the music and sat down to the instrument. The others listened, and were sufficiently surprised to hear how perfectly Ottilie had taught herself the piece — but far more surprised were they at the way in which she contrived to adapt herself to Edward's style of playing. Adapt herself, is not the right expression — Charlotte's skill and power enabled her, in order to please her husband, to keep up with him when he went too fast, and hold in for him if he hesitated ; but Ottilie, who had several times heard them play the sonata together, seemed to have learnt it according to the idea·in which they accompanied each other — she had so completely made his defects her own, that a kind of living whole resulted from it, which did not move indeed according to exact rule, but the effect of which was in the highest degree pleasant and delightful. The composer himself would have been pleased to hear his work disfigured in a manner so charming.

Charlotte and the Captain watched this strange unexpected occurrence in silence, with the kind of feeling with which we often observe the actions of children — unable exactly to approve of them, from the serious consequences which may follow, and yet without being able to find fault, perhaps with a kind of envy. For, indeed, the regard of these two for one another was growing also, as well as that of the others — and it was perhaps only the more perilous because they were both stronger, more certain of themselves, and better able to restrain themselves.

The Captain had already begun to feel that a habit which he could not resist was threatening to bind him to Charlotte. He forced himself to stay away at the hour when she commonly used to be at the works; by getting up very early in the morning he contrived to finish there whatever he had to do, and went back to the castle to his work in his own room. The first day or two Charlotte thought it was an accident — she looked for him in every place where she thought he could possibly be. Then she thought she understood him — and admired him all the more.

Avoiding, as the Captain now did, being alone with Charlotte, the more industriously did he labor to hurry forward the preparations for keeping her rapidly-approaching birthday with all splendor. While he was bringing up the new road from below -behind the village, he made the men, under pretence that he wanted stones, begin working at the top as well, and work down, to meet the others; and he had calculated his arrangements so that the two should exactly meet on the eve of the day. The excavations for the new house were already done; the rock was blown away with gunpowder; and a fair foundation-stone had been hewn, with a hollow chamber, and a flat slab adjusted to cover it.

This outward activity, these little mysterious purposes of friendship, prompted by feelings which more or less they were obliged to repress, rather prevented the little party when together from being as lively as usual. Edward, who felt that there was a sort of void, one evening called upon the Captain to fetch his violin — Charlotte should play the piano, and he should accompany her. The Captain was unable to refuse the general request, and they executed together one of the most difficult pieces of music with an ease, and freedom, and feeling, which could not but afford themselves, and the two who were listening to them, the greatest delight. They promised themselves a frequent repetition of it, as well as further practice to-

gether. " They do it better than we, Ottilie," said Edward;
" we will admire them — but we can enjoy ourselves together too."

CHAPTER IX.

THE birthday was come, and everything was ready.
The wall was all complete which protected the raised
village road against the water, and so was the walk;
passing the church, for short time it followed the path
which had been laid out by Charlotte, and then winding
upwards among the rocks, inclined first under the summer-house to the right and then, after a wide sweep, passed
back above it to the right again, and so by degrees out
on to the summit.

A large party had assembled for the occasion. They
went first to church, where they found the whole congregation collected together in their holiday dresses. After
service, they filed out in order; first the boys, then the
young men, then the old: after them came the party from
the castle, with their visitors and retinue; and the village
maidens, young girls, and women, brought up the rear.

At the turn of the walk, a raised stone seat had been
contrived, where the Captain made Charlotte and the
visitors stop and rest. From here they could see over
the whole distance from the beginning to the end —
the troops of men who had gone up before them, the file
of women following, and now drawing up to where they
were. It was lovely weather, and the whole effect was

4

singularly beautiful. Charlotte was taken by surprise, she
was touched, and she pressed the Captain's hand warmly.

They followed the crowd who had slowly ascended,
and were now forming a circle round the spot where the
future house was to stand. The lord of the castle, his
family, and the principal strangers were now invited to
descend into the vault, where the fountain-stone, supported
on one side, lay ready to be let down. A well-dressed
mason, a trowel in one hand and a hammer in the
other, came forward, and with much grace spoke an
address in verse, of which in prose we can give but an
imperfect rendering.

"Three things," he began, "are to be looked to in a
building — that it stand on the right spot; that it be
securely founded; that it be successfully executed. The
first is the business of the master of the house — his and
his only. As in the city the prince and the council alone
determined where a building shall be, so in the country
it is the right of the lord of the soil that he shall say,
'Here my dwelling shall stand; here, and nowhere
else.'"

Edward and Ottilie were standing opposite one another, as these words were spoken; but they did not venture
to look up and exchange glances.

"To the third, the execution, there is neither art nor
handicraft which must not in some way contribute.
But the second, the founding, is the province of the
mason; and, boldly to speak it out, it is the head and
front of all the undertaking — a solemn thing it is — and
our bidding you descend hither is full of meaning. You
are celebrating your festival in the deep of the earth.
Here within this hollow spot, you show us the honor of
appearing as witnesses of our mysterious craft. Presently

we shall lower down this carefully-hewn stone into its place; and soon these earth-walls, now ornamented with fair and worthy persons, will be no more accessible — but will be closed in for ever!

"This foundation-stone, which with its angles typifies the just angles of the building, with the sharpness of its moulding, the regularity of it, and with the truth of its lines to the horizontal and perpendicular, the uprightness and equal height of all the walls, we might now without more ado let down — it would rest in its place with its own weight. But even here there shall not fail of lime and means to bind it. For as human beings who may be well inclined to each other by nature, yet hold more firmly together when the law cements them, so are stones also, whose forms may already fit together, united far better by these binding forces. It is not seemly to be idle among the working, and here you will not refuse to be our fellow laborer," — with these words he reached the trowel to Charlotte, who threw mortar with it under the stone — several of the others were then desired to do the same, and then it was at once let fall. Upon which the hammer was placed next in Charlotte's, and then in the others' hands, to strike six times with it, and conclude, in this expression, the wedlock of the stone with the earth.

"The work of the mason," went on the speaker, "now under the free sky as we are, if it be not done in concealment, yet must pass into concealment — the soil will be laid smoothly in, and thrown over this stone, and with the walls which we rear into the daylight we in the end are seldom remembered. The works of the stone-cutter and the carver remain under the eyes; but for us it is not to complain when the plasterer blots out the last trace of our hands, and appropriates our work to himself; when he overlays it, and smoothes it, and colors it.

"Not from regard for the opinion of others, but from respect for himself, the mason will be faithful in his calling. There is none who has more need to feel in himself the consciousness of what he is. When the house is finished, when the soil is smoothed, and the surface plastered over, and the outside all overwrought with ornament, he can even see in yet through all disguises, and still recognize those exact and careful adjustments, to which the whole is indebted for its being and for its persistence.

"But as the man who commits some evil deed has to fear, that, notwithstanding all precautions, it will one day come to light — so too must he expect who has done some good thing in secret, that it also, in spite of himself, will appear in the day; and therefore we make this foundation-stone at the same time a stone of memorial. Here, in these various hollows which have been hewn into it, many things are now to be buried, as a witness to some far-off world — these metal cases hermetically sealed contain documents in writing; matters of various note are engraved on these plates; in these fair glass bottles we bury the best old wine, with a note of the year of its vintage. We have coins too of many kinds, from the mint of the current year. All this we have received through the liberality of him for whom we build. There is space yet remaining, if guest or spectator desires to offer anything to the after-world!"

After a slight pause the speaker looked round; but, as is commonly the case on such occasions, no one was prepared; they were all taken by surprise. At last, a merry-looking young officer set the example, and said, "If

I am to contribute anything which as yet is not to be found in this treasure-chamber, it shall be a pair of buttons from my uniform — I don't see why they do not deserve to go down to posterity!" No sooner said than done, and then a number of persons found something of the same sort which they could do; the young ladies did not hesitate to throw in some of their side hair combs — smelling bottles and other trinkets were not spared. Only Ottilie hung back; till a kind word from Edward roused her from the abstraction in which she was watching the various things being heaped in. Then she unclasped from her neck the gold chain on which her father's picture had hung, and with a light gentle hand laid it down on the other jewels. Edward rather disarranged the proceedings, by at once, in some haste, having the cover let fall, and fastened down.

The young mason who had been most active through all this, again took his place as orator, and went on, "We lay down this stone for ever, for the establishing the present and the future possessors of this house. But in that we bury this treasure together with it, we do it in the remembrance — in this most enduring of works — of the perishableness of all human things. We remember that a time may come when this cover so fast sealed shall again be lifted: and that can only be when all shall again be destroyed which as yet we have not brought into being.

"But now — now that it at once may begin to be, back with our thoughts out of the future — back into the present. At once, after the feast which we have this day kept together, let us on with our labor; let no one of all those trades which are to work on our foundation, through us keep unwilling holiday. Let the building rise swiftly to its height, and out of the windows, which as yet have no existence, may the master of the house, with his family and with his guests, look forth with a glad heart over his broad lands. To him and to all here present herewith be health and happiness."

With these words he drained a richly cut tumbler at a draught, and flung it into the air, thereby to signify the excess of pleasure by destroying the vessel which had served for such a solemn occasion. This time, however, it fell out otherwise. The glass did not fall back to the earth and indeed without a miracle.

In order to get forward with the buildings, they had already thrown out the whole of the soil at the opposite corner; indeed, they had begun to raise the wall, and for this purpose had reared a scaffold as high as was absolutely necessary. On the occasion of the festival, boards had been laid along the top of this, and a number of spectators were allowed to stand there. It had been meant principally for the advantage of the workmen themselves. The glass had flown up there, and had been caught by one of them, who took it as a sign of good luck for himself. He waved it round without letting it out of his hand, and the letters E and O were to be seen very richly cut upon it, running one into the other. It was one of the glasses which had been executed for Edward when he was a boy.

The scaffoldings were again deserted, and the most active among the party climbed up to look round them, and could not speak enough in praise of the beauty of the prospect on all sides. How many new discoveries does not a person make when on some high point he ascends but a single story higher. Inland many fresh villages came in sight. The line of the river could be traced like

a thread of silver; indeed, one of the party thought that
he distinguished the spires of the capital. On the other
side, behind the wooded hill, the blue peaks of the far-off
mountains were seen rising, and the country immediately
about them was spread out like a map.

"If the three ponds," cried some one, " were but thrown
together to make a single sheet of water, there would be
everything here which is noblest and most excellent."

"That might easily be effected," the Captain said. " In
early times they must have formed all one lake among the
hills here."

" Only I must beseech you to spare my clump of planes
and poplars that stand so prettily by the centre pond,"
said Edward. " See," — he turned to Ottilie, bringing her
a few steps forward, and pointing down, — " those trees I
planted myself."

" How long have they been standing there?" asked
Ottilie.

"Just about as long as you have been in the world,"
replied Edward. " Yes, my dear child, I planted them
when you were still lying in your cradle."

The party now betook themselves back to the castle.
After dinner was over they were invited to walk through
the village to take a glance at what had been done there
as well. At a hint from the Captain, the inhabitants had
collected in front of the houses. They were not standing
in rows, but formed in natural family groups, partly occupied at their evening work, part out enjoying themselves
on the new benches. They had determined, as an agreeable duty which they imposed upon themselves, to have
everything in its present order and cleanliness, at least
every Sunday and holiday.

A little party, held together by such feelings as had

grown up among our friends, is always unpleasantly interrupted by a large concourse of people. All four were delighted to find themselves again alone in the large drawing-room, but this sense of home was a little disturbed by a letter which was brought to Edward, giving notice of fresh guests who were to arrive the following day.

"It is as we supposed," Edward cried to Charlotte. "The Count will not stay away; he is coming to-morrow."

"Then the Baroness, too, is not far off," answered Charlotte.

"Doubtless not," said Edward. "She is coming, too, to-morrow, from another place. They only beg to be allowed to stay for a night; the next day they will go on together."

"We must prepare for them in time, Ottilie," said Charlotte.

"What arrangement shall I desire to be made?" Ottilie asked.

Charlotte gave a general direction, and Ottilie left the room.

The Captain inquired into the relation in which these two persons stood towards one another, and with which he was only very generally acquainted. They had some time before, both being already married, fallen violently in love with one another; a double marriage was not to be interfered with without attracting attention. A divorce was proposed. On the Baroness' side it could be effected, on that of the Count it could not. They were obliged seemingly to separate, but their position towards one another remained unchanged, and though in the winter at the Residence they were unable to be together, they indemnified themselves in the summer, while making tours and staying at watering-places.

They were both slightly older than Edward and Charlotte, and had been intimate with them from early times at court. The connection had never been absolutely broken off, although it was impossible to approve of their proceedings. On the present occasion their coming was most unwelcome to Charlotte; and if she had looked closely into her reasons for feeling it so, she would have found it was on account of Ottilie. The poor innocent girl should not have been brought so early in contact with such an example.

"It would have been more convenient if they had not come till a couple of days later," Edward was saying, as Ottilie re-entered, "till we had finished with this business of the farm. The deed of sale is complete. One copy of it I have here, but we want a second, and our old clerk has fallen ill." The Captain offered his services, and so did Charlotte, but there was something or other to object to both of them.

"Give it to me," cried Ottilie, a little hastily.

"You will never be able to finish it," said Charlotte.

"And really I must have it early the day after to-morrow, and it is long," Edward added.

"It shall be ready," Ottilie cried; and the paper was already in her hands.

The next morning, as they were looking out from their highest windows for their visitors, whom they intended to go some way and meet, Edward said, "Who is that yonder, riding slowly along the road?"

The Captain described accurately the figure of the horseman.

"Then it is he," said Edward; " the particulars, which
4*

you can see better than I, agree very well with the general figure, which I can see too. It is Mittler; but what is he doing, coming riding at such a pace as that?"

The figure came nearer, and Mittler it veritably was. They received him with warm greetings as he came slowly up the steps.

"Why did you not come yesterday? Edward cried, as he approached.

"I do not like your grand festivities," answered he; " but I am come to-day to keep my friend's birthday with you quietly."

"How are you able to find time enough? asked Edward, with a laugh.

"My visit, if you can value it, you owe to an observation which I made yesterday. I was spending a right happy afternoon in a house where I had established peace, and then I heard that a birthday was being kept here. Now this is what I call selfish, after all, said I to myself: you will only enjoy yourself with those whose broken peace you have mended. Why cannot you for once go and be happy with friends who keep the peace for themselves? No sooner said than done. Here I am, as I determined with myself that I would be."

"Yesterday you would have met a large party here; to-day you will find but a small one," said Charlotte; " you will meet the Count and the Baroness, with whom you have had enough to do already, I believe."

Out of the middle of the party, who had all four come down to welcome him, the strange man dashed in the keenest disgust, seizing at the same time his hat and whip. "Some unlucky star is always over me," he cried, " directly I try to rest and enjoy myself. What business have I going out of my proper character? I ought never to have come, and now I am persecuted away. Under one roof with those two I will not remain, and you take care of yourselves. They bring nothing but mischief; their nature is like leaven, and propagates its own contagion."

They tried to pacify him, but it was in vain. "Whoever strikes at marriage," he cried ; — " whoever, either by word or act, undermines this, the foundation of all moral society, that man has to settle with me, and if I cannot become his master, I take care to settle myself out of his way. Marriage is the beginning and the end of all culture. It makes the savage mild; and the most cultivated has no better opportunity for displaying his gentleness. Indissoluble it must be, because it brings so much happiness that what small exceptional unhappiness it may bring counts for nothing in the balance. And what do men mean by talking of unhappiness? Impatience it is which from time to time comes over them, and then they fancy themselves unhappy. Let them wait till the moment is gone by, and then they will bless their good fortune that what has stood so long continues standing. There never can be any adequate ground for separation. The condition of man is pitched so high, in its joys and in its sorrows, that the sum which two married· people owe to one another defies calculation. It is an infinite debt, which can only be discharged through all eternity.

" Its annoyances marriage may often have ; I can well believe that, and it is as it should be. We are all married to our consciences, and there are times when we should be glad to be divorced from them; mine gives me more annoyance than ever a man or a woman can give."

All this he poured out with the greatest vehemence: he would very likely have gone on speaking longer, had not the sound of the postilions' horns given notice of the arrival of the visitors, who, as if on a concerted arrangement, drove into the castle-court from opposite sides at the same moment. Mittler slipped away as their host hastened to receive them, and desiring that his horse might be brought out immediately, rode angrily off.

CHAPTER X.

THE visitors were welcomed and brought in. They were delighted to find themselves again in the same house and in the same rooms where in early times they had passed many happy days, but which they had not seen for a long time. Their friends too were very glad to see them. The Count and the Baroness had both those tall fine figures which please in middle life almost better than in youth. If something of the first bloom had faded off them, yet there was an air in their appearance which was always irresistibly attractive. Their manners too were thoroughly charming. Their free way of taking hold of life and dealing with it, their happy humor, and apparent easy unembarrassment, communicated itself at once to the rest; and a lighter atmosphere hung about the whole party, without their having observed it stealing on them.

The effect made itself felt immediately on the entrance of the new-comers. They were fresh from the fashionable world, as was to be seen at once, in their dress, in their equipment, and in everything about them; and they formed a contrast not a little striking with our friends, their country style, and the vehement feelings which were at work underneath among them. This, however, very soon disappeared in the stream of past recollection and present interests, and a rapid, lively conversation soon united them all. After a short time they again separated. The ladies withdrew to their own apartments, and there found amusement enough in the many things which they had to tell each other, and in setting to work at the same time to examine the new fashions, the spring dresses, bonnets, and such like; while the gentlemen were employing themselves looking at the new travelling chariots, trotting out the horses, and beginning at once to bargain and exchange.

They did not meet again till dinner; in the mean time they had changed their dress. And here, too, the newly-arrived pair showed to all advantage. Everything they wore was new, and in a style which their friends at the castle had never seen, and yet, being accustomed to it themselves, it appeared perfectly natural and graceful.

The conversation was brilliant and well sustained, as, indeed, in the company of such persons everything and nothing appears to interest. They spoke in French that the attendants might not understand what they said, and swept in happiest humor over all that was passing in the great or the middle world. On one particular subject they remained, however, longer than was desirable! It was occasioned by Charlotte asking after one of her early friends, of whom she had to learn, with some distress, that she was on the point of being separated from her husband.

"It is a melancholy thing," Charlotte said, "when we

fancy our absent friends are finally settled, when we believe persons very dear to us to be provided for for life,
suddenly to hear that their fortunes are cast loose once
more; that they have to strike into a fresh path of life,
and very likely a most insecure one."

"Indeed, my dear friend," the Count answered, "it is
our own fault if we allow ourselves to be surprised at
such things.   We please ourselves with imagining matters
of this earth, and particularly matrimonial connections, as
very enduring; and as concerns this last point, the plays
which we see over and over again help to mislead us;
being, as they are, so untrue to the course of the world.
In a comedy we see a marriage as the last aim of a desire which is hindered and crossed through a number of
acts, and at the instant when it is reached the curtain
falls, and the momentary satisfaction continues to ring on
in our ears.   But in the world it is very different.   The
play goes on still behind the scenes, and when the curtain
rises again we may see and hear, perhaps, little enough
of the marriage."

"It cannot be so very bad, however," said Charlotte,
smiling.   "We see people who have gone off the boards
of the theatre, ready enough to undertake a part upon
them again."

"There is nothing to say against that," said the Count.
"In a new character a man may readily venture on a
second trial; and when we know the world we see clearly
that it is only this positive eternal duration of marriage in
a world where everything is in motion, which has anything
unbecoming about it.   A certain friend of mine whose
humor displays itself principally in suggestions for new
laws, maintained that every marriage should be concluded
only for five years.   Five, he said, was a sacred number

— pretty and uneven. Such a period would be long enough for people to learn one another's character, bring a child or two into the world, quarrel, separate, and what was best, get reconciled again. He would often exclaim, 'How happily the first part of the time would pass away!' Two or three years, at least, would be perfect bliss. On one side or other there would not fail to be a wish to have the relation continue longer, and the amiability would increase the nearer they got to the parting time. The indifferent, even the dissatisfied party, would be softened and gained over by such behavior; they would forget, as in pleasant company the hours pass always unobserved, how the time went by, and they would be delightfully surprised when, after the term had run out, they first observed that they had unknowingly prolonged it."

Charming and pleasant as all this sounded, and deep (Charlotte felt it to her soul) as was the moral significance which lay below it, expressions of this kind, on Ottilie's account, were most distasteful to her. She knew very well that nothing was more dangerous than the licentious conversation which treats culpable or semi-culpable actions as if they were common, ordinary, and even laudable, and of such undesirable kind assuredly were all which touched on the sacredness of marriage. She endeavored, therefore, in her skilful way, to give the conversation another turn, and when she found that she could not, it vexed her that Ottilie had managed everything so well that there was no occasion for her to leave the table. In her quiet observant way a nod or a look was enough for her to signify to the head servant whatever was to be done, and everything went off perfectly, although there were a couple of strange men in livery in the way, who were rather a trouble than

a convenience. And so the Count, without feeling Charlotte's hints, went on giving his opinions on the same
subject. Generally, he was little enough apt to be tedious
in conversation; but this was a thing which weighed so
heavily on his heart, and the difficulties which he found in
getting separated from his wife were so great that it had
made him bitter against everything which concerned the
marriage bond, — that very bond which, notwithstanding,
he was so anxiously desiring between himself and the
Baroness.

" The same friend," he went on, " has another law which
he proposes. A marriage shall only be held indissoluble
when either both parties, or at least one or the other,
enter into it for the third time. Such persons must be
supposed to acknowledge beyond a doubt that they find
marriage indispensable for themselves; they have had
opportunities of thoroughly knowing themselves; of
knowing how they conducted themselves in their earlier
unions; whether they have any peculiarities of temper,
which are a more frequent cause of separation than bad
dispositions. People would then observe one another
more closely; they would pay as much attention to the
married as the unmarried, no one being able to tell how
things may turn out."

" That would add no little to the interest of society,"
said Edward. " As things are now, when a man is married
nobody cares any more either for his virtues or for his
vices."

" Under this arrangement," the Baroness struck in,
laughing, " our good hosts have passed successfully over
their two steps, and may make themselves ready for their
third."

" Things have gone happily with them," said the Count.

"In their case death has done with a good will what in others the consistorial courts do with a very bad one."

"Let the dead rest," said Charlotte, with a half serious look.

"Why so," persevered the Count, "when we can remember them with honor? They were generous enough to content themselves with less than their number of years for the sake of the larger good which they could leave behind them."

"Alas! that in such cases," said the Baroness, with a suppressed sigh, "happiness is only bought with the sacrifice of our fairest years."

"Indeed, yes," answered the Count; "and it might drive us to despair, if it were not the same with everything in this world. Nothing goes as we hope. Children do not fulfil what they promise; young people very seldom; — and if they keep their word, the world does not keep its word with them."

Charlotte, who was delighted that the conversation had taken a turn at last, replied cheerfully,

"Well, then, we must content ourselves with enjoying what good we are to have in fragments and pieces, as we can get it; and the sooner we can accustom ourselves to this the better."

"Certainly," the Count answered, "you too have had the enjoyment of very happy times. When I look back upon the years when you and Edward were the loveliest couple at the court, I see nothing now to be compared with those brilliant times, and such magnificent figures. When you two used to dance together, all eyes were turned upon you, fastened upon you, while you saw nothing but each other."

"So much has changed since those days," said Char-

lotte, " that we can listen to such pretty things about
ourselves without our modesty being shocked at them."

" I often privately found fault with Edward," said the
Count, " for not being more firm. Those singular parents
of his would certainly have given way at last; and ten
fair years is no trifle to gain."

" I must take Edward's part," struck in the Baroness.
" Charlotte was not altogether without fault — not altogether free from what we must call prudential considerations; and although she had a real, hearty love for Edward,
and did in her secret soul intend to marry him, I can bear
witness how sorely she often tried him; and it was through
this that he was at last unluckily prevailed upon to leave
her and go abroad, and try to forget her."

Edward bowed to the Baroness, and seemed grateful for
her advocacy.

" And then I must add this," she continued, " in excuse
for Charlotte. The man who was at that time suing for
her, · had for a long time given proofs of his constant
attachment to her; and, when one came to know him
well, was a far more loveable person than the rest of you
may like to acknowledge."

" My dear friend," the Count replied, a little pointedly,
" confess, now, that he was not altogether indifferent to
yourself, and that Charlotte had more to fear from you
than from any other rival. I find it one of the highest
traits in women, that they continue so long in their regard
for a man, and that absence of no duration will serve to
disturb or remove it."

" This fine feature, men possess, perhaps, even more,"
answered the Baroness. " At any rate, I have observed
with you, my dear Count, that no one has more influence
over you than a lady to whom you were once attached.

I have seen you take more trouble to do things when a certain person has asked you, than the friend of this moment would have obtained of you, if she had tried."

"Such a change as that one must bear the best way one can," replied the Count. "But as to what concerns Charlotte's first husband, I could not endure him, because he parted so sweet a pair from one another — a really predestined pair, who, once brought together, have no reason to fear the five years, or be thinking of a second or third marriage."

"We must try," Charlotte said, "to make up for what we then allowed to slip from us."

"Aye, and you must keep to that," said the Count; "your first marriages," he continued, with some vehemence, "were exactly marriages of the true detestable sort. And, unhappily, marriages generally, even the best, have (forgive me for using a strong expression) something awkward about them. They destroy the delicacy of the relation; everything is made to rest on the broad certainty out of which one side or other, at least, is too apt to make their own advantage. It is all a matter of course; and they seem only to have got themselves tied together, that one or the other, or both, may go their own way the more easily."

At this moment, Charlotte, who was determined once for all that she would put an end to the conversation, made a bold effort at turning it, and succeeded. It then became more general. She and her husband and the Captain were able to take a part in it. Even Ottilie had to give her opinion; and the dessert was enjoyed in the happiest humor. It was particularly beautiful, being composed almost entirely of the rich summer fruits in elegant baskets, with epergnes of lovely flowers arranged in exquisite taste.

The new laying-out of the park came to be spoken of; and immediately after dinner they went to look at what was going on. Ottilie withdrew, under pretence of having household matters to look to; in reality, it was to set to work again at the transcribing. The Count fell into conversation with the Captain, and Charlotte afterwards joined them. When they were at the summit of the height, the Captain good-naturedly ran back to fetch the plan, and in his absence the Count said to Charlotte,

"He is an exceedingly pleasing person. He is very well-informed, and his knowledge is always ready. His practical power, too, seems methodical and vigorous. What he is doing here would be of great importance in some higher sphere."

Charlotte listened to the Captain's praises with an inward delight. She collected herself, however, and composedly and clearly confirmed what the Count had said. But she was not a little startled when he continued:

"This acquaintance falls most opportunely for me. I know of a situation for which he is perfectly suited, and I shall be doing the greatest favor to a friend of mine, a man of high rank, by recommending to him a person who is so exactly everything which he desires."

Charlotte felt as if a thunder-stroke had fallen on her. The Count did not observe it: women, being accustomed at all times to hold themselves in restraint, are always able, even in the most extraordinary cases, to maintain an apparent composure; but she heard not a word more of what the Count said, though he went on speaking.

"When I have made up my mind upon a thing," he

added, "I am quick about it. I have put my letter together already in my head, and I shall write it immediately. You can find me some messenger, who can ride off with it this evening."

Charlotte was suffering agonies. Startled with the proposal, and shocked at herself, she was unable to utter a word. Happily, the Count continued talking of his plans for the Captain, the desirableness of which was only too apparent to Charlotte.

It was time that the Captain returned. He came up and unrolled his design before the Count. But with what changed eyes Charlotte now looked at the friend whom she was to lose. In her necessity, she bowed and turned away, and hurried down to the summer-house. Before she was half way there, the tears were streaming from her eyes, and she flung herself into the narrow room in the little hermitage, and gave herself up to an agony, a passion, a despair, of the possibility of which, but a few moments before, she had not had the slightest conception.

Edward had gone with the Baroness in the other direction towards the ponds. This ready-witted lady, who liked to be in the secret about everything, soon observed, in a few conversational feelers which she threw out, that Edward was very fluent and free-spoken in praise of Ottilie. She contrived in the most natural way to lead him out by degrees so completely, that at last she had not a doubt remaining that here was not merely an incipient fancy, but a veritable, full-grown passion.

Married women, if they have no particular love for one another, yet are silently in league together, especially against young girls. The consequences of such an inclination presented themselves only too quickly to her

world-experienced spirit. Added to this, she had been
already, in the course of the day, talking to Charlotte
about Ottilie; she had disapproved of her remaining in
the country, particularly being a girl of so retiring a
character; and she had proposed to take Ottilie with her
to the residence of a friend, who was just then bestowing
geat expense on the education of an only daughter, and
who was only looking about to find some well-disposed
companion for her, — to put her in the place of a second
child, and let her share in every advantage. Charlotte
had taken time to consider. But now this glimpse of the
Baroness into Edward's heart changed what had been
but a suggestion at once into a settled determination;
and the more rapidly she made up her mind about it, the
more she outwardly seemed to flatter Edward's wishes.
Never was there any one more self-possessed than this
lady; and to have mastered ourselves in extraordinary
cases, disposes us to treat even a common case with
dissimulation — it makes us inclined, as we have had to
do so much violence to ourselves, to extend our control
over others, and hold ourselves in a degree compensated
in what we outwardly gain for what we inwardly have
been obliged to sacrifice. To this feeling there is often
joined a kind of secret, spiteful pleasure in the blind,
unconscious ignorance with which the victim walks on
into the snare. It is not the immediately doing as we
please which we enjoy, but the thought of the surprise
and exposure which is to follow. And thus was the
Baroness malicious enough to invite Edward to come
with Charlotte and pay her a visit at the grape-gathering;
and, to his question whether they might bring Ottilie
with them, to frame an answer which, if he pleased, he
might interpret to his wishes.

Edward had already begun to pour out his delight at the beautiful scenery, the broad river, the hills, the rocks, the vineyard, the old castle, the water-parties, and the jubilee at the grape-gathering, the wine pressing, etc., in all of which, in the innocence of his heart, he was only exuberating in the anticipation of the impression which these scenes were to make on the fresh spirit of Ottilie. At this moment they saw her approaching, and the Baroness said quickly to Edward, that he had better say nothing to her of this intended autumn expedition — things which we set our heart upon so long before, so often failing to come to pass. Edward gave his promise; but he obliged his companion to move more quickly to meet her; and at last, when they came very close, he ran on several steps in advance. A heartfelt happiness expressed itself in his whole being. He kissed her hand as he pressed into it a nosegay of wild flowers, which he had gathered on his way.

The Baroness felt bitter to the heart at the sight of it. At the same time that she was able to disapprove of what was really objectionable in this affection, she could not bear to see what was sweet and beautiful in it thrown away on such a poor paltry girl.

When they had collected again at the supper table, an entirely different temper was spread over the party. The Count, who had in the meantime written his letter and dispatched a messenger with it, occupied himself with the Captain, whom he had been drawing out more and more — spending the whole evening at his side, talking of serious matters. The Baroness, who sat on the Count's right, found but small amusement in this; nor did Edward find any more. The latter, first because he was thirsty, and then because he was excited, did not spare

the wine, and attached himself entirely to Ottilie, whom
he had made sit by him.   On the other side, next to the
Captain, sat Charlotte; for her it was hard, it was almost
impossible, to conceal the emotion under which she was
suffering.

The Baroness had sufficient time to make her observations at leisure. She perceived Charlotte's uneasiness,
and occupied as she was with Edward's passion for Ottilie,
she easily satisfied herself that her abstraction and distress
were owing to her husband's behavior; and she set herself to consider in which way she could best compass her
ends.

Supper was over, and the party remained divided.
The Count, whose object was to probe the Captain to
the bottom, had to try many turns before he could arrive at what he wished with so quiet, so little vain, but
so exceedingly laconic a person. They walked up
and down together on one side of the saloon, while Edward, excited with wine and hope, was laughing with
Ottilie at a window, and Charlotte and the Baroness were
walking backwards and forwards, without speaking, on
the other side. Their being so silent, and their standing
about in this uneasy, listless way, had its effect at last in
breaking up the rest of the party   The ladies withdrew
to their rooms, the gentlemen to the other wing of the
castle; and so this day appeared to be concluded.

CHAPTER XI.

EDWARD went with the Count to his room. They continued talking, and he was easily prevailed upon to stay a little longer there. The Count lost himself in old times, spoke eagerly of Charlotte's beauty, which, as a critic, he dwelt upon with much warmth.

" A pretty foot is a great gift of nature," he said. " It is a grace which never perishes. I observed it to-day, as she was walking. I should almost have liked to have kissed her shoe, and repeat that somewhat barbarous but significant practice of the Sarmatians, who know no better way of showing reverence for any one they love or re- spect, than by using his shoe to drink his health out of."

The point of the foot did not remain the only subject of praise between two old acquaintances; they went from the person back upon old stories and adventures, and came on the hindrances which at that time people had thrown in the way of lovers' meetings — what trouble they had taken, what arts they had been obliged to de- vise, only to be able to tell each other that they loved.

"Do you remember," continued the Count, " an adven- ture in which I most unselfishly stood your friend when their High Mightinesses were on a visit to your uncle, and were all together in that great, straggling castle. The day went in festivities and glitter of all sorts; and a part of the night at least in pleasant conversation."

" And you, in the meantime, had observed the back-way which led to the court ladies' quarters," said Edward, " and so managed to effect an interview for me with my beloved."

5

"And she," replied the Count, "thinking more of propriety than of my enjoyment, had kept a frightful old duenna with her. So that, while you two, between looks and words, got on extremely well together, my lot, in the meanwhile, was far from pleasant."

"It was only yesterday," answered Edward, " when we heard that you were coming, that I was talking over the story with my wife, and describing our adventure on returning. We missed the road, and got into the entrance-hall from the garden. Knowing our way from thence so well as we did, we supposed we could get along easily enough. But you remember our surprise on opening the door. The floor was covered over with mattresses, on which the giants lay in rows stretched out and sleeping. The single sentinel at his post looked wonderingly at us; but we, in the cool way young men do things, strode quietly on over the outstretched boots, without disturbing a single one of the snoring children of Anak."

"I had the strongest inclination to stumble," the Count said, "that there might be an alarm given. What a resurrection we should have witnessed."

At this moment the castle clock struck twelve.

"It is deep midnight," the Count added, laughing, "and just the proper time; I must ask you, my dear Baron, to show me a kindness. Do you guide me to-night, as I guided you then. I promised the Baroness that I would see her before going to bed. We have had no opportunity of any private talk together the whole day. We have not seen each other for a long time, and it is only natural that we should wish for a confidential hour. If you will show me the way there, I will manage to get back again; and in any case, there will be no boots for me to stumble over."

"I shall be very glad to show you such a piece of hospitality," answered Edward; "only the three ladies are together in the same wing. Who knows whether we shall not find them still with one another, or make some other mistake, which may have a strange appearance?"

"Do not be afraid," said the Count; "the Baroness expects me. She is sure by this time to be in her own room, and alone."

"Well, then, the thing is easy enough," Edward answered.

He took a candle, and lighted the Count down a private staircase leading into a long gallery. At the end of this, he opened a small door. They mounted a winding flight of stairs, which brought them out upon a narrow landing-place; and then, putting the candle in the Count's hand, he pointed to a tapestried door on the right, which opened readily at the first trial, and admitted the Count, leaving Edward outside in the dark.

Another door on the left led into Charlotte's sleeping-room. He heard her voice, and listened. She was speaking to her maid. "Is Ottilie in bed?" she asked. "No," was the answer; "she is sitting writing in the room below." "You may light the night-lamp," said Charlotte; "I shall not want you any more. It is late. I can put out the candle, and do whatever I may want else myself."

It was a delight to Edward to hear that Ottilie was writing still. She is working for me, he thought triumphantly. Through the darkness, he fancied he could see her sitting all alone at her desk. He thought he would go to her, and see her; and how she would turn to receive him. He felt a longing, which he could not resist, to be near her once more. But, from where he was, there was no way to the apartments which she

occupied. He now found himself immediately at his
wife's door. A singular change of feeling came over him.
He tried the handle, but the bolts were shot. He knocked
gently. Charlotte did not hear him. She was walking
rapidly up and down in the large dressing-room adjoining. She was repeating over and over what, since the
Count's unexpected proposal, she had often enough had
to say to herself. The Captain seemed to stand before
her. At home, and everywhere, he had become her all
in all. And now he was to go; and it was all to be
desolate again. She repeated whatever wise things one
can say to oneself; she even anticipated, as people so
often do, the wretched comfort, that time would come at
last to her relief; and then she cursed the time which
would have to pass before it could lighten her sufferings —
she cursed the dead, cold time when they would be
lightened. At last she burst into tears; they were the
more welcome, since tears with her were rare. She flung
herself on the sofa, and gave herself up unreservedly to
her sufferings. Edward, meanwhile, could not take himself from the door. He knocked again ; and a third time
rather louder; so that Charlotte, in the stillness of the
night, distinctly heard it, and started up in fright. Her
first thought was — it can only be, it must be, the Captain; her second, that it was impossible, She thought
she must have been deceived. But surely she had heard
it ; and she wished, and she feared to have heard it.
She went into her sleeping-room, and walked lightly up
to the bolted tapestry-door. She blamed herself for her
fears. " Possibly it may be the Baroness wanting something," she said to herself; and she called out quietly and
calmly, " Is anybody there ? " A light voice answered,
"It is I." " Who ? " returned Charlotte, not being able

to make out the voice. She thought she saw the Captain's figure standing at the door. In a rather louder tone, she heard the word "Edward!" She drew back the bolt, and her husband stood before her. He greeted her with some light jest. She was unable to reply in the same tone. He complicated the mysterious visit by his mysterious explanation of it.

" Well, then," he said at last, "I will confess, the real reason why I am come is, that I have made a vow to kiss your shoe this evening."

"It is long since you thought of such a thing as that," said Charlotte.

" So much the worse," he answered ; " and so much the better."

She had thrown herself back in an arm-chair, to prevent him from seeing the slightness of her dress. He flung himself down before her, and she could not prevent him from giving her shoe a kiss. And when the shoe came off in his hand, he caught her foot and pressed it tenderly against his breast.

Charlotte was one of those women who, being of a naturally calm temperament, continue in marriage, without any purpose or any effort, the air and character of lovers. She was never expressive towards her husband; generally, indeed, she rather shrank from any warm demonstration on his part. It was not that she was cold, or at all hard and repulsive, but she remained always like a loving bride, who draws back with a kind of shyness even from what is permitted. And so Edward found her this evening, in a double sense. How sorely did she not long that her husband would go; the figure of his friend seemed to hover in the air and reproach her. But what should have had the effect of driving

Edward away only attracted him the more. There
were visible traces of emotion about her. She had been
crying; and tears, which with weak persons detract
from their graces, add immeasurably to the attractiveness
of those whom we know commonly as strong and
self-possessed.

Edward was so agreeable, so gentle, so pressing; he
begged to be allowed to stay with her. He did not
demand it, but half in fun, half in earnest, he tried to
persuade her; he never thought of his rights. At last, as
if in mischief, he blew out the candle.

In the dim lamplight, the inward affection, the imagination, maintained their rights over the real;— it was
Ottilie that was resting in Edward's arms; and the
Captain, now faintly, now clearly, hovered before Charlotte's soul. And so, strangely intermingled, the absent
and the present flowed in a sweet enchantment one into
the other.

And yet the present would not let itself be robbed of
its own unlovely right. They spent a part of the night
talking and laughing at all sorts of things, the more
freely, as the heart had no part in it. But when Edward
awoke in the morning, on his wife's breast, the day
seemed to stare in with a sad, awful look, and the sun to
be shining in upon a crime. He stole lightly from her
side; and she found herself, with strange enough feelings, when she awoke, alone.

CHAPTER XII.

WHEN the party assembled again at breakfast, an attentive observer might have read in the behavior of its various members the different things which were passing in their inner thoughts and feelings. The Count and the Baroness met with the air of happiness which a pair of lovers feel, who, after having been forced to endure a long separation, have mutually assured each other of their unaltered affection. On the other hand, Charlotte and Edward equally came into the presence of the Captain and Ottilie with a sense of shame and remorse. For such is the nature of love that it believes in no rights except its own, and all other rights vanish away before it. Ottilie was in child-like spirits. For her — she was almost what might be called open. The Captain appeared serious. His conversation with the Count, which had roused in him feelings that for some time past had been at rest and dormant, had made him only too keenly conscious that here he was not fulfilling his work, and at bottom was but squandering himself in a half-activity of idleness.

Hardly had their guests departed, when fresh visitors were announced — to Charlotte most welcomely, all she wished for being to be taken out of herself, and to have her attention dissipated. They annoyed Edward, who was longing to devote himself to Ottilie; and Ottilie did not like them either; the copy which had to be finished the next morning early being still incomplete. They staid a long time, and immediately that they were gone she hurried off to her room.

It was now evening. Edward, Charlotte, and the
Captain had accompanied the strangers some little way
on foot, before the latter got into their carriage, and
previous to returning home they agreed to take a walk
along the water-side.

A boat had come, which Edward had had fetched from
a distance, at no little expense; and they decided that
they would try whether it was easy to manage. It was
made fast on the bank of the middle pond, not far from
some old ash trees, on which they calculated to make an
effect in their future improvements. There was to be a
landing-place made there, and under the trees a seat was
to be raised, with some wonderful architecture about it:
it was to be the point for which people were to make
when they went across the water.

"And where had we better have the landing-place on
the other side?" said Edward. "I should think under
my plane trees."

"They stand a little too far to the right," said the
Captain. "You are nearer the castle if you land further
down. However, we must think about it."

The Captain was already standing in the stern of the
boat, and had taken up an oar; Charlotte got in, and
Edward with her — he took the other oar; but as he was
on the point of pushing off, he thought of Ottilie — he
recollected that this water-party would keep him out
late; who could tell when he would get back? He
made up his mind shortly and promptly; sprang back to
the bank, and reaching the other oar to the Captain,
hurried home — making excuses to himself as he ran.

Arriving there he learnt that Ottilie had shut herself
up — she was writing. In spite of the agreeable feeling
that she was doing something for him, it was the keenest

mortification to him not to be able to see her. His impatience increased every moment. He walked up and down the large drawing-room; he tried a thousand things, and could not fix his attention upon any. He was longing to see her alone, before Charlotte came back with the Captain. It was dark by this time, and the candles were lighted.

At last she came in beaming with loveliness: the sense that she had done something for her friend had lifted all her being above itself. She put down the original and her transcript on the table before Edward.

"Shall we collate them?" she said, with a smile.

Edward did not know what to answer. He looked at her — he looked at the transcript. The first few sheets were written with the greatest carefulness in a delicate woman's hand — then the strokes appeared to alter, to become more light and free — but who can describe his surprise as he ran his eyes over the concluding page? "For heaven's sake," he cried, "what is this? this is my hand!" He looked at Ottilie, and again at the paper: the conclusion, especially, was exactly as if he had written it himself. Ottilie said nothing, but she looked at him with her eyes full of the warmest delight. Edward stretched out his arms. "You love me!" he cried: "Ottilie, you love me!" They fell on each other's breast — which had been the first to catch the other it would have been impossible to distinguish.

From that moment the world was all changed for Edward. He was no longer what he had been, and the world was no longer what it had been. They parted — he held her hands; they gazed in each other's eyes. They were on the point of embracing each other again.

5*

Charlotte entered with the Captain. Edward inwardly
smiled at their excuses for having stayed out so long.
Oh! how far too soon you have returned, he said to himself.

They sat down to supper. They talked about the
people who had been there that day. Edward, full of
love and ecstasy, spoke well of every one — always sparing, often approving. Charlotte, who was not altogether
of his opinion remarked this temper in him, and jested
with him about it — he who had always the sharpest
thing to say on departed visitors, was this evening so
gentle and tolerant.

With fervor and heartfelt conviction, Edward cried,
"One has only to love a single creature with all one's
heart, and the whole world at once looks lovely!"

Ottilie dropped her eyes on the ground, and Charlotte
looked straight before her.

The Captain took up the word, and said, "It is the
same with deep feelings of respect and reverence; we first
learn to recognize what there is that is to be valued in
the world, when we find occasion to entertain such sentiments towards a particular object."

Charlotte made an excuse to retire early to her room,
where she could give herself up to thinking over what
had passed in the course of the evening between herself
and the Captain.

When Edward sprang on shore, and, pushing off the
boat, had himself committed his wife and his friend to the
uncertain element, Charlotte found herself face to face with
the man on whose account she had been already secretly
suffering so bitterly, sitting in the twilight before her, and
sweeping along the boat with the sculls in easy motion.
She felt a depth of sadness, very rare with her, weighing

on her spirits. The undulating movement of the boat, the splash of the oars, the faint breeze playing over the watery mirror, the sighing of the reeds, the long flight of the birds, the fitful twinkling of the first stars — there was something spectral about it all in the universal stillness. She fancied her friend was bearing her away to set her on some far-off shore, and leave her there alone; strange emotions were passing through her, and she could not give way to them and weep.

The Captain was describing to her the manner in which, in his opinion, the improvements should be continued. He praised the construction of the boat; it was so convenient, he said, because one person could so easily manage it with a pair of oars. She should herself learn how to do this; there was often a delicious feeling in floating along alone upon the water, one's own ferryman and steersman.

The parting which was impending, sank on Charlotte's heart as he was speaking. Is he saying this on purpose? She thought to herself. Does he know it yet? Does he suspect it? or is it only accident; and is he unconsciously foretelling me my fate?

A weary, impatient heaviness took hold of her; she begged him to make for land as soon as possible, and return with her to the castle.

It was the first time that the Captain had been upon the water, and, though generally he had acquainted himself with its depth, he did not know accurately the particular spots. Dusk was coming on; he directed his course to a place where he thought it would be easy to get on shore, and from which he knew the footpath which led to the castle was not far distant. Charlotte, however, repeated her wish to get to land quickly, and the place which he thought of being at a short distance, he gave it up, and exerting himself as much as he possibly could, made straight for the bank. Unhappily the water was shallow, and he ran aground some way off from it. From the rate at which he was going the boat was fixed fast, and all his efforts to move it were in vain. What was to be done? There was no alternative but to get into the water and carry his companion ashore.

It was done without difficulty or danger. He was strong enough not to totter with her, or give her any cause for anxiety; but in her agitation she had thrown her arms about his neck. He held her fast, and pressed her to himself — and at last laid her down upon a grassy bank, not without emotion and confusion .... she still lay upon his neck .... he caught her up once more in his arms and pressed a warm kiss upon her lips. The next moment he was at her feet: he took her hand, and held it to his mouth, and cried,

"Charlotte, will you forgive me?"

The kiss which he had ventured to give, and which she had all but returned to him, brought Charlotte to herself again — she pressed his hand — but she did not attempt to raise him up. She bent down over him, and laid her hand upon his shoulder, and said,

"We cannot now prevent this moment from forming an epoch in our lives; but it depends on us to bear ourselves in a manner which shall be worthy of us. You must go away, my dear friend; and you are going. The Count has plans for you, to give you better prospects — I am glad, and I am sorry. I did not mean to speak of it till it was certain: but this moment obliges me to tell you my secret ..... Since it does not depend on ourselves to alter our feelings, I can only forgive you, I can only

forgive myself, if we have the courage to alter our situation." She raised him up, took his arm to support herself,
and they walked back to the castle without speaking.

But now she was standing in her own room, where she
had to feel and to know that she was Edward's wife. Her
strength and the various discipline in which through life
she had trained herself, came to her assistance in the conflict. Accustomed as she had always been to look steadily
into herself and to control herself, she did not now find it
difficult, with an earnest effort, to come to the resolution
which she desired. She could almost smile when she
remembered the strange visit of the night before. Suddenly she was seized with a wonderful instinctive feeling,
a thrill of fearful delight which changed into holy hope
and longing. She knelt earnestly down, and repeated
the oath which she had taken to Edward before the altar.

Friendship, affection, renunciation, floated in glad,
happy images before her. She felt restored to health and
to herself. A sweet weariness came over her. She lay
down, and sunk into a calm, quiet sleep.

CHAPTER XIII.

EDWARD, on his part, was in a very different temper.
So little he thought of sleeping that it did not once
occur to him even to undress himself. A thousand times
he kissed the transcript of the document, but it was the
beginning of it, in Ottilie's childish, timid hand; the end
he scarcely dared to kiss, for he thought it was his own

hand which he saw. Oh, that it were another document! he whispered to himself; and, as it was, he felt it was the sweetest assurance that his highest wish would be fulfilled. Thus it remained in his hands, thus he continued to press it to his heart, although disfigured by a third name subscribed to it. The waning moon rose up over the wood. The warmth of the night drew Edward out into the free air. He wandered this way and that way; he was at once the most restless and the happiest of mortals. He strayed through the gardens — they seemed too narrow for him; he hurried out into the park, and it was too wide. He was drawn back toward the castle; he stood under Ottilie's window. He threw himself down on the steps of the terrace below. "Walls and bolts," he said to himself, "may still divide us, but our hearts are not divided. If she were here before me, into my arms she would fall, and I into hers; and what can one desire but that sweet certainty!" All was stillness round him; not a breath was moving; — so still it was, that he could hear the unresting creatures underground at their work, to whom day or night are alike. He abandoned himself to his delicious dreams; at last he fell asleep, and did not wake till the sun with his royal beams was mounting up in the sky and scattering the early mists.

He found himself the first person awake on his domain. The laborers seemed to be staying away too long: they came; he thought they were too few, and the work set out for the day too slight for his desires. He inquired for more workmen; they were promised, and in the course of the day they came. But these, too, were not enough for him to carry his plans out as rapidly as he wished. To do the work gave him no pleasure any longer; it should all be done. And for whom? The paths should be gravelled that Ottilie might walk pleasantly upon them; seats should be made at every spot and corner that Ottilie might rest on them. The new park house was hurried forward. It should be finished for Ottilie's birthday. In all he thought and all he did, there was no more moderation. The sense of loving and of being loved, urged him out into the unlimited. How changed was now to him the look of all the rooms, their furniture, and their decorations! He did not feel as if he was in his own house any more. Ottilie's presence absorbed everything, He was utterly lost in her; no other thought ever rose before him; no conscience disturbed him; every restraint which had been laid upon his nature burst loose. His whole being centered upon Ottilie. This impetuosity of passion did not escape the Captain, who longed, if he could, to prevent its evil consequences. All those plans which were now being hurried on with this immoderate speed, had been drawn out and calculated for a long, quiet, easy execution. The sale of the farm had been completed; the first instalment had been paid. Charlotte, according to the arrangement, had taken possession of it. But the very first week after, she found it more than usually necessary to exercise patience and resolution, and to keep her eye on what was being done. In the present hasty style of proceeding, the money which had been set apart for the purpose would not go far.

Much had been begun, and much yet remained to be done. How could the Captain leave Charlotte in such a situation? They consulted together, and agreed that it would be better that they themselves should hurry on the works, and for this purpose employ money which could be made good again at the period fixed for the discharge

of the second instalment of what was to be paid for the
farm. It could be done almost without loss. They
would have a freer hand. Everything would progress
simultaneously. There were laborers enough at hand,
and they could get more accomplished at once, and arrive swiftly and surely at their aim. Edward gladly gave
his consent to a plan which so entirely coincided with his
own views.

During this time Charlotte persisted with all her heart
in what she had determined for herself, and her friend stood
by her with a like purpose, manfully. This very circumstance, however, produced a greater intimacy between
them. They spoke openly to one another of Edward's
passion, and consulted what had better be done. Charlotte kept Ottilie more about herself, watching her nar-
rowly; and the more she understood her own heart, the
deeper she was able to penetrate into the heart of the
poor girl. She saw no help for it, except in sending her
away.

It now appeared a happy thing to her that Luciana had
gained such high honors at the school; for her great
aunt, as soon as she heard of it, desired to take her entirely to herself, to keep her with her, and bring her out
into the world. Ottilie could, therefore, return thither.
The Captain would leave them well provided for, and
everything would be as it had been a few months before;
indeed, in many respects better. Her own position in
Edward's affection, Charlotte thought she could soon recover; and she settled it all, and laid it all out before
herself so sensibly that she only strengthened herself
more completely in her delusion, as if it were possible for
them to return within their old limits, — as if a bond

which had been violently broken could again be joined together as before.

In the mean time Edward felt very deeply the hindrances which were thrown in his way. He soon observed that they were keeping him and Ottilie separate; that they made it difficult for him to speak with her alone, or even to approach her, except in the presence of others. And while he was angry about this, he was angry at many things besides. If he caught an opportunity for a few hasty words with Ottilie, it was not only to assure her of his love, but to complain of his wife and of the Captain. He never felt that with his own irrational haste he was on the way to exhaust the cash-box. He found bitter fault with them because in the execution of the work they were not keeping to the first agreement, and yet he had been himself a consenting party to the second; indeed, it was he who had occasioned it and made it necessary.

Hatred is a partisan, but love is even more so. Ottilie also estranged herself from Charlotte and the Captain. As Edward was complaining one day to Ottilie of the latter, saying that he was not treating him like a friend, or, under the circumstances, acting quite uprightly, she answered unthinkingly, "I have once or twice had a painful feeling that he was not quite honest with you. I heard him say once to Charlotte, 'If Edward would but spare us that eternal flute of his! He can make nothing of it, and it is too disagreeable to listen to him.' You may imagine how it hurt me, when I like accompanying you so much."

She had scarcely uttered the words when her conscience whispered to her that she had much better have been silent. However, the thing was said. Edward's features

worked violently. Never had anything stung him more.
He was touched on his tenderest point. It was his
amusement; he followed it like a child. He never made
the slightest pretensions; what gave him pleasure should
be treated with forbearance by his friends. He never
thought how intolerable it is for a third person to have
his ears lacerated by an unsuccessful talent. He was
indignant; he was hurt in a way which he could not
forgive. He felt himself discharged from all obligations.

The necessity of being with Ottilie, of seeing her,
whispering to her, exchanging his confidence with her,
increased with every day. He determined to write to
her, and ask her to carry on a secret correspondence
with him. The strip of paper on which he had, laconically
enough, made his request, lay on his writing-table, and
was swept off by a draught of wind as his valet entered
to dress his hair. The latter was in the habit of trying
the heat of the iron by picking up any scraps of paper
which might be lying about. This time his hand fell on
the billet; he twisted it up hastily, and it was burnt.
Edward observing the mistake, snatched it out of his
hand. After the man was gone, he sat himself down to
write it over again. The second time it would not run
so readily off his pen. It gave him a little uneasiness; he
hesitated, but he got over it. He squeezed the paper
into Ottilie's hand the first moment he was able to approach her. Ottilie answered him immediately. He put
the note unread in his waistcoat pocket, which, being
made short in the fashion of the time, was shallow, and
did not hold it as it ought. It worked out, and fell without his observing it on the ground. Charlotte saw it,

picked it up, and after giving a hasty glance at it, reached it to him.

"Here is something in your handwriting," she said, "which you may be sorry to lose."

He was confounded. Is she dissembling? he thought to himself. Does she know what is in the note, or is she deceived by the resemblance of the hand? He hoped, he believed the latter. He was warned — doubly warned; but those strange accidents, through which a higher intelligence seems to be speaking to us, his passion was not able to interpret. Rather, as he went further and further on, he felt the restraint under which his friend and his wife seemed to be holding him the more intolerable. His pleasure in their society was gone. His heart was closed against them, and though he was obliged to endure their society, he could not succeed in re-discovering or re-animating within his heart anything of his old affection for them. The silent reproaches which he was forced to make to himself about it, were disagreeable to him. He tried to help himself with a kind of humor which, however, being without love, was also without its usual grace.

Over all such trials, Charlotte found assistance to rise in her own inward feelings. She knew her own determination. Her own affection, fair and noble as it was she would utterly renounce.

And sorely she longed to go to the assistance of the other two. Separation, she knew well, would not alone suffice to heal so deep a wound. She resolved that she would speak openly about it to Ottilie herself. But she could not do it. The recollection of her own weakness stood in her way. She thought she could talk generally to her about the sort of thing. But general expressions about " the sort of thing," fitted her own case equally well, and she could not bear to touch it. Every hint which she would give Ottilie, recoiled back on her own heart. She would warn, and she was obliged to feel that she might herself still be in need of warning.

She contented herself, therefore, with silently keeping the lovers more apart, and by this gained nothing. The slight hints which frequently escaped her had no effect upon Ottilie; for Ottilie had been assured by Edward that Charlotte was devoted to the Captain, that Charlotte herself wished for a separation, and he was at this moment considering the readiest means by which it could be brought about.

Ottilie, led by the sense of her own innocence along the road to the happiness for which she longed, only lived for Edward. Strengthened by her love for him in all good, more light and happy in her work for his sake, and more frank and open towards others, she found herself in a heaven upon earth.

So all together, each in his or her own fashion, reflecting or unreflecting, they continued on the routine of their lives. All seemed to go its ordinary way, as, in monstrous cases, when everything is at stake, men will still live on, as if it were all nothing.

CHAPTER XIV.

IN the mean time a letter came from the Count to the Captain — two, indeed — one which he might produce, holding out fair, excellent prospects in the distance; the other containing a distinct offer of an immediate situation, a place of high importance and responsibility at the Court, his rank as Major, a very considerable salary, and other advantages. A number of circumstances, however, made it desirable that for the moment he should not speak of it, and consequently he only informed his friends of his distant expectations, and concealed what was so nearly impending.

He went warmly on, at the same time, with his present occupation, and quietly made arrangements to secure the works being all continued without interruption after his departure. He was now himself desirous that as much as possible should be finished off at once, and was ready to hasten things forward to prepare for Ottilie's birthday. And so, though without having come to any express understanding, the two friends worked side by side together. Edward was now well pleased that the cash-box was filled by their having taken up money. The whole affair went forward at fullest speed.

The Captain had done his best to oppose the plan of throwing the three ponds together into a single sheet of water. The lower embankment would have to be made much stronger, the two intermediate embankments to be taken away, and altogether, in more than one sense, it seemed a very questionable proceeding. However, both these schemes had been already undertaken; the soil which was removed above, being carried at once down to where it was wanted. And here there came opportunely on the scene a young architect, an old pupil of the Captain, who partly by introducing workmen who understood work of this nature, and partly by himself, whenever it was possible, contracting for the work itself,

advanced things not a little, while at the same time they
could feel more confidence in their being securely and
lastingly executed. In secret this was a great pleasure
to the Captain. He could now be confident that his
absence would not be so severely felt. It was one of the
points on which he was most resolute with himself, never
to leave anything which he had taken in hand uncom-
pleted, unless he could see his place satisfactorily supplied. And he could not but hold in small respect,
persons who introduce confusion around themselves only
to make their absence felt, and are ready to disturb in
wanton selfishness what they will not be at hand to
restore.

So they labored on, straining every nerve to make
Ottilie's birthday splendid, without any open acknowledgment that this was what they were aiming at, or,
indeed, without their directly acknowledging it to themselves. Charlotte wholly free from jealousy as she was,
could not think it right to keep it as a real festival.
Ottilie's youth, the circumstances of her fortune, and her
relationship to their family, were not at all such as made
it fit that she should appear as the queen of the day;
and Edward would not have it talked about, because
everything was to spring out, as it were, of itself, with a
natural and delightful surprise.

They, therefore, came all of them to a sort of tacit understanding that on this day, without further circumstance, the new house in the park was to be opened, and
they might take the occasion to invite the neighborhood
and give a holiday to their own people. Edward's passion, however, knew no bounds. Longing as he did to
give himself to Ottilie, his presents and his promises must
be infinite. The birthday gifts which on the great occa-

sion. he was to offer to her seemed, as Charlotte had
arranged them, far too insignificant. He spoke to his valet,
who had the care of his wardrobe, and who consequently
had extensive acquaintance among the tailors and mercers
and fashionable milliners; and he, who not only understood himself what valuable presents were, but also the
most graceful way in which they should be offered, immediately ordered an elegant box, covered with red mo-
rocco and studded with steel nails, to be filled with
presents worthy of such a shell. Another thing, too, he
suggested to Edward. Among the stores at the castle
was a small show of fireworks which had never been let
off. It would be easy to get some more, and have something really fine. Edward caught the idea, and his servant promised to see to its being executed. This matter
was to remain a secret.

While this was going on, the Captain, as the day drew
nearer, had been making arrangements for a body of police to be present — a precaution which he always thought
desirable when large numbers of men are to be brought
together. And, indeed, against beggars, and against all
other inconveniences by which the pleasure of a festival
can be disturbed, he had made effectual provision.

Edward.and his confidant, on the contrary, were mainly
occupied with their fireworks. They were to be let off
on the side of the middle water in front of the great ash-
tree. The party were to be collected on the opposite
side, under the planes, that at a sufficient distance from
the scene, in ease and safety, they might see them to the
best effect, with the reflections on the water, the water-
rockets, and floating-lights, and all the other designs.

Under some other pretext, Edward had the ground
underneath the plane-trees cleared of bushes and grass

and moss. And now first could be seen the beauty of their forms, together with their full height and spread, right up from the earth. He was delighted with them. It was just this very time of the year that he had planted them. How long ago could it have been? he said to himself. As soon as he got home, he turned over the old diary books, which his father, especially when in the country, was very careful in keeping. He might not find an entry of this particular planting, but another important domestic matter, which Edward well remembered, and which had occurred on the same day, would surely be mentioned. He turned over a few volumes. The circumstance he was looking for was there. How amazed, how overjoyed he was, when he discovered the strangest coincidence! The day and the year on which he had planted those trees, was the very day, the very year, when Ottilie was born.

CHAPTER XV.

THE long-wished-for morning dawned at last on Edward; and very soon a number of guests arrived. They had sent out a large number of invitations, and many who had missed the laying of the foundation-stone, which was reported to have been so charming, were the more careful not to be absent on the second festivity.

Before dinner the carpenter's people appeared, with music, in the court of the castle. They bore an immense garland of flowers, composed of a number of single

wreaths, winding in and out, one above the other; salut-
ing the company, they made request, according to custom,
for silk handkerchiefs and ribbons, at the hands of the
fair sex, with which to dress themselves out. When the
castle party went into the dining-hall, they marched off
singing and shouting, and after amusing themselves a
while in the village, and coaxing many a ribbon out of the
women there, old and young, they came at last, with
crowds behind them and crowds expecting them, out
upon the height where the park-house was now standing.
After dinner, Charlotte rather held back her guests. She
did not wish that there should be any solemn or formal
procession, and they found their way in little parties,
broken up, as they pleased, without rule or order, to the
scene of action. Charlotte staid behind with Ottilie, and
did not improve matters by doing so. For Ottilie being
really the last that appeared, it seemed as if the trumpets
and the clarionets had only been waiting for her, and as
if the gayeties had been ordered to commence directly on
her arrival.

To take off the rough appearance of the house, it had
been hung with green boughs and flowers. They had
dressed it out in an architectural fashion, according to a
design of the Captain's; only that, without his knowledge,
Edward had desired the Architect to work in the date
upon the cornice in flowers, and this was necessarily permitted to remain. The Captain had only arrived on the
scene in time to prevent Ottilie's name from figuring in
splendor on the gable. The beginning, which had been
made for this, he contrived to turn skilfully to some other
use, and to get rid of such of the letters as had been
already finished.

The garland was set up, and was to be seen far and
6

wide about the country. The flags and the ribbons
fluttered gayly in the air; and a short oration was, the
greater part of it, dispersed by the wind. The solemnity
was at an end. There was now to be a dance on the
smooth lawn in front of the building, which had been en-
closed with boughs and branches. A gayly-dressed working mason took Edward up to a smart-looking girl of the
village, and called himself upon Ottilie, who stood out
with him. These two couples speedily found others to
follow them, and Edward contrived pretty soon to change
partners, catching Ottilie, and making the round with
her. The younger part of the company joined merrily in
the dance with the people, while the elder among them
stood and looked on.

Then, before they broke up and walked about, an order
was given that they should all collect again at sunset
under the plane-trees. Edward was the first upon the
spot, ordering everything, and making his arrangements
with his valet, who was to be on the other side, in company with the firework-maker, managing his exhibition
of the spectacle.

The Captain was far from satisfied at some of the
preparations which he saw made; and he endeavored to
get a word with Edward about the crush of spectators
which was to be expected. But the latter, somewhat
hastily; begged that he might be allowed to manage this
part of the day's amusements himself.

The upper end of the embankment having been recently raised, was still far from compact. It had been
staked, but there was no grass upon it, and the earth was
uneven and insecure. The crowd pressed on, however,
in great numbers. The sun went down, and the castle
party was served with refreshments under the plane-trees,

to pass the time till it should have become sufficiently dark. The place was approved of beyond measure, and they looked forward to frequently enjoying the view over so lovely a sheet of water, on future occasions.

A calm evening, a perfect absence of wind, promised everything in favor of the spectacle, when suddenly loud and violent shrieks were heard. Large masses of the earth had given way on the edge of the embankment, and a number of people were precipitated into the water. The pressure from the throng had gone on increasing till at last it had become more than the newly-laid soil would bear, and the bank had fallen in. Everybody wanted to obtain the best place, and now there was no getting either backwards or forwards.

People ran this and that way, more to see what was going on than to render assistance. What could be done when no one could reach the place?

The Captain, with a few determined persons, hurried down and drove the crowd off the embankment back upon the shore; in order that those who were really of service might have free room to move. One way or another they contrived to seize hold of such as were sinking; and with or without assistance all who had been in the water were got out safe upon the bank, with the exception of one boy, whose struggles in his fright, instead of bringing him nearer to the embankment, had only carried him further from it. His strength seemed to be failing — now only a hand was seen above the surface, and now a foot. By an unlucky chance the boat was on the opposite shore filled with fireworks — it was a long business to unload it, and help was slow in coming. The Captain's resolution was taken; he flung off his coat; all eyes were directed towards him, and his sturdy vigorous figure gave every one hope and confidence: but a cry of surprise rose out of the crowd as they saw him fling himself into the water — every eye watched him as the strong swimmer swiftly reached the boy, and bore him, although to appearance dead, to the embankment.

Now came up the boat. The Captain stepped in and examined whether there were any still missing, or whether they were all safe. The surgeon was speedily on the spot, and took charge of the inanimate boy. Charlotte joined them, and entreated the Captain to go now and take care of himself, to hurry back to the castle and change his clothes. He would not go, however, till persons on whose sense he could rely, who had been close to the spot at the time of the accident, and who had assisted in saving those who had fallen in, assured him that all were safe.

Charlotte saw him on his way to the house, and then she remembered that the wine and the tea, and everything else which he could want, had been locked up, for fear any of the servants should take advantage of the disorder of the holiday, as on such occasions they are too apt to do. She hurried through the scattered groups of her company, which were loitering about the plane-trees. Edward was there, talking to every one — beseeching every one to stay. He would give the signal directly, and the fireworks should begin. Charlotte went up to him, and entreated him to put off an amusement which was no longer in place, and which at the present moment no one could enjoy. She reminded him of what ought to be done for the boy who had been saved, and for his preserver.

"The surgeon will do whatever is right, no doubt," replied Edward. "He is provided with everything which he can want, and we should only be in the way if we crowded about him with our anxieties."

Charlotte persisted in her opinion, and made a sign to Ottilie, who at once prepared to retire with her. Edward seized her hand, and cried, "We will not end this day in a lazaretto. She is too good for a sister of mercy. Without us, I should think, the half-dead may wake, and the living dry themselves."

Charlotte did not answer, but went. Some followed her — others followed these : in the end, no one wished to be the last, and all followed. Edward and Ottilie found themselves alone under the plane-trees. He insisted that stay he would, earnestly, passionately, as she entreated him to go back with her to the castle. "No, Ottilie!" he cried; "the extraordinary is not brought to pass in the smooth common way — the wonderful accident of this evening brings us more speedily together. You are mine — I have often said it to you, and sworn it to you. We will not say it and swear it any more — we will make it BE."

The boat came over from the other side. The valet was in it — he asked, with some embarrassment, what his master wished to have done with the fireworks?

"Let them off!" Edward cried to him: "let them off! — It was only for you that they were provided, Ottilie, and you shall be the only one to see them! Let me sit beside you, and enjoy them with you." Tenderly, timidly, he sat down at her side, without touching her.

Rockets went hissing up — cannon thundered — Roman candles shot out their blazing balls — squibs flashed and darted — wheels spun round, first singly, then in pairs, then all at once, faster and faster, one after the other, and more and more together. Edward, whose bosom was on fire, watched the blazing spectacle with eyes gleaming with delight; but Ottilie, with her delicate and nervous feelings, in all this noise and fitful blazing and flashing, found more to distress her than to please. She leant shrinking against Edward, and he, as she drew to him and clung to him, felt the delightful sense that she belonged entirely to him.

The night had scarcely reassumed its rights, when the moon rose and lighted their path as they walked back. A figure, with his hat in his hand, stepped across their way, and begged in alms of them — in the general holiday he said that he had been forgotten. The moon shone upon his face, and Edward recognized the features of the importunate beggar; but, happy as he then was, it was impossible for him to be angry with any one. He could not recollect that, especially for that particular day, begging had been forbidden under the heaviest penalties — he thrust his hand into his pocket, took the first coin which he found, and gave the fellow a piece of gold. His own happiness was so unbounded that he would have liked to have shared it with every one.

In the mean time all had gone well at the castle. The skill of the surgeon, every thing which was required being ready at hand, Charlotte's assistance — all had worked together, and the boy was brought to life again. The guests dispersed, wishing to catch a glimpse or two of what was to be seen of the fireworks from the distance; and, after a scene of such confusion, were glad to get back to their own quiet homes.

The Captain also, after having rapidly changed his dress, had taken an active part in what required to be done. It was now all quiet again, and he found himself alone with Charlotte — gently and affectionately he now told her that his time for leaving them approached. She had gone through so much that evening, that this discovery made but a slight impression upon her — she had seen how her friend could sacrifice himself; how he had saved another, and had himself been saved. These strange incidents seemed to foretell an important future to her — but not an unhappy one.

Edward, who now entered with Ottilie, was informed at once of the impending departure of the Captain. He suspected that Charlotte had known longer how near it was; but he was far too much occupied with himself, and with his own plans, to take it amiss, or care about it.

On the contrary, he listened attentively, and with signs of pleasure, to the account of the excellent and honorable position in which the Captain was to be placed. The course of the future was hurried impetuously forward by his own secret wishes. Already he saw the Captain married to Charlotte, and himself married to Ottilie. It would have been the richest present which any one could have made him, on the occasion of the day's festival!

But how surprised was Ottilie, when, on going to her room, she found upon the table the beautiful box! Instantly she opened it; inside, all the things were so nicely packed and arranged, that she did not venture to take them out, she scarcely even ventured to lift them. There were muslin, cambric, silk, shawls and lace, all rivalling each other in delicacy, beauty, and costliness — nor were ornaments forgotten. The intention had been, as she saw well, to furnish her with more than one complete suit of clothes: but it was all so costly, so little like what she had been accustomed to, that she scarcely dared, even in thought, to believe it could be really for her.

CHAPTER XVI.

THE next morning the Captain had disappeared, having left a grateful, feeling letter addressed to his friends upon his table. He and Charlotte had already taken a half leave of each other the evening before — she felt that the parting was for ever, and she resigned herself to it; for in the Count's second letter, which the Captain had at last shown to her, there was a hint of a prospect of an advantageous marriage, and, although he had paid no attention to it at all, she accepted it for as good as certain, and gave him up firmly and fully.

Now, therefore, she thought that she had a right to require of others the same control over themselves which she had exercised herself: it had not been impossible to her, and it ought not to be impossible to them. With this feeling she began the conversation with her husband; and she entered upon it the more openly and easily, from a sense that the question must now, once for all, be decisively set at rest.

" Our friend has left us," she said; " we are now once more together as we were — and it depends upon ourselves whether we choose to return altogether into our old position."

Edward, who heard nothing except what flattered his own passion, believed that Charlotte, in these words, was alluding to her previous widowed state, and, in a roundabout way, was making a suggestion for a separation; so that he answered, with a laugh, " Why not? all we want is to come to an understanding." But he found himself sorely enough undeceived, as Charlotte continued, " And we have now a choice of opportunities for placing Ottilie in another situation. Two openings have offered themselves for her, either of which will do very well. Either she can return to the school, as my daughter has left it and is with her great-aunt; or she can be received into a desirable family, where, as the companion of an only child, she will enjoy all the advantages of a solid education."

Edward, with a tolerably successful effort at commanding himself, replied, "Ottilie has been so much spoilt, by living so long with us here, that she will scarcely like to leave us now."

"We have all of us been too much spoilt," said Charlotte; "and yourself not least. This is an epoch which requires us seriously to bethink ourselves. It is a solemn warning to us to consider what is really for the good of all the members of our little circle — and we ourselves must not be afraid of making sacrifices."

"At any rate I cannot see that it is right that Ottilie should be made a sacrifice," replied Edward; "and that would be the case if we were now to allow her to be sent away among strangers. The Captain's good genius has sought him out here — we can feel easy, we can feel happy, at seeing him leave us; but who can tell what may be before Ottilie? There is no occasion for haste."

"What is before us is sufficiently clear," Charlotte answered, with some emotion; and as she was determined to have it all out at once, she went on: "You love Ottilie; every day you are becoming more attached to her. A reciprocal feeling is rising on her side as well, and feeding itself in the same way. Why should we not acknowledge in words what every hour makes obvious? and are we not to have the common prudence to ask ourselves in what it is to end?"

"We may not be able to find an answer on the moment," replied Edward, collecting himself; "but so much may be said, that if we cannot exactly tell what will come of it, we may resign ourselves to wait and see what the future may tell us about it."

No great wisdom is required to prophesy here," answered Charlotte; "and, at any rate, we ought to feel that you and I are past the age when people may walk blindly where they should not or ought not to go. There is no one else to take care of us — we must be our own friends, our own managers. No one expects us to commit ourselves in an outrage upon decency: no one expects that we are going to expose ourselves to censure or to ridicule."

"How can you so mistake me?" said Edward, unable to reply to his wife's clear, open words. "Can you find it a fault in me, if I am anxious about Ottilie's happiness? I do not mean future happiness — no one can count on that — but what is present, palpable, and immediate. Consider, don't deceive yourself; consider frankly Ottilie's case, torn away from us, and sent to live among strangers. I, at least, am not cruel enough to propose such a change for her!"

Charlotte saw too clearly into her husband's intentions, through this disguise. For the first time she felt how far he had estranged himself from her. Her voice shook a little — "Will Ottilie be happy if she divides us?" she said. "If she deprives me of a husband, and his children of a father!"

"Our children, I should have thought, were sufficiently provided for," said Edward, with a cold smile; adding, rather more kindly, "but why at once expect the very worst?"

"The very worst is too sure to follow this passion of yours," returned Charlotte: "do not refuse good advice while there is yet time; do not throw away the means which I propose to save us. In troubled cases those must work and help who see the clearest — this time it is I. Dear, dearest Edward! listen to me — can you propose to me, that now at once I shall renounce my happiness! renounce my fairest rights! renounce you!"

"Who says that?" replied Edward, with some embarrassment.

"You, yourself," answered Charlotte; "in determining to keep Ottilie here, are you not acknowledging everything which must arise out of it? I will urge nothing on you — but if you cannot conquer yourself, at least you will not be able much longer to deceive yourself."

Edward felt how right she was. It is fearful to hear spoken out, in words, what the heart has gone on long permitting to itself in secret. To escape only for a moment, Edward answered, "It is not yet clear to me what you want."

"My intention," she replied, "was to talk over with you these two proposals — each of them has its advantages. The school would be best suited to her, as she now is; but the other situation is larger, and wider, and promises more, when I think what she may become." She then detailed to her husband circumstantially what would lie before Ottilie in each position, and concluded with the words, "For my own part I should prefer the lady's house to the school, for more reasons than one; but particularly because I should not like the affection, the love indeed, of the young man there, which Ottilie has gained, to increase."

Edward appeared to approve; but it was only to find

some means of delay. Charlotte, who desired to commit
him to a definite step, seized the opportunity, as Edward
made no immediate opposition, to settle Ottilie's departure, for which she had already privately made all
preparations, for the next day.

Edward shuddered — he thought he was betrayed.
His wife's affectionate speech he fancied was an artfully
contrived trick to separate him for ever from his happiness. He appeared to leave the thing entirely to her;
but in his heart his resolution was already taken. To
gain time to breathe, to put off the immediate intolerable
misery of Ottilie's being sent away, he determined to
leave his house. He told Charlotte he was going; but he
had blinded her to his real reason, by telling her that he
would not be present at Ottilie's departure; indeed, that,
from that moment, he would see her no more. Charlotte,
who believed that she had gained her point, approved
most cordially. He ordered his horse, gave his valet the
necessary directions what to pack up, and where he
should follow him; and then, on the point of departure,
he sat down and wrote :

"EDWARD TO CHARLOTTE.

"The misfortune, my love, which has befallen us, may
or may not admit of remedy; only this I feel, that if I
am not at once to be driven to despair, I must find some
means of delay for myself, and for all of us. In making
myself the sacrifice, I have a right to make a request. I
am leaving my home, and I only return to it under hap-
pier and more peaceful auspices. While I am away, you
keep possession of it — *but with Ottilie.* I choose to know
that she is with you, and not among strangers. Take
care of her; treat her as you have treated her — only

more lovingly, more kindly, more tenderly! I promise
that I will not attempt any secret intercourse with her.—
Leave me, as long a time as you please, without knowing
anything about you. I will not allow myself to be anxious — nor need you be uneasy about me; only, with all
my heart and soul, I beseech you, make no attempt to
send Ottilie away, or to introduce her into any other situation. Beyond the circle of the castle and the park,
placed in the hands of strangers, she belongs to me, and I
will take possession of her! If you have any regard for
my affection, for my wishes, for my sufferings, you will
leave me alone to my madness: and if any hope of recovery from it should ever hereafter offer itself to me I will
not resist."

This last sentence ran off his pen — not out of his
heart. Even when he saw it upon the paper, he began
bitterly to weep. That he, under any circumstances,
should renounce the happiness — even the wretchedness
— of loving Ottilie! He only now began to feel what
he was doing — he was going away without knowing
what was to be the result. At any rate he was not to
see her again *now* — with what certainty could he promise himself that he would ever see her again? But the
letter was written — the horses were at the door; every
moment he was afraid he might see Ottilie somewhere,
and then his whole purpose would go to the winds. He
collected himself — he remembered, that, at any rate,
he would be able to return at any moment he pleased;
and that, by his absence he would have advanced nearer
to his wishes: on the other side, he pictured Ottilie to
himself forced to leave the house if he stayed. He sealed
the letter, ran down the steps, and sprang upon his horse.

As he rode past the hotel, he saw the beggar to whom

he had given so much money the night before, sitting under the trees; the man was busy enjoying his dinner,
and, as Edward passed, stood up and made him the hum-
blest obeisance.   That figure had appeared to him yesterday, when Ottilie was on his arm; now it only served as
a bitter reminiscence of the happiest hour of his life.   His
grief redoubled.   The feeling of what he was leaving behind was intolerable.   He looked again at the beggar.
"Happy wretch!" he cried, "you can still feed upon the
arms of yesterday — and I cannot any more on the happiness of yesterday!"

CHAPTER XVII.

OTTILIE heard some one ride away, and went to the
window in time just to catch a sight of Edward's
back.   It was strange, she thought, that he should have
left the house without seeing her, without having even
wished her good morning.   She grew uncomfortable, and
her anxiety did not diminish when Charlotte took her out
for a long walk, and talked of various other things; but not
once, and apparently on purpose, mentioning her husband.
When they returned she found the table laid only with
two covers.

It is unpleasant to miss even the most trifling thing to
which we have been accustomed.   In serious things such
a loss becomes miserably painful.   Edward and the Captain were not there.   The first time, for a long while,
Charlotte sat at the head of the table herself — and it

seemed to Ottilie as if she was deposed. The two ladies
sat opposite each other; Charlotte talked, without the
least embarrassment, of the Captain and his appointment,
and of the little hope there was of seeing him again for a
long time. The only comfort Ottilie could find for herself was in the idea that Edward had ridden after his
friend, to accompany him a part of his journey.

On rising from table, however, they saw Edward's
travelling carriage under the window. Charlotte, a little
as if she was put out, asked who had it brought round
there. She was told it was the valet, who had some
things there to pack up. It required all Ottilie's self-
command to conceal her wonder and her distress.

The valet came in, and asked if they would be so good
as to let him have a drinking cup of his master's, a pair
of silver spoons, and a number of other things, which
seemed to Ottilie to imply that he was gone some distance, and would be away for a long time.

Charlotte gave him a very cold dry answer. She did
not know what he meant—he had everything belonging
to his master under his own care. What the man
wanted was to speak a word to Ottilie, and on some
pretence or other to get her out of the room; he made
some clever excuse, and persisted in his request so far
that Ottilie asked if she should go to look for the things
for him? But Charlotte quietly said that she had better
not. The valet had to depart, and the carriage rolled
away.

It was a dreadful moment for Ottilie. She understood
nothing—comprehended nothing. She could only feel
that Edward had been parted from her for a long time.
Charlotte felt for her situation, and left her to herself.

We will not attempt to describe what she went

through, or how she wept. She suffered infinitely. She prayed that God would help her only over this one day. The day passed, and the night, and when she came to herself again she felt herself a changed being.

She had not grown composed. She was not resigned, but after having lost what she had lost, she was still alive, and there was still something for her to fear. Her anxiety, after returning to consciousness, was at once lest, now that the gentlemen were gone, she might be sent away too. She never guessed at Edward's threats, which had secured her remaining with her aunt. Yet Charlotte's manner served partially to reassure her. The latter exerted herself to find employment for the poor girl, and hardly ever,—never, if she could help it,—left her out of her sight; and although she knew well how little words can do against the power of passion, yet she knew, too, the sure though slow influence of thought and reflection, and therefore missed no opportunity of inducing Ottilie to talk with her on every variety of subject.

It was no little comfort to Ottilie when one day Charlotte took an opportunity of making (she did it on purpose) the wise observation, "How keenly grateful people were to us when we were able by stilling and calming them to help them out of the entanglements of passion! Let us set cheerfully to work," she said, "at what the men have left incomplete: we shall be preparing the most charming surprise for them when they return to us, and our temperate proceedings will have carried through and executed what their impatient natures would have spoilt."

"Speaking of temperance, my dear aunt, I cannot help saying how I am struck with the intemperance of men, particularly in respect of wine. It has often pained and distressed me, when I observed how, for hours together, clearness of understanding, judgment, considerateness, and whatever is most amiable about them, will be utterly gone, and instead of the good which they might have done if they had been themselves, most disagreeable things sometimes threaten. How often may not wrong, rash determinations have arisen entirely from that one cause!"

Charlotte assented, but she did not go on with the subject. She saw only too clearly that it was Edward of whom Ottilie was thinking. It was not exactly habitual with him, but he allowed himself much more frequently than was at all desirable to stimulate his enjoyment and his power of talking and acting by such indulgence. If what Charlotte had just said had set Ottilie thinking again about men, and particularly about Edward, she was all the more struck and startled when her aunt began to speak of the impending marriage of the Captain as of a thing quite settled and acknowledged. This gave a totally different aspect to affairs from what Edward had previously led her to entertain. It made her watch every expression of Charlotte's, every hint, every action, every step. Ottilie had become jealous, sharp-eyed, and suspicious, without knowing it.

Meanwhile, Charlotte with her clear glance looked through the whole circumstances of their situation, and made arrangements which would provide, among other advantages, full employment for Ottilie. She contracted her household, not parsimoniously, but into narrower dimensions; and, indeed, in one point of view, these moral aberrations might be taken for a not unfortunate accident. For in the style in which they had been going on, they had fallen imperceptibly into extravagance; and from a want of seasonable reflection, from the rate at which they had been living, and from the variety of schemes into which they had been launching out, their fine fortune, which had been in excellent condition, had been shaken, if not seriously injured.

The improvements which were going on in the park she did not interfere with; she rather sought to advance whatever might form a basis for future operations. But here, too, she assigned herself a limit. Her husband on his return should still find abundance to amuse himself with.

In all this work she could not sufficiently value the assistance of the young architect. In a short time the lake lay stretched out under her eyes, its new shores turfed and planted with the most discriminating and excellent judgment. The rough work at the new house was all finished. Everything which was necessary to protect it from the weather she took care to see provided, and there for the present she allowed it to rest in a condition in which what remained to be done could hereafter be readily commenced again. Thus hour by hour she recovered her spirits and her cheerfulness. Ottilie only seemed to have done so. She was only for ever watching, in all that was said and done, for symptoms which might show her whether Edward would be soon returning: and this one thought was the only one in which she felt any interest.

It was, therefore, a very welcome proposal to her when it was suggested that they should get together the boys of the peasants, and employ them in keeping the park clean and neat. Edward had long entertained the idea. A pleasant-looking sort of uniform was made for them, which they were to put on in the evenings, after they had been properly cleaned and washed. The wardrobe was

kept in the castle; the more sensible and ready of the
boys themselves were entrusted with the management of
it — the Architect acting as chief director. In a very
short time, the children acquired a kind of character. It
was found easy to mould them into what was desired;
and they went through their work not without a sort of
manœuvre. As they marched along, with their garden
shears, their long-handled pruning knives, their rakes,
their little spades and hoes, and sweeping brooms: others
following after these with baskets to carry off the stones
and rubbish; and others, last of all, trailing along the
heavy iron roller — it was a thoroughly pretty, delightful
procession. The Architect observed in it a beautiful series of situations and occupations to ornament the frieze
of a garden house. Ottilie, on the other hand, could see
nothing in it but a kind of parade, to salute the master of
the house on his near return.

And this stimulated her, and made her wish to begin
something of the sort herself. They had before endeavored to encourage the girls of the village in knitting, and
sewing, and spinning, and whatever else women could do;
and since what had been done for the improvement of
the village itself, there had been a perceptible advance in
these descriptions of industry. Ottilie had given what
assistance was in her power, but she had given it at random, as opportunity or inclination prompted her; now
she thought she would go to work more satisfactorily and
methodically. But a company is not to be formed out of
a number of girls, as easily as out of a number of boys.
She followed her good sense, and, without being exactly
conscious of it, her efforts were solely directed towards
connecting every girl as closely as possible each with her
own home, her own parents, brothers and sisters: and

she succeeded with many of them. One lively little creature only was incessantly complained of as showing no
capacity for work, and as never likely to do any thing if
she were left at home.

Ottilie could not be angry with the girl, for to herself
the little thing was especially attached — she clung to her,
went after her, and ran about with her, whenever she was
permitted — and then she would be active and cheerful
and never tire. It appeared to be a necessity of the child's
nature to hang about a beautiful mistress. At first, Ottilie
allowed her to be her companion; then she herself began
to feel a sort of affection for her; and, at last, they never
parted at all, and Nanny attended her mistress wherever
she went.

The latter's footsteps were often bent towards the garden, where she liked to watch the beautiful show of fruit.
It was just the end of the raspberry and cherry season,
the few remains of which were no little delight to Nanny.
On the other trees there was a promise of a magnificent
bearing for the autumn, and the gardener talked of nothing but his master; and how he wished that he might be
at home to enjoy it. Ottilie could listen to the good old
man for ever! He thoroughly understood his business;
and Edward — Edward — Edward — was for ever the
theme of his praise!

Ottilie observed, how well all the grafts which had
been budded in the spring had taken. "I only wish,"
the gardener answered, "my good master may come to
enjoy them. If he were here this autumn, he would see
what beautiful sorts there are in the old castle garden,
which the late lord, his honored father, put there. I
think the fruit gardeners that are now don't succeed as
well as the Carthusians used to do. We find many fine

names in the catalogue, and then we bud from them, and bring up the shoots, and, at last, when they come to bear, it is not worth while to have such trees standing in our garden."

Over and over again, whenever the faithful old servant saw Ottilie, he asked when his master might be expected home; and when Ottilie had nothing to tell him, he would look vexed, and let her see in his manner that he thought she did not care to tell him: the sense of uncertainty which was thus forced upon her became painful beyond measure, and yet she could never be absent from these beds and borders. What she and Edward had sown and planted together were now in full flower, requiring no further care from her, except that Nanny should be at hand with the watering-pot; and who shall say with what sensations she watched the later flowers, which were just beginning to show, and which were to be in the bloom of their beauty on Edward's birthday, the holiday to which she had looked forward with such eagerness, when these flowers were to have expressed her affection and her gratitude to him!—but the hopes which she had formed of that festival were dead now, and doubt and anxiety never ceased to haunt the soul of the poor girl.

Into real open, hearty understanding with Charlotte, there was no more a chance of her being able to return; for, indeed, the position of these two ladies was very different. If things could remain in their old state—if it were possible that they could return again into the smooth, even way of calm ordered life, Charlotte gained everything; she gained happiness for the present, and a happy future opened before her. On the other hand, for Ottilie all was lost—one may say, all; for she had first found in Edward what life and happiness meant; and, in her present position, she felt an infinite and dreary chasm of which before she could have formed no conception. A heart which seeks, feels well that it wants something; a heart which has lost, feels that something is gone — its yearning and its longing changes into uneasy impatience — and a woman's spirit, which is accustomed to waiting and to enduring, must now pass out from its proper sphere; become active, and attempt and do something to make its own happiness.

Ottilie had not given up Edward — how could she? — although Charlotte, wisely enough, in spite of her conviction to the contrary, assumed it as a thing of course, and resolutely took it as decided that a quiet rational regard was possible between her husband and Ottilie. How often, however, did not Ottilie remain at nights, after bolting herself into her room, on her knees before the open box, gazing at the birthday presents, of which as yet she had not touched a single thing — not cut out or made up a single dress! How often with the sunrise did the poor girl hurry out of the house, in which she once had found all her happiness, away into the free air, into the country which then had had no charms for her. — Even on the solid earth she could not bear to stay; she would spring into the boat, and row out into the middle of the lake, and there, drawing out some book of travels, lie rocked by the motion of the waves, reading and dreaming that she was far away, where she would never fail to find her friend — she remaining ever nearest to his heart, and he to hers.

CHAPTER XVIII.

IT may be easily supposed that the strange, busy gentleman, whose acquaintance we have already made — Mittler — as soon as he received information of the disorder which had broken out among his friends, felt desirous, though neither side had as yet called on him for assistance, to fulfil a friend's part toward them, and do what he could to help them in their misfortune. He thought it advisable, however, to wait first a little while; knowing too well, as he did, that it was more difficult to come to the aid of cultivated persons in their moral perplexities, than of the uncultivated. He left them, therefore, for some time to themselves; but at last he could withhold no longer, and he hastened to seek out Edward, on whose traces he had already lighted. His road led him to a pleasant, pretty valley, with a range of green, sweetly-wooded meadows, down the centre of which ran a never-failing stream, sometimes winding slowly along, then tumbling and rushing among rocks and stones. The hills sloped gently up on either side, covered with rich corn-fields and well-kept orchards. The villages were at proper distances from each other. The whole had a peaceful character about it, and the detached scenes seemed designed expressly, if not for painting, at least for life.

At last a neatly-kept farm, with a clean, modest dwelling-house, situated in the middle of the garden, fell under his eye. He conjectured that this was Edward's present abode; and he was not mistaken.

Of this our friend in his solitude we have only thus

much to say — that in his seclusion he was resigning himself utterly to the feeling of his passion, thinking out plan after plan, and feeding himself with innumerable hopes. · He could not deny that he longed to see Ottilie there; that he would like to carry her off there, to tempt her there; and whatever else (putting, as he now did, no check upon his thoughts) pleased to suggest itself, whether permitted or unpermitted. Then his imagination wandered up and down, picturing every sort of possibility. If he could not have her there, if he could not lawfully possess her, he would secure to her the possession of the property for her own. There she should live for herself, silently, independently; she should be happy in that spot — sometimes his self-torturing mood would lead him further — be happy in it, perhaps, with another.

So days flowed away in increasing oscillation between hope and suffering, between tears and happiness — between purposes, preparations, and despair. The sight of Mittler did not surprise him; he had long expected that he would come; and now that he did, he was partly welcome to him. He believed that he had been sent by Charlotte. He had prepared himself with all manner of excuses and delays; and if these would not serve, with decided refusals; or else, perhaps, he might hope to learn something of Ottilie, — and then he would be dear to him as a messenger from heaven.

Not a little vexed and annoyed was Edward, therefore, when he understood that Mittler had not come from the castle at all, but of his own free accord. His heart closed up, and at first the conversation would not open itself. Mittler, however, knew very well that a heart that is occupied with love has an urgent necessity to express itself — to pour out to a friend what is passing within it; and he allowed himself, therefore, after a few speeches backwards and forwards, for this once to go out of his character, and play the confidant in place of the mediator. He had calculated justly. He had been finding fault in a good-natured way with Edward, for burying himself in that lonely place, upon which Edward replied:

"I do not know how I could spend my time more agreeably. I am always occupied with her; I am always close to her. I have the inestimable comfort of being able to think where Ottilie is at each moment — where she is going, where she is standing, where she is reposing. I see her moving and acting before me as usual; ever doing or designing something which is to give me pleasure. But this will not always answer; for how can I be happy away from her? And then my fancy begins to work; I think what Ottilie should do to come to me; I write sweet, loving letters in her name to myself, and then I answer them, and keep the sheets together. I have promised that I will take no steps to seek her; and that promise I will keep. But what binds her, that she should make no advances to me? Has Charlotte had the barbarity to exact a promise, to exact an oath from her, not to write to me, not to send me a word, a hint, about herself? Very likely she has. It is only natural; and yet to me it is monstrous, it is horrible. If she loves me — as I think, as I know that she does — why does she not resolve, why does she not venture to fly to me, and throw herself into my arms? I often think she ought to do it; and she could do it. If I ever hear a noise in the hall, I look towards the door. It must be her — she is coming — I look up to see her. Alas! because the possible is impossible, I let myself imagine that the impossible must become possible. At night, when I lie awake, and the lamp

7

flings an uncertain light about the room, her form, her spirit, a sense of her presence, sweeps over me, approaches me, seizes me. It is but for a moment; it is that I may have an assurance that she is thinking of me, that she is mine. Only one pleasure remains to me. When I was with her I never dreamed of her; now when I am far away, and, oddly enough, since I have made the acquaintance of other attractive persons in this neighborhood, for the first time, her figure appears to me in my dreams, as if she would say to me, 'Look on them, and on me. You will find none more beautiful, more lovely than I.' And so she is present in every dream I have. In whatever happens to me with her, we are woven in and in together. Now we are subscribing a contract together. There is her hand, and there is mine; there is her name, and there is mine; and they move one into the other, and seem to devour each other. Sometimes she does something which injures the pure idea which I have of her; and then I feel how intensely I love her, by the indescribable anguish which it causes me. Again, unlike herself, she will rally and vex me; and then at once the figure changes — her sweet, round, heavenly face draws out; it is not her, it is another; but I lie vexed, dissatisfied and wretched. Laugh not, dear Mittler, or laugh on as you will. I am not ashamed of this attachment, of this — if you please to call it so — foolish, frantic passion. No, I never loved before. It is only now that I know what to love means. Till now, what I have called life was nothing but its prelude — amusement, sport to kill the time with. I never lived till I knew her, till I loved her — entirely and only loved her. People have often said of me, not to my face, but behind my back, that in most things I was but a botcher and a bungler. It may be so; for I had not then found in what I could show myself a master. I should like to see the man who outdoes me in the talent of love. A miserable life it is, full of anguish and tears; but it is so natural, so dear to me, that I could hardly change it for another."

Edward had relieved himself slightly by this violent unloading of his heart. But in doing so every feature of his strange condition had been brought out so clearly before his eyes, that, overpowered by the pain of the struggle, he burst into tears, which flowed all the mo e freely as his heart had been made weak by telling it all.

Mittler, who was the less disposed to put a check on his inexorable good sense and strong, vigorous feeling, because by this violent outbreak of passion on Edward's part he saw himself driven far from the purpose of his coming, showed sufficiently decided marks of his disapprobation. Edward should act as a man, he said; he should remember what he owed to himself as a man. He should not forget that the highest honor was to command ourselves in misfortune; to bear pain, if it must be so, with equanimity and self-collectedness. That was what we should do, if we wished to be valued and looked up to as examples of what was right.

Stirred and penetrated as Edward was with the bitterest feelings, words like these could but have a hollow, worthless sound.

"It is well," he cried, "for the man who is happy, who has all that he desires, to talk; but he would be ashamed of it if he could see how intolerable it was to the sufferer. Nothing short of an infinite endurance would be enough, and easy and contented as he was, what could he know of an infinite agony? There are cases," he continued, "yes, there are, where comfort is a lie, and despair is a duty. Go, heap your scorn upon the noble Greek, who well knows how to delineate heroes, when in their anguish he lets those heroes weep. He has even a proverb, ' Men who can weep are good.' Leave me, all you with dry heart and dry eye. Curses on the happy, to whom the wretched serve but for a spectacle. When body and soul are torn in pieces with agony, they are to bear it — yes, to be noble and bear it, if they are to be allowed to go off the scene with applause. Like the gladiators, they must die gracefully before the eyes of the multitude. My dear Mittler, I thank you for your visit; but really you would oblige me much, if you would go out and look about you in the garden. We will meet again. I will try to compose myself, and become more like you."

Mittler was unwilling to let a conversation drop which it might be difficult to begin again, and still persevered. Edward, too, was quite ready to go on with it; besides that of itself, it was tending towards the issue which he desired.

" Indeed," said the latter, " this thinking and arguing backwards and forwards leads to nothing. In this very conversation I myself have first come to understand myself! I have first felt decided as to what I must make up my mind to do. My present and my future life I see before me; I have to choose only between misery and happiness. Do you, my best friend, bring about the separation which must take place, which, in fact, is already made; gain Charlotte's consent for me. I will not enter upon the reasons why I believe there will be the less difficulty in prevailing upon her. You, my dear friend, must go. Go, and give us all peace; make us all happy."

Mittler hesitated. Edward continued:

" My fate and Ottilie's cannot be divided, and shall

not be shipwrecked. Look at this glass; our initials are engraved upon it. A gay reveller flung it into the air, that no one should drink of it more. It was to fall on the rock and be dashed to pieces; but it did not fall; it was caught. At a high price I bought it back, and now I drink out of it daily — to convince myself that the connection between us cannot be broken; that destiny has decided."

"Alas, alas!" cried Mittler, "what must I not endure with my friends? Here comes superstition, which of all things I hate the worst — the most mischievous and accursed of all the plagues of mankind. We trifle with prophecies, with forebodings, and dreams, and give a seriousness to our every-day life with them; but when the seriousness of life itself begins to show, when everything around us is heaving and rolling, then come in these spectres to make the storm more terrible."

"In this uncertainty of life," cried Edward, "poised as it is between hope and fear, leave the poor heart its guiding-star. It may gaze towards it, if it cannot steer towards it."

"Yes, I might leave it; and it would be very well," replied Mittler, "if there were but one consequence to expect; but I have always found that nobody will attend to symptoms of warning. Man cares for nothing except what flatters him and promises him fair; and his faith is alive exclusively for the sunny side."

Mittler, finding himself carried off into the shadowy regions, in which the longer he remained in them, the more uncomfortable he always felt, was the more ready to assent to Edward's eager wish that he should go to Charlotte. Indeed, if he stayed, what was there further which at that moment he could urge on Edward? To gain time, to inquire in what state things were with the ladies, was the best thing which even he himself could suggest as at present possible.

He hastened to Charlotte, whom he found as usual, calm and in good spirits. She told him readily of everything which had occurred; for from what Edward had said he had only been able to gather the effects. On his own side, he felt his way with the utmost caution. He could not prevail upon himself even cursorily to mention the word separation. It was a surprise, indeed, to him, but from his point of view an unspeakably delightful one, when Charlotte, at the end of a number of unpleasant things, finished with saying:

"I must believe, I must hope, that things will all work round again, and that Edward will return to me. How can it be otherwise, as soon as I become a mother?"

"Do I understand you right?" returned Mittler.

"Perfectly," Charlotte answered.

"A thousand times blessed be this news!" he cried, clasping his hands together. "I know the strength of this argument on the mind of a man. Many a marriage have I seen first cemented by it, and restored again when broken. Such a good hope as this is worth more than a thousand words. Now indeed it is the best hope which we can have. For myself, though," he continued, "I have all reason to be vexed about it. In this case I can see clearly no self-love of mine will be flattered. I shall earn no thanks from you by my services; I am in the same case as a certain medical friend of mine, who succeeds in all cures which he undertakes with the poor for the love of God; but can seldom do anything for the rich who will pay him. Here, thank God, the thing cures itself, after all my talking and trying had proved fruitless."

Charlotte now asked him if he would carry the news to Edward; if he would take a letter to him from her, and then see what should be done. But he declined undertaking this. "All is done," he cried; "do you write your letter — any messenger will do as well as I — I will come back to wish you joy. I will come to the christening!"

For this refusal she was vexed with him — as she frequently was. His eager impetuous character brought about much good; but his over-haste was the occasion of many a failure. No one was more dependent than he on the impressions which he formed on the moment.

Charlotte's messenger came to Edward, who received him half in terror. The letter was to decide his fate, and it might as well contain No as Yes. He did not venture, for a long time, to open it. At last he tore off the cover, and stood petrified at the following passage, with which it concluded:

"Remember the night-adventure when you visited your wife as a lover — how you drew her to you, and clasped her as a well-beloved bride in your arms. In this strange accident let us revere the providence of heaven, which has woven a new link to bind us, at the moment when the happiness of our lives was threatening to fall asunder and to vanish."

What passed from that moment in Edward's soul it would be difficult to describe! Under the weight of such a stroke, old habits and fancies come out again to assist to kill the time and fill up the chasms of life. Hunting and fighting are an ever-ready resource of this kind for a nobleman; Edward longed for some outward peril, as a

counterbalance to the storm within him. He craved for
death, because the burden of life threatened to become
too heavy for him to bear. It comforted him to think
that he would soon cease to be, and so would make those
whom he loved happy by his departure.

No one made any difficulty in his doing what he pur-
posed — because he kept his intention a secret. He made
his will with all due formalities. It gave him a very
sweet feeling to secure Ottilie's fortune — provision was
made for Charlotte, for the unborn child, for the Captain,
and for the servants. The war, which had again broken
out, favored his wishes : he had disliked exceedingly the
half-soldiering which had fallen to him in his youth, and
that was the reason why he had left the service. Now it
gave him a fine exhilarating feeling to be able to rejoin it,
under a commander of whom it could be said, that under
his conduct death was likely, and victory was sure.

Ottilie, when Charlotte's secret was made known to her,
bewildered by it, like Edward, and more than he, retired
into herself— she had nothing further to say: hope she
could not, and wish she dared not.   A glimpse into what
was passing in her we can gather from her Diary, some
passages of which we think to communicate.

PART II.

CHAPTER I.

THERE often happens to us in common life what, in an epic poem, we are accustomed to praise as a stroke of art in the poet; namely, that when the chief figures go off the scene, conceal themselves or retire into inactivity, some other or others, whom hitherto we have scarcely observed, come forward and fill their places. And these putting out all their force, at once fix our attention and sympathy on themselves, and earn our praise and admiration.

Thus, after the Captain and Edward were gone, the Architect, of whom we have spoken, appeared every day a more important person. The ordering and executing of a number of undertakings depended entirely upon him, and he proved himself thoroughly understanding and business-like in the style in which he went to work; while in a number of other ways he was able also to make himself of assistance to the ladies, and find amusement for their weary hours. His outward air and appearance were of the kind which win confidence and awake affection. A youth in the full sense of the word, well formed, tall, perhaps a little too stout; modest without being timid, and easy without being obtrusive, there was no work and no trouble which he was not delighted to take upon himself; and as he could keep accounts with great facility, the whole economy of the household soon

7*

was no secret to him, and everywhere his salutary influence made itself felt. Any stranger who came he was
commonly set to entertain, and he was skilful either at
declining unexpected visits, or at least so far preparing
the ladies for them as to spare them any disagreeableness.

Among others, he had one day no little trouble with a
young lawyer, who had been sent by a neighboring nobleman to speak about a matter which, although of no particular moment, yet touched Charlotte to the quick. We
have to mention this 'incident, because it gave occasion
for a number of things which otherwise might perhaps
have remained long untouched.

We remember certain alterations which Charlotte had
made in the churchyard. The entire body of the monuments had been removed from their places, and had been
ranged along the walls of the church, leaning against the
string-course. The remaining space had been levelled,
except a broad walk which led up to the church, and
past it to the opposite gate; and it had been all sown
with various kinds of trefoil, which had shot up and
flowered most beautifully.

The new graves were to follow one after another in a
regular order from the end, but the spot on each occasion
was to be carefully smoothed over and again sown. No
one could deny that on Sundays and holidays, when the
people went to church, the change had given it a most
cheerful and pleasant appearance. At the same time the
clergyman, an old man and clinging to old customs, who
at first had not been especially pleased with the alteration, had become thoroughly delighted with it, all the
more because when he sat out like Philemon with his
Baucis under the old linden trees at his back door, instead

of the humps and mounds he had a beautiful clean lawn to look out upon ; and which, moreover, Charlotte having secured the use of the spot to the parsonage, was no little convenience to his household.

Notwithstanding this, however, many members of the congregation had been displeased that the means of marking the spots where their forefathers rested had been removed, and all memorials of them thereby obliterated. However well preserved the monuments might be, they could only show who had been buried, but not where he had been buried, and the *where*, as many maintained, was everything.

Of this opinion was a family in the neighborhood, who for many years had been in possession of a considerable vault for a general resting-place of themselves and their relations, and in consequence had settled a small annual sum for the use of the church. And now this young lawyer had been sent to cancel this settlement, and to show that his client did not intend to pay it any more, because the condition under which it had been hitherto made had not been observed by the other party, and no regard had been paid to objection and remonstrance. Charlotte, who was the originator of the alteration herself, chose to speak to the young man, who in a decided though not a violent manner, laid down the grounds on which his client proceeded, and gave occasion in what he said for much serious reflection.

"You see," he said, after a slight introduction, in which he sought to justify his peremptoriness; "you see, it is right for the lowest as well as for the highest to mark the spot which holds those who are dearest to him. The poorest peasant who buries a child, finds it some consolation to plant a light wooden cross upon the grave, and hang a garland upon it, to keep alive the memorial, at least as long as the sorrow remains; although such a mark, like the mourning, will pass away with time. Those better off change the cross of wood into iron, and fix it down and guard it in various ways; and here we have endurance for many years. But because this too will sink at last and become invisible, those who are able to bear the expense see nothing fitter than to raise a stone which shall promise to endure for generations, and which can be restored and be made fresh again by posterity. Yet this stone it is not which attracts us; it is that which is contained beneath it, which is entrusted, where it stands, to the earth. It is not the memorial so much of which we speak, as of the person himself; not of what once was, but of what is. Far better, far more closely, can I embrace some dear departed one in the mound which rises over his bed, than in a monumental writing which only tells us that once he was. In itself, indeed, it is but little; but around it, as around a central mark, the wife, the husband, the kinsman, the friend, after their departure, shall gather in again; and the living shall have the right to keep far off all strangers, and evil-wishers from the side of the dear one who is sleeping there.

"And, therefore, I hold it quite fair and fitting that my principal shall withdraw his grant to you. It is, indeed, but too reasonable that he should do it, for the members of his family are injured in a way for which no compensation could be even proposed. They are deprived of the sad sweet feelings of laying offerings on the remains of their dead, and of the one comfort in their sorrow of one day lying down at their side."

"The matter is not of that importance," Charlotte answered, "that we should disquiet ourselves about it with the vexation of a law-suit. I regret so little what I have done, that I will gladly myself indemnify the church for what it loses through you. Only I must confess candidly to you, your arguments have not convinced me; the pure feeling of an universal equality at last, after death, seems to me more composing than this hard determined persistance in our personalities and in the conditions and circumstances of our lives. " What do you say to it ? " she added, turning to the Architect.

" It is not for me," replied he, " either to argue, or to attempt to judge in such a case. Let me venture, however, to say what my own art and my own habits of thinking suggest to me. Since we are no longer so happy as to be able to press to our breasts the in-urned remains of those we have loved, since we are neither wealthy enough, nor of cheerful heart enough to preserve them undecayed in large elaborate sarcophagi; since, indeed, we cannot even find place any more for ourselves and ours in the churches, and are banished out into the open air, we all, I think, ought to approve the method which you, my gracious lady, have introduced. If the members of a common congregation are laid out side by side, they are resting by the side of, and among their kindred; and, if the earth be once to receive us all, I can find nothing more natural or more desirable than that. the mounds, which, if they are thrown up, are sure to sink slowly in again together, should be smoothed off at once, and the covering, which all bear alike, will press lighter upon each."

" And is it all, is it all to pass away," said Ottilie, " without one token of remembrance, without anything to call back the past ? "

" By no means," continued the Architect: " it is not from remembrance, it is from *place* that men should be

set free. The architect, the sculptor, are highly interested
that men should look to their art — to their hand, for a
continuance of their being; and, therefore, I should wish
to see well-designed, well-executed monuments; not·
sown up and down by themselves at random, but erected
all in a single spot, where they can promise themselves
endurance. Inasmuch as even the good and the great
are contented to surrender the privilege of resting in
person in the churches, *we* may, at least, erect there or
in some fair hall near the burying-place, either monuments or monumental writings. A thousand forms might
be suggested for them, and a thousand ornaments with
which they might be decorated."

"If the artists are so rich," replied Charlotte, "then tell
me how it is that they are never able to escape from little
obelisks, dwarf pillars, and urns for ashes: Instead of
your thousand forms of which you boast, I have never
seen anything but a thousand repetitions."

"It is very generally so with us," returned the Architect, "but it is not universal: and very likely the right
taste and the proper application of it may be a peculiar
art. In this case especially we have this great difficulty,
that the monument must be something cheerful and yet
commemorate a solemn subject; while its matter is
melancholy, it must not itself be melancholy. As regards
designs for monuments of all kinds, I have collected
numbers of them, and I will take some opportunity of
showing them to you; but at all times the fairest memorial of a man remains some likeness of himself. This,
better than anything else, will give a notion of what he
was; it is the best text for many or for few notes, only it
ought to be made when he is at his best age, and that is
generally neglected; no one thinks of preserving forms

while they are alive, and if it is done at all, it is done carelessly and incompletely: and then comes death; a cast is taken swiftly off the face; this mask is set upon a block of stone, and that is what is called a bust. How seldom is the artist in a position to put any real life into such things as these!"

"You have contrived," said Charlotte, "without perhaps knowing it or wishing it, to lead the conversation altogether in my favor. The likeness of a man is quite independent; everywhere that it stands, it stands for itself, and we do not require it to mark the site of a particular grave. But I must acknowledge to you to having a strange feeling; even to likenesses I have a kind of disinclination. Whenever I see them they seem to be silently reproaching me. They point to something far away from us, — gone from us; and they remind me how difficult it is to pay right honor to the present. If we think how many people we have seen and known, and consider how little we have been to them and how little they have been to us, it is no very pleasant reflection. We have met a man of genius without having enjoyed much with him, — a learned man without having learnt from him, — a traveller without having been instructed, — a man to love without having shown him any kindness.

"And, unhappily, this is not the case only with accidental meetings. Societies, and families behave in the same way towards their dearest members, towns towards their worthiest citizens, people towards their most admirable princes, nations towards their most distinguished men.

"I have heard it asked why we heard nothing but good spoken of the dead, while of the living it is never

without some exception.   It should be answered, because
from the former we have nothing more to fear, while the
latter may still, here or there, fall in our way.   So un-
real is our anxiety to preserve the memory of others, —
generally no more than a mere selfish amusement; and
the real, holy, earnest feeling, would be what should
prompt us to be more diligent and assiduous in our
attentions toward those who still are left to us."

CHAPTER II.

UNDER the stimulus of this accident, and of the conversations which arose out of it, they went the following day to look over the burying-place, for the ornamenting of which and relieving it in some degree of its
sombre look, the architect made many a happy proposal.
His interest too, had to extend itself to the church as
well; a building which had caught his attention from the
moment of his arrival.

It had been standing for many centuries, built in old
German style, the proportions good, the decorating elaborate and excellent; and one might easily gather that the
architect of the neighboring monastery had left the stamp
of his art and of his love on this smaller building also; it
worked on the beholder with a solemnity and a sweetness,
although the change in its internal arrangements for the
Protestant service, had taken from it something of its repose and majesty.

The Architect found no great difficulty in prevailing

on Charlotte to give him a considerable sum of money
to restore it externally and internally, in the original
spirit, and thus, as he thought, to bring it into harmony
with the resurrection-field which lay in front of it. He
had himself much practical skill, and a few laborers who
were still busy at the lodge, might easily be kept together,
until this pious work too should be completed.

The building itself, therefore, with all its environs, and
whatever was attached to it, was now carefully and
thoroughly examined; and then showed itself, to the
greatest surprise and delight of the architect, a little side
chapel, which nobody had thought of, beautifully and
delicately proportioned, and displaying still greater care
and pains in its decoration. It contained at the same
time many remnants, carved and painted, of the implements used in the old services, when the different festivals
were distinguished by a variety of pictures and cere-
monies, and each was celebrated in its own peculiar
style.

It was impossible for him not at once to take this
chapel into his plan; and he determined to bestow especial pains on the restoring of this little spot, as a memorial of old times, and of their taste. He saw exactly
how he would like to have the vacant surfaces of the
walls ornamented, and delighted himself with the prospect of exercising his talent for painting upon them; but
of this, at first, he made a secret to the rest of the party.

Before doing anything else, he fulfilled his promise of
showing the ladies the various imitations of, and designs
from, old monuments, vases, and other such things which
he had made; and when they came to speak of the simple barrow-sepulchres of the northern nations, he brought
a collection of weapons and implements which had been

found in them. He had got them exceedingly nicely
and conveniently arranged in drawers and compartments
laid on boards cut to fit them, and covered over with
cloth; so that these solemn old things, in the way he
treated them, had a smart, dressy appearance, and it was
like looking into the box of a trinket merchant.

Having once begun to show his curiosities, and finding
them prove serviceable to entertain our friends in their
loneliness; every evening he would produce one or other
of his treasures. They were most of them of German ori-
gin — pieces of metal, old coins, seals, and such like. All
these things directed the imagination back upon old times;
and when at last they came to amuse themselves with the
first specimens of printing, woodcuts, and the earliest
copper-plate engraving, and when the church, in the same
spirit, was growing out, every day, more and more in form
and color like the past, they had almost to ask themselves
whether they really were living in a modern time, whether
it were not a dream, that manners, customs, modes of life,
and convictions were all really so changed.

After such preparation, a great portfolio, which at last
he produced, had the best possible effect. It contained
indeed, principally only outlines and figures, but as these
had been traced upon original pictures, they retained perfectly their ancient character, and most captivating indeed
this character was to the spectators. All the figures
breathed only the purest feeling; every one, if not noble,
at any rate was good; cheerful composure, ready recognition of One above us, to whom all reverence is due;
silent devotion, in love and tranquil explanation, was expressed on every face, on every jesture. The old bald-
headed man, the curly-pated boy, the light-hearted youth,
the earnest man, the glorified saint, the angel hovering in

the air, all seemed happy in an innocent, satisfied, pious expectation. The commonest object had a trait of celestial life; and every nature seemed adapted to the service of God, and to be, in some way or other, employed upon it.

Towards such a region most of them gazed as towards a vanished golden age, or on some lost paradise; only perhaps Ottilie had a chance of finding herself among beings of her own nature. Who could offer any opposition when the Architect asked to be allowed to paint the spaces between the arches and the walls of the chapel in the style of these old pictures; and thereby leave his own distinct memorial at a place where life had gone so pleasantly with him?

He spoke of it with some sadness, for he could see, in the state in which things were, that his sojourn in such delightful society could not last for ever; indeed, that perhaps it would now soon be ended.

For the rest, these days were not rich in incidents; yet full of occasion for serious entertainment. We therefore take the opportunity of communicating something of the remarks which Ottilie noted down among her manuscripts, to which we cannot find a fitter transition than through a simile which suggested itself to us on contemplating her exquisite pages.

There is, we are told, a curious contrivance in the service of the English marine. The ropes in use in the royal navy, from the largest to the smallest, are so twisted that a red thread runs through them from end to end, which cannot be extracted without undoing the whole: and by which the smallest pieces may be recognized as belonging to the crown.

Just so is there drawn through Ottilie's diary, a thread

of attachment and affection which connects it all together, and characterizes the whole. And thus these remarks, these observations, these extracted sentences, and whatever else it may contain, were, to the writer, of peculiar meaning. Even the few separate pieces which we select and transcribe will sufficiently explain our meaning.

FROM OTTILIE'S DIARY.

"To rest hereafter at the side of those whom we love is the most delightful thought which man can have when once he looks out beyond the boundary of life. What a sweet expression is that — 'He was gathered to his fathers!'"

––––––––

"Of the various memorials and tokens which bring nearer to us the distant and the separated — none is so satisfactory as a picture. To sit and talk to a beloved picture, even though it be unlike, has a charm in it, like the charm which there sometimes is in quarrelling with a friend. We feel, in a strange sweet way, that we are divided and yet cannot separate."

––––––––

"We entertain ourselves often with a present person as with a picture. He need not speak to us, he need not look at us, or take any notice of us; we look at him, we feel the relation in which we stand to him; such relation can even grow without his doing anything towards it, without his having any feeling of it: he is to us exactly as a picture."

––––––––

"One is never satisfied with a portrait of a person that one knows. I have always felt for the portrait-painter on this account. One so seldom requires of people what is impossible and of them we do really require what is impossible; they must gather up into their picture the relation of every body to its subject, all their likings and all dislikings; they must not only paint a man as they see him, but as every one else sees him.. It does not surprise me if such artists become by degrees stunted, but indifferent, and all of one idea; and indeed it would not matter what came of it, if it were not that in consequence we have to go without the pictures of so many persons near and dear to us."

"It is too true, the Architect's collection of weapons and old implements, which were found with the bodies of their owners, covered with great hills of earth and rock, proves to us how useless is man's so great anxiety to preserve his personality after he is dead; and so inconsistent people are! the Architect confesses to have himself opened these barrows of his forefathers, and yet goes on occupying himself with memorials for posterity."

"But after all why should we take it so much to heart? is all that we do, done for eternity? Do we not put on our dress in the morning, to throw it off again at night? Do we not go abroad to return home again? And why should we not wish to rest by the side of our friends, though it were but for a century?"

"When we see the many grave-stones which have fallen in, which have been defaced by the footsteps of the congregation, which lie buried under the ruins of the churches, that have themselves crumbled together over them, we may fancy the life after death to be as a second life, into which a man enters in the figure, or the picture, or the inscription, and lives longer there than when he was really alive. But this figure also, this second existence, dies out too, sooner or later. Time will not allow himself to be cheated of his rights with the monuments of men or with themselves."

CHAPTER III.

IT causes us so agreeable a sensation to occupy ourselves with what we can only half do, that no person ought to find fault with the dilettante, when he is spending his time over an art which he can never learn; nor blame the artist if he chooses to pass out over the border of his own art, and amuse himself in some neighboring field. With such complacency of feeling we regard the preparation of the Architect for the painting the chapel. The colors were got ready, the measurements taken; the cartoons designed. He had made no attempt at originality, but kept close to his outlines; his only care was to make a proper distribution of the sitting and floating figures, so as tastefully to ornament his space with them.

The scaffoldings were erected. The work went forward; and as soon as anything had been done on which the eye could rest, he could have no objection to Charlotte and Ottilie coming to see how he was getting on.

The life-like faces of the angels, their robes waving against the blue sky-ground, delighted the eye, while their still and holy air calmed and composed the spirit, and produced the most delicate effect.

The ladies ascended the scaffolding to him, and Ottilie had scarcely observed how easily and regularly the work was being done, than the power which had been fostered in her by her early education at once appeared to develop. She took a brush, and with a few words of direction, painted a richly folding robe, with as much delicacy as skill.

Charlotte, who was always glad when Ottilie would occupy or amuse herself with anything, left them both in the chapel, and went to follow the train of her own thoughts, and work her way for herself through her cares and anxieties which she was unable to communicate to a creature.

When ordinary men allow themselves to be worked up by common every-day difficulties into fever fits of passion, we can give them nothing but a compassionate smile. But we look with a kind of awe on a spirit in which the seed of a great destiny has been sown, which must abide the unfolding of the germ, and neither dare nor can do anything to precipitate either the good or the ill, either the happiness or the misery, which is to arise out of it.

. Edward had sent an answer by Chorlotte's messenger, who had come to him in his solitude. It was written with kindness and interest, but it was rather composed and serious than warm and affectionate. He had vanished almost immediately after, and Charlotte could learn no news about him; till at last she accidentally found his name in the newspaper, where he was mentioned with honor among those who had most distinguished themselves in a late important engagement. She now understood

the method which he had taken; she perceived that he
had escaped from great danger; only she was convinced
at the same time that he would seek out greater; and it
was all too clear to her that in every sense he would
hardly be withheld from any extremity.

She had to bear about this perpetual anxiety in her
thoughts, and turn which way she would, there was no
light in which she could look at it that would give her
comfort.

Ottilie, never dreaming of anything of this, had taken
to the work in the chapel with the greatest interest, and
she had easily obtained Charlotte's permission to go on
with it regularly. So now all went swiftly forward, and
the azure heaven was soon peopled with worthy inhabitants. By continual practice both Ottilie and the architect had gained more freedom with the last figures; they
became perceptibly better. The faces, too, which had
been all left to the architect to paint, showed by degrees
a very singular peculiarity. They began all of them to
resemble Ottilie. The neighborhood of the beautiful girl
had made so strong an impression on the soul of the
young man, who had no variety of faces preconceived in
his mind, that by degrees, on the way from the eye to
the hand, nothing was lost, and both worked in exact
harmony together. Enough; one of the last faces
succeeded perfectly; so that it seemed as if Ottilie herself was looking down out of the spaces of the sky.

They had finished with the arching of the ceiling.
The walls they proposed to leave plain, and only to cover
them over with a bright brown color. The delicate pillars and the quaintly-moulded ornaments were to be
distinguished from them by a dark shade. But as in
such things one thing ever leads on to another, they

determined at least on having festoons of flowers and fruit, which should as it were unite together heaven and earth. Here Ottilie was in her element. The gardens provided the most perfect patterns; and although the wreaths were as rich as they could make them, it was all finished sooner than they had supposed possible.

It was still looking rough and disorderly. The scaffolding poles had been run together, the planks thrown one on the top of the other; the uneven pavement was yet more disfigured by the particolored stains of the paint which had been spilt over it.

The Architect begged that the ladies would give him a week to himself, and during that time would not enter the chapel; at the end of it, one fine evening, he came to them, and begged them both to go and see it. He did not wish to accompany them, he said, and at once took his leave.

"Whatever surprise he may have designed for us," said Charlotte, as soon as he was gone, "I cannot myself just now go down there. You can go by yourself, and tell me all about it. No doubt he has been doing something which we shall like. I will enjoy it first in your description, and afterwards it will be the more charming in the reality."

Ottilie, who knew well that in many cases Charlotte took care to avoid everything which could produce emotion, and particularly disliked to be surprised, set off down the walk by herself, and looked round involuntarily for the Architect, who however was nowhere to be seen, and must have concealed himself somewhere. She walked into the church, which she found open. This had been finished before; it had been cleaned up, and service had been performed in it. She went on to the chapel door; its heavy mass, all overlaid with iron, yielded easily to her touch, and she found an unexpected sight in a familiar spot.

A solemn beautiful light streamed in through the one tall window. It was filled with stained glass, gracefully put together. The entire chapel had thus received a strange tone, and a peculiar genius was thrown over it. The beauty of the vaulted ceiling and the walls was set off by the elegance of the pavement, which was composed of peculiarly shaped tiles, fastened together with gypsum, and forming exquisite patterns as they lay. This and the colored glass for the windows the Architect had prepared without their knowledge, and a short time was sufficient to have it put in its place.

Seats had been provided as well. Among the relics of the old church some finely carved chancel chairs had been discovered, which now were standing about at convenient places along the walls.

The parts which she knew so well now meeting her as an unfamiliar whole, delighted Ottilie. She stood still, walked up and down, looked and looked again; at last she seated herself in one of the chairs, and it seemed, as she gazed up and down, as if she was, and yet was not — as if she felt and did not feel — as if all this would vanish from before her, and she would vanish from herself; and it was only when the sun left the window, on which before it had been shining full, that she awoke to possession of herself, and hastened back to the castle.

She did not hide from herself the strange epoch at which this surprise had occurred to her. It was the evening of Edward's birthday. Very differently she had hoped to keep it. How was not everything to be dressed out for this festival? and now all the splendor of the autumn flowers remained ungathered. Those sunflowers still turned their faces to the sky; those asters still looked out with quiet, modest eye; and whatever of them all had been wound into wreaths had served as patterns for the decorating a spot which, if it was not to remain a mere artist's fancy, was only adapted as a general mausoleum.

And then she had to remember the impetuous eagerness with which Edward had kept her birthday-feast. She thought of the newly-erected lodge, under the roof of which they had promised themselves so much enjoyment. The fireworks flashed and hissed again before her eyes and ears; the more lonely she was, the more keenly her imagination brought it all before her. But she felt herself only the more alone. She no longer leant upon his arm, and she had no hope ever any more to rest herself upon it.

FROM OTTILIE'S DIARY.

"I have been struck with an observation of the young architect.

"In the case of the creative artist, as in that of the artisan, it is clear that man is least permitted to appropriate to himself what is most entirely his own. His works forsake him as the birds forsake the nest in which they were hatched.

"The fate of the Architect is the strangest of all in this way. How often he expends his whole soul, his whole heart and passion, to produce buildings into which he himself may never enter. The halls of kings owe their magnificence to him; but he has no enjoyment of them in their splendor. In the temple he draws a partition line between himself and the Holy of Holies; he may never more set his foot upon the steps which he has laid down for the heart-thrilling ceremonial; as the goldsmith may only adore from afar off the *monstrance* whose enamel and whose jewels he has himself set together. The builder surrenders to the rich man, with the key of his palace, all pleasure and all right there, and never shares with him in the enjoyment of it. And must not art in this way, step by step, draw off from the artist, when the work, like a child who is provided for, has no more to fall back upon its father? And what a power there must be in art itself, for its own self-advancing, when it has been obliged to shape itself almost solely out of what was open to all, only out of what was the property of every one, and therefore also of the artist!"

"There is a conception among old nations which is awful, and may almost seem terrible. They pictured their fore-fathers to themselves sitting round on thrones, in enormous caverns, in silent converse; when a new comer entered, if he were worthy enough, they rose up, and inclined their heads to welcome him. Yesterday, as I was sitting in the chapel, and other carved chairs stood round like that in which I was, the thought of this came over me with a soft, pleasant feeling. Why cannot you stay sitting here? I said to myself; stay here sitting meditating with yourself long, long, long, till at last your friends come, and you rise up to them, and with a gentle inclination direct them to their places. The colored window panes convert the day into a solemn twilight; and some one should set up for us an ever-burning lamp, that the night might not be utter darkness."

"We may imagine ourselves in what situation we

please, we always conceive ourselves as *seeing*. I believe
men only dream that they may not cease to see. Some
day, perhaps, the inner light will come out from within
us, and we shall not any more require another.

"The year dies away, the wind sweeps over the stub-
ble, and there is nothing left to stir under its touch. But
the red berries on yonder tall tree seem as if they would
still remind us of brighter things; and the stroke of the
thrasher's flail awakes the thought how much of nourishment and life lies buried in the sickled ear."

CHAPTER IV.

HOW strangely, after all this, with the sense so vividly
impressed on her of mutability and perishableness,
must Ottilie have been affected by the news which could
not any longer be kept concealed from her, that Edward
had exposed himself to the uncertain chances of war!
Unhappily, none of the observations which she had occasion to make upon it escaped her. But it is well for us
that man can only endure a certain degree of unhappiness;
what is beyond that, either annihilates him, or passes by
him, and leaves him apathetic. There are situations in
which hope and fear run together, in which they mutually
destroy one another, and lose themselves in a dull indifference. If it were not so, how could we bear to know of
those who are most dear to us being in hourly peril, and
yet go on as usual with our ordinary everyday life?

It was therefore as if some good genius was caring for

Ottilie, that, all at once, this stillness, in which she seemed
to be sinking from loneliness and want of occupation, was
suddenly invaded by a wild army, which, while it gave
her externally abundance of employment, and so took
her out of herself, at the same time awoke in her the
consciousness of her own power.

Charlotte's daughter, Luciana, had scarcely left the
school and gone out into the great world; scarcely had
she found herself at her aunt's house in the midst of a
large society, than her anxiety to please produced its
effect in really pleasing; and a young, very wealthy man,
soon experienced a passionate desire to make her his
own. His large property gave him a right to have the ·
best of everything for his use, and nothing seemed to be
wanting to him except a perfect wife, for whom, as for
the rest of his good fortune, he should be the envy of the
world.

This incident in her family had been for some time
occupying Charlotte. It had engaged all her attention,
and taken up her whole correspondence, except so far as
this was directed to the obtaining news of Edward; so
that latterly Ottilie had been left more than was usual to
herself. She knew, indeed, of an intended visit from
Luciana. She had been making various changes and
arrangements in the house in preparation for it; but she
had no notion that it was so near. Letters, she supposed,
would first have to pass, settling the time, and then un-
settling it; and then a final fixing: when the storm broke
suddenly over the castle and over herself.

Up drove, first, lady's maids and men-servants, their
carriage loaded with trunks and boxes. The household
was already swelled to double or to treble its size, and
then appeared the visitors themselves. There was the

great aunt, with Luciana and some of her friends; and then the bridegroom with some of his friends. The entrance-hall was full of things — bags, portmanteaus, and leather articles of every sort. The boxes had to be got out of their covers, and that was infinite trouble; and of luggage and of rummage there was no end. At intervals, moreover, there were violent showers, giving rise to much inconvenience. Ottilie encountered all this confusion with the easiest equanimity, and her happy talent showed in its fairest light. In a very little time she had brought things to order, and disposed of them. Every one found his room, — every one had his things exactly as they wished, and all thought themselves well attended to, because they were not prevented from attending on themselves.

The journey had been long and fatiguing, and they would all have been glad of a little rest after it. The bridegroom would have liked to pay his respects to his mother-in-law, express his pleasure, his gratitude, and so on. But Luciana could not rest. She had now arrived at the happiness of being able to mount a horse. The bridegroom had beautiful horses, and mount they must on the spot. Clouds and wind, rain and storm, they were nothing to Luciana, and now it was as if they only lived to get wet through, and to dry themselves again. If she took a fancy to go out walking, she never thought what sort of dress she had on, or what her shoes were like, she must go and see the grounds of which she had heard so much; what could not be done on horseback, she ran through on foot. In a little while she had seen everything, and given her opinion about everything; and with such rapidity of character it was not easy to contradict or oppose her. The whole household had much to suf-

fer, but most particularly the lady's maids, who were at
work from morning to night, washing, and ironing, and
stitching.

As soon as she had exhausted the house and the park,
she thought it was her duty to pay visits all round the
neighborhood. As they rode and drove very fast, all
round the neighborhood was a considerable distance.
The castle was flooded with return visits, and that they
might not miss one another, it soon came to days being
fixed for them.

Charlotte, in the mean time, with her aunt, and the
man of business of the bridegroom, were occupied in
determining about the settlements, and it was left to
Ottilie, with those under her, to take care that all this
crowd of people were properly provided for. Game-
keepers and gardeners, fishermen and shopdealers, were
set in motion, Luciana always showing herself like the
blazing nucleus of a comet with its long tail trailing
behind it. The ordinary amusements of the parties soon
became too insipid for her taste. Hardly would she leave
the old people in peace at the card-table. Whoever
could by any means be set moving (and who could resist
the charm of being pressed by her into service?) must
up, if not to dance, then to play at forfeits, or some other
game, where they were to be victimized and tormented.
Notwithstanding all that, however, and although afterwards the redemption of the forfeits had to be settled
with herself, yet of those who played with her, never
any one, especially never any man, let him be of what
sort he would, went quite empty-handed away. Indeed,
some old people of rank who were there she succeeded
in completely winning over to herself, by having contrived to find out their birthdays or christening days,

and marking them with some particular celebration. In all this she showed a skill not a little remarkable. Every one saw himself favored, and each considered himself to be the one most favored, a weakness of which the oldest person of the party was the most notably guilty.

It seemed to be a sort of pride with her, that men who had anything remarkable about them — rank, character, or fame — she must and would gain for herself. Gravity and seriousness she made give way to her, and, wild strange creature as she was, she found favor even with discretion itself. Not that the young were at all cut short in consequence. Everybody had his share, his day his hour, in which she contrived to charm and to enchain him. It was therefore natural enough that before long she should have had the Architect in her eye, looking out so unconsciously as he did from under his long black hair, and standing so calm and quiet in the back-ground. To all her questions she received short sensible answers; but he did not seem inclined to allow himself to be carried away further, and at last, half provoked, half in malice, she resolved that she would make him the hero of a day, and so gain him for her court.

It was not for nothing that she had brought that quantity of luggage with her. Much, indeed, had followed her afterwards. She had provided herself with an endless variety of dresses. When it took her fancy she would change her dress three or four times a day, usually wearing something of an ordinary kind, but making her appearance suddenly at intervals in a thorough masquerade dress, as a peasant girl or a fish maiden, as a fairy or a flower-girl; and this would go on from morning till night. Sometimes she would even disguise herself as an old woman, that her young face might peep out the fresher

8*

from under the cap; and so utterly in this way did she confuse and mix together the actual and the fantastic, that people thought they were living with a sort of drawing-room witch.

But the principal use which she had for these disguises were pantomimic tableaux and dances, in which she was skilful in expressing a variety of character. A cavalier in her suite had taught himself to accompany her action on the piano with the little music which was required; they needed only to exchange a few words and they at once understood one another.

One day, in a pause of a brilliant ball, they were called upon suddenly to extemporize (it was on a private hint from themselves) one of these exhibitions. Luciana seemed embarrassed, taken by surprise; and contrary to her custom let herself be asked more than once. She could not decide upon her character, desired the party to choose, and asked, like an improvisatore, for a subject. At last her piano-playing companion, with whom it had been all previously arranged, sat down at the instrument, and began to play a mourning march, calling on her to give them the Artemisia which she had been studying so admirably. She consented; and after a short absence reappeared, to the sad tender music of the dead march, in the form of the royal widow, with measured step, carrying an urn of ashes before her. A large black tablet was borne in after her, and a carefully cut piece of chalk in a gold pencil case.

One of her adorers and adjutants, into whose ear she whispered something, went directly to call the Architect, to desire him, and if he would not come to drag him up, as master-builder, to draw the grave for the mausoleum, and to tell him at the same time that he was not to play the statist, but enter earnestly into his part as one of the performers.

Embarrassed as the Architect outwardly appeared (for in his black, close-fitting, modern civilian's dress, he formed a wonderful contrast with the gauze crape fringes, tinsel tassels, and crown,) he very soon composed himself internally, and the scene became all the more strange. With the greatest gravity he placed himself in front of the tablet, which was supported by a couple of pages, and drew carefully an elaborate tomb, which indeed would have suited better a Lombard than a Carian prince; but it was in such beautiful proportions, so solemn in its parts, so full of genius in its decoration, that the spectators watched it growing with delight, and wondered at it when it was finished.

All this time he had not once turned towards the queen, but had given his whole attention to what he was doing. At last he inclined his head before her, and signified that he believed he had now fulfilled her commands. She held the urn out to him, expressing her desire to see it represented on the top of the monument. He complied, although unwillingly, as it would not suit the character of the rest of his design. Luciana was now at last released from her impatience. Her intention had been by no means to get a scientific drawing out of him. If he had only made a few strokes, sketched out something which should have looked like a monument, and devoted the rest of his time to her, it would have been far more what she had wished, and would have pleased her a great deal better. His manner of proceeding had thrown her into the greatest embarrassment. For although in her sorrow, in her directions, in her gestures, in her approbation of the work as it slowly rose before her, she had

tried to manage some sort of change of expression, and
although she had hung about close to him, only to place
herself into some sort of relation to him, yet he had kept
himself throughout too stiff, so that too often she had
been driven to take refuge with her urn; she had to
press it to her heart and look up to heaven, and at last,
a situation of that kind having a necessary tendency to
intensify, she made herself more like a widow of Ephesus
than a queen of Caria. The representation had to
lengthen itself out and became tedious. The piano-forte
player, who had usually patience enough, did not know
into what tune he could escape. He thanked God when
he saw the urn standing on the pyramid, and fell involuntarily as the queen was going to express her gratitude,
into a merry air; by which the whole thing lost its
character, the company however being throughly cheered
up by it, who forthwith divided, some going up to
express their delight and admiration of the lady for her
excellent performance, and some praising the Architect
for his most artistlike and beautiful drawing.

The bridegroom especially paid marked attention to
the Architect. "I am vexed," he said, "that the drawing should be so perishable; you will permit me however
to have it taken to my room, where I should much like
to talk to you about it."

"If it would give you any pleasure," said the Architect, "I can lay before you a number of highly finished
designs for buildings and monuments of this kind, of
which this is but a mere hasty sketch."

Ottilie was standing at no great distance, and went up
to them. "Do not forget," she said to the Architect,
"to take an opportunity of letting the Baron see your

collection. He is a friend of art and antiquity. I should like you to become better acquainted."

Luciana was passing at the moment. "What are they speaking of?" she asked.

"Of a collection of works of art," replied the Baron, "which this gentleman possesses, and which he is good enough to say that he will show us."

"Oh, let him bring them immediately," cried Luciana, "you will bring them, will you not?" she added, in a soft and sweet tone, taking both his hands in hers.

"The present is scarcely a fitting time," the Architect answered.

"What!" Luciana cried, in a tone of authority; "you will not obey the command of your queen!" and then she begged him again with some piece of absurdity.

"Do not be obstinate," said Ottilie, in a scarcely audible voice.

The Architect left them with a bow, which said neither yes nor no.

He was hardly gone, when Luciana was flying up and down the saloon with a greyhound. "Alas!" she exclaimed, as she ran accidentally against her mother, "am I not an unfortunate creature? I have not brought my monkey with me. They told me I had better not; but I am sure it was nothing but the laziness of my people, and it is such a delight to me. But I will have it brought after me; and somebody shall go and fetch it. If I could only see a picture of the dear creature, it would be a comfort to me; I certainly will have his picture taken, and it shall never be out of my sight."

"Perhaps I can comfort you," replied Charlotte. "There is a whole volume full of the most wonderful ape faces in the library, which you can have fetched if you like."

Luciana shrieked for joy. The great folio was produced instantly. The sight of these hideous creatures, so
like to men, and with the resemblance even more carica-
tured by the artist, gave Luciana the greatest delight.
Her amusement with each of the animals, was to find
some one of her acquaintance whom it resembled. "Is
that not like my uncle?" she remorselessly exclaimed;
"and here, look, here is my milliner M., and here is Par-
son S., and here the image of that creatnre ——— bodily!
After all, these monkeys are the real *incroyables*, and it
is inconceivable why they are not admitted into the best
society."

It was in the best society that she said this, and yet no
one took it ill of her. People had become accustomed to
allow her so many liberties in her prettinesses, that at last
they came to allow them in what was unpretty.

During this time, Ottilie was talking to the bridegroom;
she was looking anxiously for the return of the Architect,
whose serious and tasteful collection was to deliver the
party from the apes; and in the expectation of it, she had
made it the subject of her conversation with the Baron,
and directed his attention on various things which he
was to see. But the Architect stayed away, and when
at last he made his appearance, he lost himself in the
crowd, without having brought anything with him, and
without seeming as if he had been asked for anything.

For a moment Ottilie became — what shall we call it?
— annoyed, put out, perplexed. She had been saying so
much about him — she had promised the bridegroom an
hour of enjoyment after his own heart; and with all the
depth of his love for Luciana, he was evidently suffering
from her present behavior.

The monkeys had to give place to a collation. Round

games followed, and then more dancing; at last, a general uneasy vacancy, with fruitless attempts at resuscitating exhausted amusements, which lasted this time, as indeed they usually did, far beyond midnight. It had already become a habit with Luciana to be never able to get out of bed in the morning or into it at night.

About this time, the incidents noticed in Ottilie's diary become more rare, while we find a larger number of maxims and sentences drawn from life and relating to life. It is not conceivable that the larger proportion of these could have arisen from her own reflection, and most likely some one had shown her varieties of them, and she had written out what took her fancy. Many, however, with an internal bearing, can be easily recognized by the red thread.

FROM OTTILIE'S DIARY.

"We like to look into the future, because the undetermined in it, which may be affected this or that way, we feel as if we could guide by our silent wishes in our own favor."

"We seldom find ourselves in a large party without thinking; the accident which brings so many here together, should bring our friends to us as well."

"Let us live in as small a circle as we will, we are either debtors or creditors before we have had time to look round."

"If we meet a person who is under an obligation to us, we remember it immediately. But how often may we meet people to whom we are ourselves under obligation, without its even occurring to us!"

"It is nature to communicate one's-self; it is culture to receive what is communicated as it is given."

"No one would talk much in society, if he only knew how often he misunderstands others."

"One alters so much what one has heard from others in repeating it, only because one has not understood it."

"Whoever indulges long in monologue in the presence of others, without flattering his listeners, provokes ill-will."

"Every word a man utters provokes the opposite opinion."

"Argument and flattery are but poor elements out of which to form a conversation."

"The pleasantest society is when the members of it have an easy and natural respect for one another."

"There is nothing in which people more betray their character than in what they find to laugh at."

"The ridiculous arises out of a moral contrast, in which two things are brought together before the mind in an innocent way."

"The foolish man often laughs where there is nothing to laugh at. Whatever touches him, his inner nature comes to the surface."

———

"The man of understanding finds almost everything ridiculous; the man of thought scarcely anything."

———

"Some one found fault with an elderly man for continuing to pay attention to young ladies. 'It is the only means,' he replied, 'of keeping one's-self young, and every body likes to do that.'"

———

"People will allow their faults to be shown them; they will let themselves be punished for them; they will patiently endure many things because of them; they only become impatient when they have to lay them aside."

———

"Certain defects are necessary for the existence of individuality. We should not be pleased, if old friends were to lay aside certain peculiarities."

———

"There is a saying, 'He will die soon,' when a man acts unlike himself."

———

"What kind of defects may we bear with and even cultivate in ourselves? Such as rather give pleasure to others than injure them."

———

"The passions are defects or excellences only in excess."

"Our passions are true phœnixes: as the old burn out, the new straight rise up out of the ashes."

———

"Violent passions are incurable diseases; the means which will cure them are what first make them thoroughly dangerous."

———

"Passion is both raised and softened by confession. In nothing, perhaps, were the middle way more desirable than in knowing what to say and what not to say to those we love."

———

CHAPTER V.

SO swept on Luciana in the social whirlpool, driving the rush of life along before her. Her court multiplied daily, partly because her impetuosity roused and attracted so many, partly because she knew how to attach the rest to her by kindness and attention. Generous she was in the highest degree; her aunt's affection for her, and her bridegroom's love, had heaped her with beautiful and costly presents. but she seemed as if nothing which she had was her own, and as if she did not know the value of the things which had streamed in upon her. One day she saw a young lady looking rather poorly dressed by the side of the rest of the party, and she did not hesitate a moment to take off a rich shawl which she was wearing and hang it over her, — doing it, at the same ti,ne, in such a humorous, graceful way that no one could refuse such a present so given. One of her courtiers always carried about a purse, with orders, whatever place they passed through, to inquire there for the most aged and most helpless persons, and give them relief, at least for the moment. In this way she gained for herself all round the country a reputation for charitableness which caused her not a little inconvenience, attracting about her far too many troublesome sufferers.

Nothing, however, so much added to her popularity as her steady and consistent kindness towards an unhappy young man, who shrank from society because, while otherwise handsome and well-formed, he had lost his right hand, although with high honor, in action. This mutilation weighed so heavily upon his spirits, it was so annoying to him that every new acquaintance he made had to be told the story of his misfortune, that he chose rather to shut himself up altogether, devoting himself to reading and other studious pursuits, and once for all would have nothing more to do with society.

She heard of the state of this young man. At once she contrived to prevail upon him to come to her, first to small parties, then to greater, and then out·into the world with her. She showed more attention to him than to any other person; particularly she endeavored, by the services which she pressed upon him, to make him sensible of what he had lost in laboring herself to supply it. At dinner, she would make him sit next to her; she cut up his food for him, that he might only have to use his fork. If people older or of higher rank prevented her from being close to him, she would stretch her attention across the entire table, and the servants were hurried off to make up to him what distance threatened to deprive

him of. At last she encouraged him to write with his
left hand. All his attempts he was to address to her,
and thus, whether far or near, she always kept herself in
correspondence with him. The young man did not know
what had happened to him, and from that moment a new
life opened out before him.

One may perhaps suppose that such behavior must
have caused some uneasiness to her bridegroom. But, in
fact, it was quite the reverse. He admired her exceedingly for her exertions, and he had the more reason for
feeling entirely satisfied about her, as she had certain
features in her character almost in excess, which kept
anything in the slightest degree dangerous utterly at
a distance. She would run about with any body, just
as she fancied; no one was free from danger of a push
or a pull, or of being made the object of some sort of
freak. But no person ever ventured to do the same to
her; no person dared to touch her, or return, in the remotest degree, any liberty which she had taken herself.
She kept every one within the strictest barriers of propriety in their behavior to herself, while she, in her own
behavior, was every moment overleaping them.

On the whole, one might have supposed it had been a
maxim with her to expose herself indifferently to praise
or blame, to regard or to dislike. If in many ways she
took pains to gain people, she commonly herself spoiled
all the good she had done by an ill tongue, which spared
no one. Not a visit was ever paid in the neighborhood,
not a single piece of hospitality was ever shown to herself and her party among the surrounding castles or man-
sions, but what on her return her excessive recklessness
let it appear that all men and all human things she was
only inclined to see on the ridiculous side.

There were three brothers who, purely out of compliment to each other, which should marry first, had been overtaken by old age before they had got the question settled; here was a little young wife with a great old husband; there, on the other hand, was a dapper little man and an unwieldy giantess. In one house, every step one took one stumbled over a child; another, however many people were crammed into it, never would seem full, because there were no children there at all. Old husbands (supposing the estate was not entailed) should get themselves buried as quickly as possible, that such a thing as a laugh might be heard again in the house. Young married people should travel: housekeeping did not sit well upon them. And as she treated the persons, so she treated what belonged to them; their houses, their furniture, their. dinner-services — everything. The ornaments of the walls of the rooms most particularly provoked her saucy remarks. From the oldest tapestry to the most modern printèd paper; from the noblest family pictures to the most frivolous new copperplate: one as well as the other had to suffer — one as well as the other had to be pulled in pieces by her satirical tongue, so that, indeed, one had to wonder how, for twenty miles round, anything continued to exist.

It was not, perhaps, exactly malice which produced all this destructiveness; wilfulness and selfishness were what ordinarily set her off upon it: but a genuine bitterness grew up in her feelings towards Ottilie.

She looked down with disdain on the calm, uninterrupted activity of the sweet girl, which every one had observed and admired, and when something was said of the care which Ottilie took of the garden and of the hothouses, she not only spoke scornfully of it, in affecting

to be surprised, if it were so, at there being neither
flowers nor fruit to be seen, not caring to consider that
they were living in the depth of winter, but every faintest scrap of green, every leaf, every bud which showed,
she chose to have picked every day and squandered on
ornamenting the rooms and tables, and Ottilie and the
gardener were not a little distressed to see their hopes
for the next year, and perhaps for a longer time, destroyed in this wanton recklessness.

As little would she be content to leave Ottilie to her
quiet work at home, in which she could live with so
much comfort. Ottilie must go with them on their
pleasure-parties and sledging-parties; she must be at the
balls which were being got up all about the neighborhood. She was not to mind the snow, or the cold, or the
night-air, or the storm; other people did not die of such
things, and why should she? The delicate girl suffered
not a little from it all, but Luciana gained nothing. For
although Ottilie went about very simply dressed, she was
always, at least so the men thought, the most beautiful
person present. A soft attractiveness gathered them all
about her; no matter whereabouts in the great rooms
she was, first or last, it was always .the same. Even
Luciana's bridegroom was constantly occupied with her;
the more so, indeed, because he desired her advice and
assistance in a matter with which he was just then engaged.

He had cultivated the acquaintance of the Architect.
On seeing his collection of works of art, he had taken
occasion to talk much with him on history and on other
matters, and especially from seeing the chapel had learnt
to appreciate his talent. The Baron was young and
wealthy. He was a collector; he wished to build. His

love for the arts was keen, his knowledge small. In the Architect he thought that he had found the man he wanted; that with his assistance there was more than one aim at which he could arrive at once. He had spoken to his bride of what he wished. She praised him for it, and was infinitely delighted with the proposal. But it was more, perhaps, that she might carry off this young man from Ottilie (for whom she fancied she saw in him a kind of inclination,) than because she thought of applying his talents to any purpose. He had shown himself, indeed, very ready to help at any of her extemporized festivities, and had suggested various resources for this thing and that. But she always thought she understood better than he what should be done, and as her inventive genius was usually somewhat common, her designs could be as well executed with the help of a tolerably handy domestic as with that of the most finished artist. Further than to an altar on which something was to be offered, or to a crowning, whether of a living head or of one of plaster of Paris, the force of her imagination could not ascend, when a birthday, or other such occasion, made her wish to pay some one an especial compliment.

Ottilie was able to give the Baron the most satisfactory answer to his inquiries as to the relation of the Architect with their family. Charlotte had already, as she was aware, been exerting herself to find some situation for him; had it not been indeed for the arrival of the party, the young man would have left them immediately on the completion of the chapel, the winter having brought all building operations to a standstill; and it was, therefore, most fortunate if a new patron could be found to assist him, and to make use of his talents.

Ottilie's own personal position with the Architect was as pure and unconcious as possible. His agreeable presence, and his industrious nature, had charmed and entertained her, as the presence of an elder brother might. Her feelings for him remained at the calm unimpassioned level of blood relationship. For in her heart there was no room for more; it was filled to overflowing with love for Edward; only God, who interpenetrates all things, could share with him the possession of that heart.

Meantime the winter sank deeper; the weather grew wilder, the roads more impracticable, and therefore it seemed all the pleasanter to spend the waning days in agreeable society. With short intervals of ebb, the crowd from time to time flooded up over the house. Officers found their way there from distant garrison towns; the cultivated among them being a most welcome addition, the ruder the inconvenience of every one. Of civilians too there was no lack; and one day the Count and the Baroness quite unexpectedly came driving up together.

Their presence gave the castle the air of a thorough court. The men of rank and character formed a circle about the Count, and the ladies yielded precedence to the Baroness. The surprise at seeing both together, and in such high spirits was not allowed to be of long continuance. It came out that the Count's wife was dead, and the new marriage was to take place as soon as ever decency would allow it.

Well did Ottilie remember their first visit, and every word which was then uttered about marriage and separation, binding and dividing, hope, expectation, disappointment, renunciation. Here were these two persons, at that time without prospect for the future, now standing before her, so near their wished-for happiness, and an involuntary sigh escaped out of her heart.

No sooner did Luciana hear that the Count was an amateur of music, than at once she must get up something of a concert. She herself would sing and accompany herself on the guitar. It was done. The instrument she did not play without skill; her voice was agreeable: as for the words one understood about as little of them as one commonly does when a German beauty sings to the guitar. However, every one assured her that she had sung with exquisite expression, and she found quite enough approbation to satisfy her. A singular misfortune befell her, however, on this occasion. Among the party there happened to be a poet, whom she hoped particularly to attach to herself, wishing to induce him to write a song or two, and address them to her. This evening, therefore, she produced scarcely anything except songs of his composing. Like the rest of the party he was perfectly courteous to her, but she had looked for more. She spoke to him several times, going as near the subject as she dared, but nothing further could she get. At last, unable to bear it any longer, she sent one of her train to him, to sound him and find out whether he had not been delighted to hear his beautiful poems so beautifully executed.

"My poems?" he replied, with amazement; pray excuse me, my dear sir," he added, "I heard nothing but the vowels, and not all of those; however, I am in duty bound to express all gratitude for so amiable an intention." The dandy said nothing, and kept his secret; the other endeavored to get himself out of the scrape by a few well-timed compliments. She did not conceal her desire

9

to have something of his which should be written for herself.

If it would not have been too ill-natured, he might
have handed her the alphabet, to imagine for herself, out
of that, such laudatory poem as would please her, and set
it to the first melody that came to hand; but she was
not to escape out of this business without mortification.
A short time after, she had to learn that the very same
evening he had written, at the foot of one of Ottilie's
favorite melodies, a most lovely poem, which was something more than complimentary.

Luciana, like all persons of her sort, who never can distinguish between where they show to advantage and
where to disadvantage, now determined to try her fortune in reciting. Her memory was good, but, if the
truth must be told, her execution was spiritless, and she
was vehement without being passionate. She recited
ballad stories, and whatever else is usually delivered in
declamation. At the same time she had contracted an
unhappy habit of accompanying what she delivered with
gestures, by which, in a disagreeable way, what is purely
epic and lyric is more confused than connected with the
dramatic.

The Count, a keensighted man, soon saw through the
party, their inclinations, dispositions, wishes, and capabilities, and by some means or other contrived to bring
Luciana to a new kind of exhibition, which was perfectly
suited to her.

" I see here," he said, " a number of persons with fine
figures, who would surely be able to imitate pictorial
emotions and postures. Suppose they were to try, if the
thing is new to them, to represent some real and well-
known picture. An imitation of this kind, if it requires

some labor in arrangement, has an inconceivably charming effect."

Luciana was quick enough in perceiving that here she was on her own ground entirely. Her fine shape, her well-rounded form, the regularity and yet expressiveness of her features, her light-brown braided hair, her long neck — she ran them all over in her mind, and calculated on their pictorial effects, and if she had only known that her beauty showed to more advantage when she was still than when she was in motion, because in the last case certain ungracefulnesses continually escaped her, she would have entered even more eagerly than she did into this natural picture-making.

They looked out the engravings of celebrated pictures, and the first which they chose was Van Dyk's Belisarius. A large well proportioned man, somewhat advanced in years, was to represent the seated, blind general. The Architect was to be the affectionate soldier standing sorrowing before him, there really being some resemblance between them. Luciana, half from modesty had chosen the part of the young woman in the background, counting out some large alms into the palm of his hand, while an old woman beside her is trying to prevent her, and representing that she is giving too much. Another woman who is in the act of giving him something, was not forgotten. Into this and other pictures they threw themselves with all earnestness. The Count gave the Architect a few hints as to the best style of arrangement, and he at once set up a kind of theatre, all necessary pains being taken for the proper lighting of it. They were already deep in the midst of their preparations, before they observed how large an outlay what they were undertaking would require, and that in the country, in the middle of winter, many things which they required it would be difficult to procure; consequently, to prevent a stoppage, Luciana had nearly her whole wardrobe cut in pieces, to supply the various costumes which the original artist had arbitrarily selected.

The appointed evening came, and the exhibition was carried out in the presence of a large assemblage, and to universal satisfaction. They had some good music to excite expectation, and the performance opened with the Belisarius. The figures were so successful, the colors were so happily distributed, and the lighting managed so skilfully, that they might really have fancied themselves in another world, only that the presence of the real instead of the apparent, produced a kind of uncomfortable sensation.

The curtain fell, and was more than once raised again by general desire. A musical interlude kept the assembly amused while preparation was going forward, to surprise them with a picture of a higher stamp; it was the well-known design of Poussin. Ahasuerus and Esther. This time Luciana had done better for herself. As the fainting, sinking queen she had put out all her charms, and for the attendant maidens who were supporting her, she had cunningly selected pretty well-shaped figures, not one among whom, however, had the slightest pretension to be compared with herself. From this picture, as from all the rest, Ottilie remained excluded. To sit on the golden throne and represent the Zeus-like monarch, Luciana had picked out the finest and handsomest man of the party, so that this picture was really of inimitable perfection.

For a third they had taken the so-called "Father's Admonition" of Terburg, and who does not know Wille's admirable engraving of this picture? One foot thrown over the other, sits a noble knightly-looking father; his daughter stands before him, to whose conscience he seems to be addressing himself. She, a fine striking figure, in a folding drapery of white satin, is only to be seen from behind, but her whole bearing appears to signify that she is collecting herself. That the admonition is not too severe, that she is not being utterly put to shame, is to be gathered from the air and attitude of the father, while the mother seems as if she were trying to conceal some slight embarrassment — she is looking into a glass of wine, which she is on the point of drinking.

Here was an opportunity for Luciana to appear in her highest splendor. Her back hair, the form of her head, neck, and shoulders, were beyond all conception beautiful; and the waist, which in the modern antique of the ordinary dresses of young ladies is hardly visible, showed to the greatest advantage in all its graceful slender elegance in the really old costume. The Architect had contrived to dispose the rich folds of the white satin with the most exquisite nature, and, without any question whatever, this living imitation far exceeded the original picture, and produced universal delight. The spectators could never be satisfied with demanding a repetition of the performance, and the very natural wish to see the face and front of so lovely a creature, when they had done looking at her from behind, at last became so decided, that a merry impatient young wit, cried out aloud the words one is accustomed to write at the bottom of a page, "Tournez, s'il vous plait," which was echoed all round the room.

The performers, however, understood their advantage too well, and had mastered too completely the idea of these works of art to yield to the most general clamor.

The daughter remained standing in her shame, without favoring the spectators with the expression of her face. The father continued to sit in his attitude of admonition, and the mother did not lift nose or eyes out of the transparent glass, in which, although she seemed to be drinking, the wine did not diminish.

We need not describe the number of smaller afterpieces; for which had been chosen Flemish public-house scenes and fair and market days.

The Count and the Baroness departed, promising to return in the first happy weeks of their approaching union. And Charlotte now had hopes, after having endured two weary months of it, of ridding herself of the rest of the party at the same time. She was assured of her daughter's happiness, as soon as the first tumult of youth and betrothal should have subsided in her; for the bridegroom considered himself the most fortunate person in the world. His income was large, his disposition moderate and rational, and now he found himself further wonderfully favored in the happiness of becoming the possessor of a young lady with whom all the world must be charmed. He had so peculiar a way of referring everything to her, and only to himself through her, that it gave him an unpleasant feeling when any newly-arrived person did not devote himself heart and soul to her, and was far from flattered if, as occasionally happened, particularly with elderly men, he neglected her for a closer intimacy with himself. Everything was settled about the Architect. On New-Year's day he was to follow him, and spend the Carnival at his house in the city, where Luciana was promising herself infinite happiness from a repetition of her charmingly successful pictures, as well as from a hundred other things; all the more as her aunt and her bridegroom seemed to make so light of the expense which was required for her amusements.

And now they were to break up. But this could not be managed in an ordinary way. They were one day making fun of Charlotte aloud, declaring that they would soon have eaten out her winter stores, when the nobleman who had represented Belisarius, being fortunately a man of some wealth, carried away by Luciana's charms, to which he had been so long devoting himself, cried out unthinkingly, " Why not manage then in the Polish fashion? you come now and eat up me, and then we will go on round the circle." No sooner said than done. Luciana willed that it should be so. The next day they all packed up and the swarm alighted on a new property. There indeed they found room enough, but few conveniences and no preparatibns to receive them. Out of this arose many *contretemps*, which entirely enchanted Luciana; their life became ever wilder and wilder. Huge hunting-parties were set on foot in the deep snow, attended with every sort of disagreeableness; women were not allowed to excuse themselves any more than men, and so they trooped on, hunting and riding, sledging and shouting, from one place to another till at last they approached the residence, and there the news of the day and the scandals and what else forms the amusement of people at courts and cities gave the imagination another direction, and Luciana with her train of attendants (her aunt had gone on some time before) swept at once into a new sphere of life.

FROM OTTILIE'S DIARY.

" We accept every person in the world as that for which he gives himself out, only he must give himself out for something. We can put up with the unpleasant more easily than we can endure the insignificant.

"We venture upon anything in society except only what involves a consequence.

"We never learn to know people when they come to us: we must go to them to find out how things stand with them.

"I find it almost natural that we should see many faults in visitors, and that directly they are gone we should judge them not in the most amiable manner. For we have, so to say, a right to measure them by our own standard. Even cautious, sensible men can scarcely keep themselves in such cases from being sharp censors.

"When, on the contrary, we are staying at the houses of others, when we have seen them in the midst of all their habits and environments among those necessary conditions from which they cannot escape, when we have seen how they affect those about them, and how they adapt themselves to their circumstances, it is ignorance, it is worse, it is ill-will, to find ridiculous what in more than one sense has a claim on our respect.

"That which we call politeness and good breeding effects what otherwise can only be obtained by violence, or not even by that.

"Intercourse with women is the element of good manners.

"How can the character, the individuality of a man co-exist with polish of manner?

"The individuality can only be properly made prominent through good manners. Every one likes what has something in it, only it must not be a disagreeable something.

"In life generally, and in society no one has such high advantages as a well-cultivated soldier.

"The rudest fighting people at least do not go out of their character, and generally behind the roughness there is a certain latent good humor, so that in difficulties it is possible to get on even with them.

"No one is more intolerable than an underbred civilian. From him one has a right to look for a delicacy, as he has no rough work to do.

"When we are living with people who have a delicate sense of propriety, we are in misery on their account when anything unbecoming is committed. So I always feel for and with Charlotte, when a person is tipping his chair. She cannot endure it.

"No one would ever come into a mixed party with spectacles on his nose, if he did but know that at once we women lose all pleasure in looking at him or listening to what he has to say.

"Free-and-easiness, where there ought to be respect, is always ridiculous. No one would put his hat down when he had scarcely paid the ordinary compliments if he knew how comical it looks.

"There is no outward sign of courtesy that does not rest on a deep moral foundation. The proper education would be that which communicated the sign and the foundation of it at the same time.

"Behavior is a mirror in which every one displays his own image.

"There is a courtesy of the heart. It is akin to love. Out of it arises the purest courtesy in the outward behavior.

"A freely offered homage is the most beautiful of all relations. And how were that possible without love?

9*

"We are never further from our wishes than when we imagine that we possess what we have desired.

"No one is more a slave than the man who thinks himself free while he is not.

"A man who has only to declare that he is free, and the next moment he feels the conditions to which he is subject.   Let him venture to declare that he is under conditions, and then he will feel that he is free.

"Against great advantages in another, there are no means of defending ourselves except love.

"There is something terrible in the sight of a highly-gifted man lying under obligations to a fool.

"'No man is a hero to his valet,' the proverb says. But that is only because it requires a hero to recognize a hero.   The valet will probably know how to value the valet-hero.

"Mediocrity has no greater consolation than in the thought that genius is not immortal.

"The greatest men are connected with their own century always through some weakness.

"One is apt to regard people as more dangerous than they are.

"Fools and modest people are alike innocuous.   It is only your half-fools and your half-wise who are really and truly dangerous.

"There is no better deliverance from the world than through art; and a man can form no surer bond with it than through art.

"Alike in the moment of our highest fortune and our deepest necessity, we require the artist.

"The business of art is with the difficult and the good.

"To see the difficult easily handled, gives us the feeling of the impossible.

"Difficulties increase the nearer we are to our end.
"Sowing is not so difficult as reaping."

CHAPTER VI.

THE very serious discomfort which this visit had caused
to Charlotte was in some way compensated to her
through the fuller insight which it had enabled her to
gain into her daughter's character. In this, her knowledge of the world was of no slight service to her. It was
not the first time that so singular a character had come
across her, although she had never seen any in which the
unusual features were so largely developed; and she had
had experience enough to show her that such persons
after having felt the discipline of life, after having gone
through something of it, and been in intercourse with
older people, may come out at last really charming and
amiable; the selfishness may soften and eager restless
activity find a definite direction for itself. And therefore,
as a mother, Charlotte was able to endure the appearance
of symptoms which for others might perhaps have been
unpleasing, from a sense that where strangers only desire
to enjoy, or at least not to have their taste offended, the
business of parents is rather to hope.

After her daughter's departure, however, she had to be
pained in a singular and unlooked-for manner, in finding
that, not so much through what there really was objectionable in her behavior, as through what was good
and praiseworthy in it, she had left an ill report of her-

self behind her. Luciana seemed to have prescribed it
as a rule to herself not only to be merry with the merry,
but miserable with the miserable; and in order to give
full swing to the spirit of contradiction in her, often to
make the happy, uncomfortable, and the sad, cheerful.
In every family among whom she came, she inquired
after such members of it as were ill or infirm, and unable
to appear in society. She would go to see them in their
rooms, enact the physician, and insist on prescribing
powerful doses for them out of her own travelling medi-
cine-chest, which she constantly took with her in her
carriage; her attempted cures, as may be supposed, either
succeeding or failing as chance happened to direct.

In this sort of benevolence she was thoroughly cruel,
and would listen to nothing that was said to her, because
she was convinced that she was managing admirably.
One of these attempts of hers on the moral side failed
very disastrously, and this it was which gave Charlotte
so much trouble, inasmuch as it involved consequences
and every one was talking about it. She never had
heard of the story till Luciana was gone: Ottilie, who
had made one of the party present at the time, had to
give her a circumstantial account of it.

One of several daughters of a family of rank had the
misfortune to have caused the death of one of her younger
sisters; it had destroyed her peace of mind, and she had
never been properly herself since. She lived in her own
room, occupying herself and keeping quiet; and she could
only bear to see the members of her own family when
they came one by one. If there were several together,
she suspected at once that they were making reflections
upon her, and upon her condition. To each of them

singly she would speak rationally enough, and talk freely
for an hour at a time.

Luciana had heard of this, and had secretly determined with herself, as soon as she got into the house,
that she would forthwith work a miracle, and restore the
young lady to society. She conducted herself in the
matter more prudently than usual, managed to introduce
herself alone to the poor sick-souled girl, and, as far as
people could understand, had wound her way into her
confidence through music. At last came her fatal mistake; wishing to make a scene, and fancying that she
had sufficiently prepared her for it, one evening she suddenly introduced the beautiful pale creature into the
midst of the brilliant glittering assembly; and perhaps
even then, the attempt might not have so utterly failed,
had not the crowd themselves, between curiosity and
apprehension, conducted themselves so unwisely, first
gathering about the invalid, and then shrinking from her
again; and with their whispers, and shaking their heads
together, confusing and agitating her. Her delicate
sensibility could not endure it. With a dreadful shriek,
which expressed, as it seemed, a horror at some monster
that was rushing upon her, she fainted. The crowd fell
back in terror on every side and, Ottilie had been one of
those who had carried back the sufferer utterly insensible
to her room.

Luciana meanwhile, just like herself, had been reading
an angry lecture to the rest of the party, without reflecting for a moment that she herself was entirely to blame,
and without letting herself be deterred by this and other
failures, from going on with her experimentalizing.

The state of the invalid herself had since that time
become more and more serious; indeed, the disorder had

increased to such a degree, that the poor thing's parents were unable to keep her any longer at home, and had been forced to confide her to the care of a public institution. Nothing remained for Charlotte, except, by the delicacy of her own attention to the family, in some degree to alleviate the pain which had been occasioned by her daughter. On Ottilie, the thing had made a deep impression. She felt the more for the unhappy girl, as she was convinced, she did not attempt to deny it to Charlotte, that by a careful treatment the disorder might have been unquestionably removed.

So there came, too, as it often happens that we dwell more on past disagreeables than on past agreeables, a slight misunderstanding to be spoken of, which had led Ottilie to a wrong judgment of the Architect, when he did not choose to produce his collection that evening, although she had so eagerly begged him to produce it. His practical refusal had remained, ever since, hanging about her heart, she herself could not tell why. Her feelings about the matter were undoubtedly just; what a young lady like Ottilie could desire, a young man like the Architect ought not to have refused. The latter, however, when she took occasion to give him a gentle reproof for it, had a very valid excuse to offer for himself.

"If you knew," he said, "how roughly even cultivated people allow themselves to handle the most valuable works of art, you would forgive me for not producing mine among the crowd. No one will take the trouble to hold a medal by the rim. They will finger the most beautiful impressions, and the smoothest surfaces; they will take the rarest coins between the thumb and forefinger, and rub them up and down, as if they

were testing the execution of the touch. Without re-
membering that a large sheet of paper ought to be held
in two hands, they will lay hold, with one, of an invaluable proof-engraving of some drawing which cannot be
replaced, like a conceited politician laying hold of a
newspaper, and passing judgment by anticipation, as he
is cutting the pages, on the occurrences of the world.
Nobody cares to recollect that if twenty people, one after
the other, treat a work of art in this way, the one-and-
twentieth will not find much to see there."

"Have not I often vexed you in this way?" asked
Ottilie. "Have not I, through my carelessness, many
times injured your treasures?"

"Never once," answered the Architect, "never. For
you it would be impossible. In you the right thing is
innate."

"In any case," replied Ottilie, "it would not be a bad
plan if in the next edition of the book of good manners,
after the chapters which tell us how we ought to eat and
drink in company, a good circumstantial chapter were
inserted, how to behave among works of art and in
museums."

"Undoubtedly," said the Architect; "and then curiosity-
collectors and amateurs would be better contented to
show their valuable treasures to the world."

Ottilie had long, long forgiven him; but as he seemed
to have taken her reproof sorely to heart, and assured her
again and again that he would gladly produce everything — that he was delighted to do anything for his
friends — she felt that she had wounded his feelings, and
that she owed him some compensation. It was not easy
for her, therefore, to give an absolute refusal to a request
which he made her in the conclusion of this conversation,

although when she called her heart into counsel about it she did not see how she could allow herself to do what he wished.

The circumstances of the matter were these: Ottilie's exclusion from the picture exhibition by Luciana's jealousy, had irritated him in the highest degree; and at the same time he had observed with regret, that at this, the most brilliant part of all the amusements at the castle, ill health had prevented Charlotte from being more than rarely present; and now he did not wish to go away, without some additional proof of his gratitude, and, for the honor of one and the entertainment of the other, preparing a far more beautiful exhibition than any of those which had preceded it. Perhaps, too, unknown to himself, another secret motive was working on him. It was so hard for him to leave the house, and to leave the family. It seemed impossible to him to go away from Ottilie's eyes, under the calm, sweet, gentle glance of which the latter part of the time he had been living almost entirely alone.

The Christmas holidays were approaching; and it became at once clear to him that the very thing which he wanted was a representation with real figures of one of those pictures of the scene in the stable,— a sacred exhibition such as at this holy season good Christians delight to offer to the divine Mother and her Child, of the manner in which she, in her seeming lowliness, was honored first by the shepherds and afterwards by kings.

He had thoroughly brought before himself how such a picture should be contrived. A fair, lovely child was found, and there would be no lack of shepherds and shepherdesses. But without Ottilie the thing could not be done. The young man had exalted her in his design

to be the mother of God, and if she refused, there was no
question but the undertaking must fall to the ground.
Ottilie, half embarrassed at the proposal, referred him and
his request to Charlotte. The latter gladly gave her
permission, and lent her assistance in overcoming and
overpersuading Ottilie's hesitation in assuming so sacred
a personality. The Architect worked day and night, that
by Christmas-eve everything might be ready.

Day and night, indeed, in the literal sense. At all
times he was a man who had but few necessities : and
Ottilie's presence seemed to be to him in the place of all
delicacies. When he was working for her, it was as if he
required no sleep ; when he was busy about her, as if he
could do without food. Accordingly by the hour of the
evening solemnity, all was complete. He had found the
means of collecting some well-toned wind instruments to
form an introduction, and produce the desired temper
of thought and feeling. But when the curtain rose,
Charlotte was taken completely by surprise. The picture
which represented itself to her had been repeated so often
in the world, that one could scarcely have expected
any new impression to be produced. But here, the
reality as representing the picture had its especial advantages. The whole space was the color rather of night
than of twilight, and there was nothing even of the
details of the scene which was obscure. The inimitable
idea that all the light should proceed from the child, the
artist had contrived to carry out by an ingenious method
of illumination which was concealed by the figures in the
foreground, who were all in shadow. Bright looking
boys and girls were standing round, their fresh faces
lighted from below ; and there were angels too, whose
own brilliancy grew pale before the divine, whose ethereal

bodies showed dim and dense, and needing other light in the presence of the body of the divine humanity. By good fortune the infant had fallen asleep in the loveliest attitude, so that nothing disturbed the contemplation when the eye rested on the seeming mother, who with infinite grace had lifted off a veil to reveal her hidden treasure. At this moment the picture seemed to have been caught and there to have remained fixed. Physically dazzled, mentally surprised, the people round appeared to have just moved to turn away their half-blinded eyes, to be glancing again towards the child with curious delight, and to be showing more wonder and pleasure than awe and reverence,— although these emotions were not forgotten, and were to be traced upon the features of some of the older spectators.

But Ottilie's figure, expression, attitude, glance, excelled all which any painter has ever represented. A man who had true knowledge of art, and had seen this spectacle, would have been in fear least any portion of it should move; he would have doubted whether anything could ever so much please him again. Unluckily, there was no one present who could comprehend the whole of this effect. The Architect alone, who, as a tall, slender shepherd, was looking in from the side over those who were kneeling, enjoyed, although he was not in the best position for seeing, the fullest pleasure. And who can describe the mien of the new-made queen of heaven? The purest humility, the most exquisite feeling of modesty, at the great honor which had undeservedly been bestowed upon her, with indescribable and immeasurable happiness, was displayed upon her features, expressing as much her own personal emotion as that of the character which she was endeavoring to represent.

Charlotte was delighted with the beautiful figures; but what had most effect on her was the child. Her eyes filled with tears, and her imagination presented to her in the liveliest colors that she might soon hope to have such another darling creature on her own lap.

They had let down the curtain, partly to give the exhibitors some little rest, partly to make an alteration in the exibition. The artist had proposed to himself to transmute the first scene of night and lowliness into a picture of splendor and glory; and for this purpose had prepared a blaze of light to fall in from every side, which this interval was required to kindle.

Ottilie, in the semi-theatrical position in which she found herself, had hitherto felt perfectly at her ease, because with the exception of Charlotte and a few members of the household, no one had witnessed this devout piece of artistic display. She was, therefore, in some degree annoyed when in the interval she learnt that a stranger had come into the saloon, and had been warmly received by Charlotte. Who it was, no one was able to tell her. She therefore made up her mind not to produce a disturbance, and to go on with her character. Candles and lamps blazed out, and she was surrounded by splendor perfectly infinite. The curtain rose. It was a sight to startle the spectators. The whole picture was one blaze of light; and instead of the full depth of shadow, there now were only the colors left remaining, which, from the skill with which they had been selected, produced a gentle softening of tone. Looking out under her long eyelashes, Ottilie perceived the figure of a man sitting by Charlotte. She did not recognize him; but the voice she fancied was that of the assistant at the school. A singular emotion came over her. How many things had

happened since she last heard the voice of that her kind
instructor! Like a flash of forked lightning the stream
of her joys and her sorrow rushed swiftly before her
soul, and the question rose in her heart. Dare you confess, dare you acknowledge it all to him? If not, how
little can you deserve to appear before him under this
sainted form; and how strange must it not seem to him
who has only known you as your natural self to see you
now under this disguise? In an instant, swift as thought,
feeling and reflection began to clash and gain within her.
Her eyes filled with tears, while she forced herself to
continue to appear as a motionless figure, and it was a
relief, indeed, to her when the child began to stir, — and
the artist saw himself compelled to give the sign that the
curtain should fall again.

If the painful feeling of being unable to meet a valued
friend had, during the last few moments, been distressing
Ottilie in addition to her other emotions, she was now in
still greater embarrassment. Was she to present herself
to him in this strange disguise? or had she better change
her dress? She did not hesitate — she did the last; and
in the interval she endeavored to collect and to compose
herself; nor did she properly recover her self-possession
until at last, in her ordinary costume, she had welcomed
the new visitor.

CHAPTER VII.

IN so far as the Architect desired the happiness of his
kind patronesses, it was a pleasure to him, now that
at last he was obliged to go, to know that he was leaving
them in good society with the estimable Assistant. At
the same time, however, when he thought of their good-
ness in its relation to himself, he could not help feeling it
a little painful to see his place so soon, and as it seemed
to his modesty, so well, so completely supplied. He had
lingered and lingered, but now he forced himself away;
what, after he was gone, he must endure as he could, at
least he could not stay to witness with his own eyes.

To the greater relief of this half-melancholy feeling,
the ladies at his departure made him a present of a waistcoat, upon which he had watched them both for some
time past at work, with a silent envy of the fortunate
unknown, to whom it was by-and-by to belong. Such
a present is the most agreeable which a true-hearted man
can receive; for while he thinks of the unwearied play
of the beautiful fingers at the making of it, he cannot
help flattering himself that in so long-sustained a labor
the feeling could not have remained utterly without an
interest in its accomplishment.

The ladies had now a new visitor to entertain, for
whom they felt a real regard, and whose stay with them
it would be their endeavor to make as agreeable as they
could. There is in all women a peculiar circle of inward
interests, which remain always the same, and from
which nothing in the world can divorce them. In outward social intercourse, on the other hand, they will

gladly and easily allow themselves to take their tone from
the person with whom at the moment they are occupied;
and thus by a mixture of impassiveness and susceptibility,
by persisting and by yielding, they continue to keep the
government to themselves, and no man in the cultivated
world can ever take it from them.

The Architect, following at the same time his own
fancy and his own inclination, had been exerting himself
and putting out his talents for their gratification and for
the purposes of his friends; and business and amusement,
while he was with them, had been conducted in this
spirit, and directed to the ends which most suited his
taste. But now in a short time, through the presence of
the Assistant, quite another sort of life was commenced.
His great gift was to talk well, and to treat in his conversation of men and human relations, particularly in
reference to the cultivation of young people. Thus arose
a very perceptible contrast to the life which had been
going on hitherto, all the more as the Assistant could not
entirely approve of their having interested themselves in
such subjects so exclusively.

Of the impersonated picture which received him on
arrival, he never said a single word. On the other hand,
when they took him to see the church and the chapel
with their new decorations, expecting to please him as
much as they were pleased themselves, he did not hesitate
to express a very contrary opinion about it.

"This mixing up of the holy with the sensuous," he
said, "is anything but pleasing to my taste; I cannot
like men to set apart certain especial places, consecrate
them, and deck them out, that by so doing they may
nourish in themselves a temper of piety. No ornaments,
not even the very simplest, should disturb in us that sense

of the Divine Being which accompanies us wherever we are, and can consecrate every spot into a temple. What pleases me is to see a home-service of God held in the saloon where people come together to eat, where they have their parties, and amuse themselves with games and dances. The highest, the most excellent in men, has no form; and one should be cautious how one gives it any form except noble action."

Charlotte, who was already generally acquainted with his mode of thinking, and in the short time he had been at the castle, had already probed it more deeply, found something also which he might do for her in his own department; and she had her garden children, whom the Architect had reviewed shortly before his departure, marshalled up into the great saloon. In their bright, clean uniforms, with their regular orderly movement, and their own natural vivacity, they looked exceedingly well. The Assistant examined them in his own way, and by a variety of questions, and by the turns which he gave them, soon brought to light the capacities and dispositions of the children; and without its seeming so, in the space of less than one hour he had really given them important instruction and assistance.

"How did you manage that?" said Charlotte, as the children marched away. "I listened with all my attention. Nothing was brought forward except things which were quite familiar, and yet I cannot tell the least how I should begin, to bring them to be discussed in so short a time so methodically, with all this questioning and answering."

"Perhaps," replied the Assistant, "we ought to make a secret of the tricks of our own handicraft. However, I will not hide from you one very simple maxim, with the

help of which you may do this, and a great deal more
than this. Take any subject, a substance, an idea, whatever you like; keep fast hold of it; make yourself thoroughly acquainted with it in all its parts, and then it will
be easy for you, in conversation, to find out, with a mass
of children, how much about it has already developed
itself in them; what requires to be stimulated, what to be
directly communicated. The answers to your questions
may be as unsatisfactory as they will, they may wander
wide of the mark; if you only take care that your counter-
question shall draw their thoughts and senses inwards
again; if you do not allow yourself to be driven from
your own position — the children will at last reflect,
comprehend, learn only what the teacher desires them to
learn, and the subject will be presented to them in the
light in which he wishes them to see it. The greatest
mistake which he can make is to allow himself to be run
away with from the subject; not to know how to keep
fast to the point with which he is engaged. Do you try
this on your own account the next time the children
come; you will find you will be greatly entertained by it
yourself."

"That is very good," said Charlotte. "The right
method of teaching is the reverse, I see, of what we must
do in life. In society we must keep the attention long
upon nothing, and in instruction the first commandment
is to permit no dissipation of it."

"Variety, without dissipation, were the best motto for
both teaching and life, if this desirable equipoise were
easy to be preserved," said the Assistant, and he was
going on further with the subject, when Charlotte called
out to him to look again at the children, whose merry
troop were at the moment moving across the court. He

expressed his satisfaction at seeing them wearing a uniform. "Men," he said, "should wear a uniform from their childhood upwards. They have to accustom themselves to work together; to lose themselves among their equals; to obey in masses, and to work on a large scale. Every kind of uniform, moreover, generates a military habit of thought, and a smart, straightforward carriage. All boys are born soldiers, whatever you do with them. You have only to watch them at their mock fights and games, their storming parties and scaling parties."

"On the other hand, you will not blame me," replied Ottilie, "if I do not insist with my girls on such unity of costume. When I introduce them to you, I hope to gratify you by a party-colored mixture."

"I approve of that, entirely," replied the other. "Women should go about in every sort of variety of dress; each following her own style and her own likings, that each may learn to feel what sits well upon her and becomes her. And for a more weighty reason as well — because it is appointed for them to stand alone all their lives, and work alone."

"That seems to me to be a paradox," answered Charlotte. "Are we then to be never anything for ourselves?"

"O, yes!" replied the assistant. "In respect of other women assuredly. But observe a young lady as a lover, as a bride, as a housewife, as a mother. She always stands isolated. She is always alone, and will be alone. Even the most empty-headed woman is in the same case. Each one of them excludes all others. It is her nature to do so; because of each one of them is required everything which the entire sex have to do. With a man it is altogether different. He would make a second man if there were none. But a woman might live to an eternity, without even so much as thinking of producing a duplicate of herself."

"One has only to say the truth in a strange way," said Charlotte, "and at last the strangest thing will seem to be true. We will accept what is good for us out of your observations, and yet as women we will hold together with women, and do common work with them too; not to give the other sex too great an advantage over us. Indeed, you must not take it ill of us, if in future we come to feel a little malicious satisfaction when our lords and masters do not get on in the very best way together."

With much care, this wise, sensible person went on to examine more closely how Ottilie proceeded with her little pupils, and expressed his marked approbation of it. "You are entirely right," he said, "in directing these children only to what they can immediately and usefully put in practice. Cleanliness, for instance, will accustom them to wear their clothes with pleasure to themselves; and everything is gained if they can be induced to enter into what they do with cheerfulness and self-reflection."

In other ways he found, to his great satisfaction, that nothing had been done for outward display; but all was inward, and designed to supply what was indispensably necessary. "In how few words," he cried, "might the whole business of education be summed up, if people had but ears to hear!"

"Will you try whether I have any ears?" said Ottilie, smiling.

"Indeed I will," answered he, "only you must not betray me. Educate the boys to be servants, and the girls to be mothers, and everything is as it should be."

"To be mothers?" replied Ottilie. "Women would

scarcely think that sufficient. They have to look forward, without being mothers, to going out into service.
And, indeed, our young men think themselves a great
deal too good for servants. One can see easily, in every
one of them, that he holds himself far fitter to be a master."

"And for that reason we should say nothing about it
to them," said the Assistant. "We flatter ourselves on
into life; but life flatters not us. How many men would
like to acknowledge at the outset, what at the end they
must acknowledge whether they like it or not? But let
us leave these considerations, which do not concern us
here.

"I consider you very fortunate in having been able to
go so methodically to work with your pupils. If your
very little ones run about with their dolls, and stitch
together a few petticoats for them; if the elder sisters
will then take care of the younger, and the whole household know how to supply its own wants, and one member
of it help the others, the further step into life will not
then be great, and such a girl will find in her husband
what she has lost in her parents.

"But among the higher ranks the problem is a sorely
intricate one. We have to provide for higher, finer, more
delicate relations; especially for such as arise out of
society. We are, therefore, obliged to give our pupils an
outward cultivation. It is indispensable, it is necessary,
and it may be really valuable, if we do not overstep the
proper measure in it. Only it is so easy, while one is
proposing to cultivate the children for a wider circle, to
drive them out into the indefinite, without keeping before
our eyes the real requisites of the inner nature. Here

lies the problem which more or less must be either solved
or blundered over by all educators.

"Many things, with which we furnish our scholars at
the school, do not please me; because experience tells
me of how little service they are likely to be in after-life.
How much is not at once stripped off; how much is not
at once committed to oblivion, as soon as the young lady
finds herself in the position of a housewife or a mother!

"In the meantime, since I have devoted myself to this
occupation, I cannot but entertain a devout hope that one
day, with the companionship of some faithful helpmate, I
may succeed in cultivating purely in my pupils that, and
that only, which they will require when they pass out
into the field of independent activity and self-reliance;
that I may be able to say to myself, in this sense is their
education completed. Another education there is indeed
which will again speedily recommence, and work on well
nigh through all the years of our life — the education
which circumstances will give us, if we do not give it to
ourselves."

How true Ottilie felt were these words! What had
not a passion, little dreamed of before, done to educate
her in the past year! What trials did she not see hovering before her if she looked forward only to the next —
to the very next, which was now so near!

It was not without a purpose that the young man had
spoken of a helpmate — of a wife; for with all his diffi-
dence, he could not refrain from thus remotely hinting at
his own wishes. A number of circumstances and accidents, indeed, combined to induce him on this visit to
approach a few steps towards his aim.

The Lady Superior of the school was advanced in
years. She had been already for some time looking

about among her fellow-laborers, male and female, for some person whom she could take into partnership with herself, and at last had made proposals to the Assistant, in whom she had the highest ground for feeling confidence. He was to conduct the business of the school with herself. He was to work with her in it, as if it was his own; and after her death, as her heir, to enter upon it as sole proprietor.

The principal thing now seemed to be, that he should find a wife who would co-operate with him. Ottilie was secretly before his eyes and before his heart. A number of difficulties suggested themselves, and yet again there were favorable circumstances on the other side to counterbalance them. Luciana had left the school; Ottilie could therefore return with less difficulty. Of the affair with Edward, some little had transpired. It passed, however, as many such things do, as a matter of indifference, and this very circumstance might make it desirable that she should leave the castle. And yet, perhaps, no decision would have been arrived at, no step would have been taken, had not an unexpected visit given a special impulse to his hesitation. The appearance of remarkable people, in any and every circle, can never be without its effects.

The Count and the Baroness, who often found themselves asked for their opinion, almost every one being in difficulty about the education of their children, as to the value of the various schools, had found it desirable to make themselves particularly acquainted with this one, which was generally so well spoken of; and under their present circumstances, they were more easily able to carry on these inquiries in company.

The Baroness, however, had something else in view as

well. While she was last at the castle, she had talked
over with Charlotte the whole affair of Edward and
Ottilie. She had insisted again and again that Ottilie
must be sent away. She tried every means to encourage
Charlotte to do it, and to keep her from being frightened
by Edward's threats. Several modes of escape from the
difficulty were suggested. Accidentally the school was
mentioned, and the Assistant and his incipient passion,
which made the Baroness more resolved than ever to
pay her intended visit there.

She went; she made acquaintance with the Assistant;
looked over the establishment, and spoke of Ottilie.
The Count also spoke with much interest of her, having
in his recent visit learnt to know her better. She had
been drawn towards him; indeed, she had felt attracted
by him; believing that she could see, that she could perceive in his solid, substantial conversation, something to
which hitherto she had been an entire stranger. In her
intercourse with Edward, the world had been utterly forgotten; in the presence of the Count, the world appeared
first worth regarding. The attraction was mutual. The
Count conceived a liking for Ottilie; he would have been
glad to have had her for a daughter. Thus a second time,
and worse than the first time, she was in the way of the
Baroness. Who knows what, in times when passions ran
hotter than they do now-a-days, this lady might not have
devised against her? As things were, it was enough if
she could get her married, and render her more innocuous for the future to the peace of mind of married women.
She therefore artfully urged the Assistant, in a delicate,
but effective manner, to set out on a little excursion to
the castle; where his plans and his wishes, of which he
made no secret to the lady, he might forthwith take steps
to realize.

With the fullest consent of the Superior he started off on his expedition, and in his heart he nourished good hopes of success. He knew that Ottilie was not ill-disposed towards him; and although it was true there was some disproportion of rank between them, yet distinctions of this kind were fast disappearing in the temper of the time. Moreover, the Baroness had made him perceive clearly that Ottilie must always remain a poor portionless maiden. To be related to a wealthy family, it was said, could be of service to nobody. For even with the largest property, men have a feeling that it is not right to deprive of any considerable sum, those who, as standing in a nearer degree of relationship, appear to have a fuller right to possession; and really it is a strange thing, that the immense privilege which a man has of disposing of his property after his death, he so very seldom uses for the benefit of those whom he loves, out of regard to established usage only appearing to consider those who would inherit his estate from him supposing he made no will at all.

Thus, while on his journey, he grew to feel himself entirely on a level with Ottilie. A favorable reception raised his hopes. He found Ottilie indeed not altogether so open with him as usual, but she was considerably matured, more developed, and, if you please, generally more conversable than he had known her. She was ready to give him the fullest insight into many things which were in any way connected with his profession; but when he attempted to approach his proper object, a certain inward shyness always held him back.

Once, however, Charlotte gave him an opportunity for saying something. In Ottilie's presence she said to him, "Well now, you have looked closely enough into everything which is going forward in my circle. How do you find Ottilie? you had better say while she is here."

Hereupon the Assistant signified, with a clear perception and composed expression, how that, in respect of a freer carriage, of an easier manner in speaking, of a higher insight into the things of the world, which showed itself more in actions than in words, he found Ottilie altered much for the better; but that he still believed it might be of serious advantage to her if she would go back for some little time to the school, in order methodically and thoroughly to make her own for ever what the world was only imparting to her in fragments and pieces, rather perplexing her than satisfying her, and often too late to be of service. He did not wish to be prolix about it. Ottilie herself knew best how much method and connection there was in the style of instruction out of which, in that case, she would be taken.

Ottilie had nothing to say against this; she could not acknowledge what it was which these words made her feel, because she was hardly able to explain it to herself. It seemed to her as if nothing in the world was disconnected so long as she thought of the one person whom she loved: and she could not conceive how, without him, anything could be connected at all.

Charlotte replied to the proposal with a wise kindness. She said that herself, as well as Ottilie, had long desired her return to the school. At that time, however, the presence of so dear a companion and helper had become indispensable to herself; still she would offer no obstacle at some future period, if Ottilie continued to wish it, to her going back there for such a time as would enable her to complete what she had begun, and to make entirely her own what had been interrupted.

The Assistant listened with delight to this qualified assent. Ottilie did not venture to say anything against it, although the very thought made her shudder. Charlotte, on her side, thought only how to gain time. She hoped that Edward would soon come back and find himself a happy father, then she was convinced all would go right; and one way or another they would be able to settle something for Ottilie.

After an important conversation which has furnished matter for after-reflection to all who have taken part in it, there commonly follows a sort of pause, which in appearance is like a general embarrassment. They walked up and down the saloon. The assistant turned over the leaves of various books, and came at last on the folio of engravings which had remained lying there since Luciana's time. As soon as he saw that it contained nothing but apes, he shut it up again.

It may have been this, however, which gave occasion to a conversation of which we find traces in Ottilie's diary.

FROM OTTILIE'S DIARY.

"It is strange how men can have the heart to take such pains with the pictures of those hideous monkeys. One lowers one's-self sufficiently when one looks at them merely as animals, but it is really wicked to give way to the inclination to look for people whom we know behind such masks."

———

"It is a sure mark of a certain obliquity, to take pleasure in caricatures and monstrous faces, and pigmies. I have to thank our kind Assistant that I have never been

10*

vexed with natural history; I could never make myself
at home with worms and beetles."

"Just now he acknowledged to me, that it was the
same with him. 'Of nature,' he said, 'we ought to know
nothing except what is actually alive immediately around
us. With the trees which blossom and put out leaves
and bear fruit in our own neighborhood, with every shrub
which we pass by, with every blade of grass on which
we tread, we stand in a real relation. They are our genuine compatriots. The birds which hop up and down
among our branches, which sing among our leaves, belong
to us; they speak to us from out childhood upwards, and
we learn to understand their language. But let a man
ask himself whether or not every strange creature, torn
out of its natural environment, does not at first sight
make a sort of painful impression upon him, which is
only deadened by custom. It is a mark of a motley, dissipated sort of life, to be able to endure monkeys, and
parrots, and black people, about one's-self.'"

"Many times when a certain longing curiosity about
these strange objects has come over me, I have envied
the traveller who sees such marvels in living, every-day
connection with other marvels. But he, too, must have
become another man. Palm-trees will not allow a man
to wander among them with impunity; and doubtless
his tone of thinking becomes very different in a land
where elephants and tigers are at home."

"The only inquirers into nature whom we care to respect, are such as know how to describe and to represent

to us the strange wonderful things which they have seen
in their proper locality, each in its own especial element.
How I should enjoy once hearing Humboldt talk!"

"A cabinet of natural curiosities we may regard like
an Egyptian burying-place, where the various plant gods
and animal gods stand about embalmed. It may be well
enough for a priest-caste to busy itself with such things
in a twilight of mystery. But in general instruction,
they have no place or business; and we must beware of
them all the more, because what is nearer to us, and
more valuable, may be so easily thrust aside by them."

"A teacher who can arouse a feeling for one single
good action, for one single good poem, accomplishes
more than he who fills our memory with rows on rows
of natural objects, classified with name and form. For
what is the result of all these, except what we know as
well without them, that the human figure pre-eminently
and peculiarly is made in the image and likeness of
God?"

"Individuals may be left to occupy themselves with
whatever amuses them, with whatever gives them pleasure, whatever they think useful; but the proper study of
mankind is man."

CHAPTER VIII.

THERE are but few men who care to occupy themselves with the immediate past. Either we are forcibly bound up in the present, or we lose ourselves in the long gone-by, and seek back for what is utterly lost, as if it were possible to summon it up again, and rehabilitate it. Even in great and wealthy families who are under large obligations to their ancestors, we commonly find men thinking more of their grandfathers than their fathers.

Such reflections as these suggested themselves to our Assistant, as, on one of those beautiful days in which the departing winter is accustomed to intimate the spring, he had been walking up and down the great old castle garden, and admiring the tall avenues of the lindens, and the formal walks and flower-beds which had been laid out by Edward's father. The trees had thriven admirably, according to the design of him who had planted them, and now when they ought to have begun to be valued and enjoyed, no one ever spoke to them. Hardly any one even went near them, and the interest and the outlay was now directed to the other side, out into the free and the open.

He remarked upon it to Charlotte on his return; she did not take it unkindly. " While life is sweeping us forwards," she replied, "we fancy that we are acting out our own impulses; we believe that we choose ourselves what we will do, and what we will enjoy. But in fact, if we look at it closely, our actions are no more than the plans, and the desires of the time which we are compelled to carry out."

"No doubt," said the Assistant. "And who is strong enough to withstand the stream of what is round him? Time passes on, and in it, opinions, thoughts, prejudices, and interests. If the youth of the son falls in the era of revolution, we may feel assured that he will have nothing in common with his father. If the father lived at a time when the desire was to accumulate property, to secure the possession of it, to narrow and to gather one's-self in, and to base one's enjoyment in separation from the world, the son will at once seek to extend himself, to communicate himself to others, to spread himself over a wide surface, and open out his closed stores."

"Entire periods," replied Charlotte, "resemble the father and son whom you have been describing. Of the state of things when every little town was obliged to have its walls and moats, when the castle of the nobleman was built in a swamp, and the smallest manor-houses were only accessible by a draw-bridge, we are scarcely able to form a conception. In our days, the largest cities take down their walls, the moats of the princes' castles are filled in; cities are no more than great *places*, and when one travels and sees all this, one might fancy that universal peace was just established, and the golden age was before the door. No one feels himself easy in a garden which does not look like the open country. There must be nothing to remind him of form and constraint, we choose to be entirely free, and to draw our breath without sense of confinement. Do you conceive it possible, my friend, that we can ever return again out of this into another, into our former condition?"

"Why should we not?" replied the Assistant. "Every condition has its own burden along with it, the most relaxed as well as the most constrained. The first presupposes abundance, and leads to extravagance. Let want re-appear, and the spirit of moderation is at once with us again. Men who are obliged to make use of their space and their soil, will speedily enough raise walls up round their gardens to be sure of their crops and plants. Out of this will arise by degrees a new 'phase of things: the useful will again gain the upper hand; and even the man of large possessions will feel at last that he must make the most of all which belongs to him. Believe me, it is quite possible that your son may become indifferent to all which you have been doing in the park, and draw in again behind the solemn walls and the tall lindens of his grandfather."

The secret pleasure which it gave Charlotte to have a son foretold to her, made her forgive the Assistant his somewhat unfriendly prophecy of how it might one day fare with her lovely, beautiful park. She therefore answered without any discomposure: "You and I are not old enough yet to have lived through very much of these contradictions; and yet when I look back into my own early youth, when I remember the style of complaints which I used then to hear from older people, and when I think at the same time of what the country and .the town then were, I have nothing to advance against what you say. But is there nothing which one can do to remedy this natural course of things? Are father and son, parents and children, to be always thus unable to understand each other? You have been so kind as to prophesy a boy to me. Is it necessary that he must stand in contradiction to his father? Must he destroy what his parents have erected, instead of completing it, instead of following on upon the same idea, and elevating it?

"There is a rational remedy for it," replied the Assistant. "But it is one which will be but seldom put in practice by men. The father should raise his son to a joint ownership with himself. He should permit him to plant and to build; and allow him the same innocent liberty which he allows to himself. One form of activity may be woven into another, but it cannot be pieced on to it. A young shoot may be readily and easily grafted with an old stem, to which no grown branch admits of being fastened.

The Assistant was glad to have the opportunity, at the moment when he saw himself obliged to take his leave, of saying something agreeable to Charlotte, and thus making himself a new link to secure her favor. He had been already too long absent from home, and yet he could not make up his mind to return there, until after a full conviction that he must allow the approaching epoch of Charlotte's confinement first to pass by, before he could look for any decision from her in respect to Ottilie. He therefore accommodated himself to the circumstances and returned with these prospects and hopes to the Superior.

Charlotte's confinement was now approaching; she kept more in her own room. The ladies who had gathered about her were her closest companions. Ottilie managed all domestic matters, hardly able, however, the while, to think what she was doing. She had indeed utterly resigned herself; she desired to continue to exert herself to the extent of her power for Charlotte, for the child, for Edward. But she could not see how it would be possible for her. Nothing could save her from utter distraction, except patiently to do the duty which each day brought with it.

A son was brought happily into the world, and the

ladies declared, with one voice, it was the very image of
its father. Only Ottilie, as she wished the new mother
joy, and kissed the child with all her heart, was unable to
see the likeness. Once already Charlotte had felt most
painfully the absence of her husband, when she had to
make preparations for her daughter's marriage. And
now the father could not be present at the birth of his
son. He could not have the choosing of the name by
which the child was hereafter to be called.

The first among all Charlotte's friends who came to
wish her joy was Mittler. He had placed expresses
ready to bring him news the instant the event took place.
He was admitted to see her, and, scarcely able to conceal
his triumph even before Ottilie, when alone with Charlotte he broke fairly out with it; and was at once ready
with means to remove all anxieties, and set aside all
immediate difficulties. The baptism should not be
delayed a day longer than necessary. The old clergyman, who had one foot already in the grave, should leave
his blessing to bind together the past and the future.
The child should be called Otto; what name would he
bear so fitly as that of his father and of his father's friend?

It required the peremptory resolution of this man to
set aside the innumerable considerations, arguments, hesi-
tations, difficulties; what this person knew, and that person knew better; the opinions, up and down, and backwards and forwards, which every friend volunteered. It
always happens on such occasions that when one inconvenience is removed, a fresh inconvenience seems to
arise; and in wishing to spare all sides, we inevitably go
wrong on one side or the other.

The letters to friends and relations were all undertaken
by Mittler, and they were to be written and sent off at

once. It was highly necessary, he thought, that the good
fortune which he considered so important for the family,
should be known as widely as possible through the ill-
natured and misinterpreting world. For indeed these
late entanglements and perplexities had got abroad
among the public, which at all times has a conviction
that whatever happens, happens only in order that it may
have something to talk about.

The ceremony of the baptism was to be observed with
all due honor, but it was to be as brief and as private as
possible. The people came together; Ottilie and Mittler
were to hold the child as sponsors. The old pastor, supported by the servants of the church, came in with slow
steps; the prayers were offered. The child lay in Ottilie's arms, and as she was looking affectionately down at
it, it opened its eyes and she was not a little startled
when she seemed to see her own eyes looking at her.
The likeness would have surprised any one. Mittler,
who next had to receive the child, started as well; he
fancying he saw in the little features a most striking likeness to the Captain. He had never seen a resemblance
so marked.

The infirmity of the good old clergyman had not permitted him to accompany the ceremony with more than
the usual liturgy.

Mittler, however, who was full of his subject, recollected his old performances when he had been in the ministry
and indeed it was one of his peculiarities that on every
sort of occasion, he always thought what he would like
to say, and how he would express himself about it.

At this time he was the less able to contain himself, as
he was now in the midst of a circle consisting entirely of
well known friends. He began therefore towards the

conclusion of the service, to put himself quietly into the
place of the clergyman ; to make cheerful speeches aloud,
expressive of his duty and his hopes as godfather, and to
dwell all the longer on the subject, as he thought he saw
in Charlotte's gratified manner that she was pleased with
his doing so.

It altogether escaped the eagerness of the orator, that
the good old man would gladly have set down; still less
did he think that he was on the way to occasion a more
serious evil.   After he had described with all his power
of impressiveness the relation in which every person present stood toward the child, thereby putting Ottilie's composure sorely to the proof, he turned at last to the old
man with the words, "And you, my worthy father, you
may now well say with Simeon, 'Lord, now lettest thou
thy servant depart in peace, for mine eyes have seen the
saviour of this house.' "

He was now in full swing towards a brilliant peroration
when he perceived the old man to whom he held out the
child, first appear a little to incline towards it, and
immediately after to totter and sink backwards.   Hardly
prevented from falling, he was lifted to a seat; but, notwithstanding the instant assistance which was rendered,
he was found to be dead.

To see thus side by side birth and death, the coffin and
the cradle, to see them and to realize them, to comprehend, not with the eye of imagination, but with the
bodily eye, at one moment these fearful opposites, was
a hard trial to the spectators; the harder, the more
utterly it had taken them by surprise. Ottilie alone stood
contemplating the slumberer, whose features still retained
their gentle sweet expression, with a kind of envy.   The

life of her soul was killed; why should the bodily life any longer drag on in weariness?

But though Ottilie was frequently led by melancholy incidents which occurred in the day, to thoughts of the past, of separation and of loss, at night she had strange visions given her to comfort her, which assured her of the existence of her beloved, and thus strengthened her, and gave her life for her own. When she laid herself down at night to rest, and was floating among sweet sensations between sleep and waking, she seemed to be looking into a clear but softly illuminated space. In this she would see Edward with the greatest distinctness, and not in the dress in which she had been accustomed to see him, but in military uniform; never in the same position, but always in a natural one, and not the least with anything fantastic about him, either standing or walking, or lying down or riding. The figure, which was painted with the utmost minuteness, moved readily before her without any effort of hers, without her willing it or exerting her imagination to produce it. Frequently she saw him surrounded with something in motion, which was darker than the bright ground; but the figures were shadowy, and she could scarcely distinguish them — sometimes they were like men, sometimes they were like horses, or like trees, or like mountains. She usually went to sleep in the midst of the apparition, and when, after a quiet night, she woke again in the morning, she felt refreshed and comforted; she could say to herself, Edward still lives, and she herself was still remaining in the closest relation towards him.

CHAPTER IX.

THE spring was come; it was late, but it therefore burst out more rapidly and more exhilaratingly than usual. Ottilie now found in the garden the fruits of her carefulness. Everything shot up and came out in leaf and flower at its proper time. A number of plants which she had been training up under glass frames and in hotbeds, now burst forward at once to meet, at last, the advances of nature; and whatever there was to do, and to take care of, it did not remain the mere labor of hope which it had been, but brought its reward in immediate and substantial enjoyment.

There was many a chasm however among the finest shoots produced by Luciana's wild ways, for which she had to console the gardener, and the symmetry of many a leafy coronet was destroyed. She tried to encourage him to hope that it would all be soon restored again, but he had too deep a feeling, and too pure an idea of the nature of his business, for such grounds of comfort to be of much service with him. Little as the gardener allowed himself to have his attention dissipated by other tastes and inclinations, he could the less bear to have the peaceful course interrupted which the plant follows towards its enduring or its transient perfection. A plant is like a self-willed man, out of whom we can obtain all which we desire, if we will only treat him his own way. A calm eye, a silent method, in all seasons of the year, and at every hour, to do exactly what has then to be done, is required of no one perhaps more than of a gardener. These qualities the good man possessed in an

eminent degree, and it was on that account that Ottilie
liked so well to work with him; but for some time past
he had not found himself able to exercise his peculiar
talent with any pleasure to himself. Whatever concerned
the fruit-gardening or kitchen-gardening, as well as whatever had in time past been required in the ornamental
gardens, he understood perfectly. One man succeeds in
one thing, another in another; he succeeded in these.
In his management of the orangery, of the bulbous
flowers, in budding shoots and growing cuttings from the
carnations and auriculas, he might challenge nature herself. But the new ornamental shrubs and fashionable
flowers remained in a measure strange to him. He had
a kind of shyness of the endless field of botany, which
had been lately opening itself, and the strange names
humming about his ears made him cross and ill-tempered.
The orders for flowers which had been made by his lord
and lady in the course of the past year, he considered so
much useless waste and extravagance. All the more, as
he saw many valuable plants disappear; and as he had
ceased to stand on the best possible terms with the
nursery gardeners, who he fancied had not been serving
him honestly.

Consequently, after a number of attempts, he had
formed a sort of a plan, in which Ottilie encouraged him
the more readily, because its first essential condition was
the return of Edward, whose absence in this, as in many
other matters, every day had to be felt more and more
seriously.

Now that the plants were ever striking new roots, and
putting out their shoots, Ottilie felt herself even more
fettered to this spot. It was just a year since she had
come there as a stranger, as a mere insignificant creature.

How much had she not gained for herself since that time! but, alas! how much had she not also since that time lost again! Never had she been so rich, and never so poor. The feelings of her loss and of her gain alternated momentarily one with another, chasing each other through her heart; and she could find no other means to help herself, except always to set to work again at what lay nearest to her, with such interest and eagerness as she could command.

That everything which she knew to be dear to Edward received especial care from her may be supposed. And why should she not hope that he himself would now soon come back again; and that when present, he would show himself grateful for all the care and pains which she had taken for him in his absence?

But there was also a far different employment which she took upon herself in his service; she had undertaken the principal charge of the child, whose immediate attendant it was all the easier for her to be, as they had determined not to put it into the hands of a nurse, but to bring it up themselves by hand with milk and water. In the beautiful season it was much out of doors, enjoying the free air, and Ottilie liked best to take it out herself, to carry the unconscious sleeping infant among the flowers and blossoms which should one day smile so brightly on its childhood, — among the young shrubs and plants, which, by their youth, seemed designed to grow up with the young lord to their after stature. When she looked about her, she did not hide from herself to what a high position that child was born; far and wide, wherever the eye could see, all would one day belong to him. How desirable, how necessary it must therefore be, that it should grow up under the eyes of its father and its mother, and renew and strengthen the union between them!

Ottilie saw all this so clearly, that she represented it to herself as conclusively decided, and for herself, as concerned with it, she never felt at all. Under this fair heaven, by this bright sunshine, at once it became clear to her, that her love if it would perfect itself, must become altogether unselfish; and there were many moments in which she believed it was an elevation which she had already attained. She only desired the well-being of her friend. She fancied herself able to resign him, and never to see him any more, if she could only know that he was happy. The one only determination which she formed for herself was never to belong to another.

They had taken care that the autumn should be no less brilliant than the spring. Sun-flowers were there, and all the other plants which are never tired of blossoming in autumn, and continue boldly on into the cold: asters especially were sown in the greatest abundance, and scattered about in all directions, to form a starry heaven upon the earth.

FROM OTTILIE'S DIARY.

"Any good thought which we have read, anything striking which we have heard, we commonly enter in our diary; but if we would take the trouble, at the same time, to copy out of our friends' letters the remarkable observations, the original ideas, the hasty word so pregnant in meaning, which we might find in them, we should then be rich indeed. We lay aside letters never to read them again, and at last we destroy them out of discretion, and so disappears the most beautiful, the most immediate breath of life, irrecoverably for ourselves and for

others. I intend to make amends in future for such neglect."

" So, then, once more the old story of the year is being
repeated over again. We are come now, thank God, again,
to its most charming chapter. The violets and the may-
flowers are its superscriptions and its vignettes. It always
makes a pleasant impression on us when we open again
at these pages in the book of life."

"We find fault with the poor, particularly with the
little ones among them, when they loiter about the streets
and beg. Do we not observe, that they begin to work
again, as soon as ever there is anything for them to do?
Hardly has nature unfolded her smiling treasures, than
the children are at once upon her track to open out a
calling for themselves. None of them beg any more;
they have each a nosegay to offer you; they were out
and gathering it before you had awakened out of your
sleep, and the supplicating face looks as sweetly at you
as the present which the hand is holding out. No person
ever looks miserable who feels that he has a right to
make a demand upon you."

"How is it that the year sometimes seems so short, and
sometimes is so long? How is it that it is so short when
it is passing, and so long as we look back over it? When
I think of the past (and it never comes so powerfully over
me as in the garden,) I feel how the perishing and the
enduring work one upon the other, and there is nothing
whose endurance is so brief as not to leave behind it some
trace of itself, something in its own likeness."

"We are able to tolerate the winter. We fancy that we can extend ourselves more freely when the trees are so spectral, so transparent. They are nothing, but they conceal nothing; but when once the germs and buds begin to show, then we become impatient for the full foliage to come out, for the landscape to put on its body, and the trees to stand before us as a form."

"Everything which is perfect in its kind, must pass out beyond and transcend its kind. It must be an inimitable something of another and a higher nature. In many of its tones the nightingale is only a bird; then it rises up above its class, and seems as if it would teach every feathered creature what singing really is."

"A life without love, without the presence of the beloved, is but poor *comédie à tiroir*. We draw out slide after slide, swiftly tiring of each, and pushing it back to make haste to the next. Even what we know to be good and important hangs but wearily together; every step is an end, and every step is a fresh beginning."

CHAPTER X.

CHARLOTTE meanwhile was well and in good spirits. She was happy in her beautiful boy, whose fair promising little form every hour was a delight to both her eyes and heart. In him she found a new link to connect

11

her with the world and with her property. Her old
activity began anew to stir in her again.

Look which way she would, she saw how much had
been done in the year that was past, and it was a pleasure
to her to contemplate it. Enlivened by the strength of
these feelings, she climbed up to the summer-house with
Ottilie and the child, and as she laid the latter down on
the little table, as on the altar of her house, and saw the
two seats still vacant, she thought of gone-by times, and
fresh hopes rose out before her for herself and for Ottilie.

Young ladies, perhaps, look timidly round them at
this or that young man, carrying on a silent examination,
whether they would like to have him for a husband; but
whoever has a daughter or a female ward to care for,
takes a wider circle in her survey. And so it fared at
this moment with Charlotte, to whom, as she thought of
how they had once sat side by side in that summer-house,
a union did not seem impossible between the Captain and
Ottilie. It had not remained unknown to her, that the
plans for the advantageous marriage, which had been
proposed to the Captain, had come to nothing.

Charlotte went on up the cliff, and Ottilie carried the
child. A number of reflections crowded upon the former.
Even on the firm land there are frequent enough ship-
wrecks, and the true wise conduct is to recover ourselves,
and refit our vessel as fast as possible. Is life to be
calculated only by its gains and losses? Who has not
made arrangement on arrangement, and has not seen them
broken in pieces? How often does not a man strike into
a road and lose it again! How often are we not turned
aside from one point which we had sharply before our eye,
but only to reach some higher stage! The traveller, to his
greatest annoyance, breaks a wheel upon his journey, and

through this unpleasant accident makes some charming acquaintance, and forms some new connection, which has an influence on all his life. Destiny grants us our wishes, but in its own way, in order to give us something beyond our wishes.

Among these and similar reflections they reached the new building on the hill, where they intended to establish themselves for the summer. The view all round them was far more beautiful than could have been supposed: every little obstruction had been removed; all the loveliness of the landscape, whatever nature, whatever the season of the year had done for it, came out in its beauty before the eye; and already the young plantations, which had been made to fill up a few openings, were beginning to look green, and to form an agreeable connecting link between parts which before stood separate.

The house itself was nearly habitable; the views particularly from the upper rooms, were of the richest variety. The longer you looked round you, the more beauties you discovered. What magnificent effects would not be produced here at the different hours of the day — by sunlight and by moonlight? Nothing could be more delightful than to come and live there, and now that she found all the rough work finished, Charlotte longed to be busy again. An upholsterer, a tapestry-hanger, a painter, who could lay on the colors with patterns, and a little gilding, were all which were required, and these were soon found, and in a short time the building was completed. Kitchen and cellar stores were quickly laid in; being so far from the castle, it was necessary to have all essentials provided; and the two ladies with the child went up and settled there. From this residence, as from a new centre point, unknown walks opened out to them; and in these high regions the free fresh air and the beautiful weather were thoroughly delightful.

Ottilie's favorite walk, sometimes alone, sometimes with the child, was down below, towards the plane-trees; along a pleasant footpath, leading directly to the point where one of the boats was kept chained in which people used to go across the water. She often indulged herself in an expedition on the water, only without the child, as Charlotte was a little uneasy about it. She never missed, however, paying a daily visit to the castle garden and the gardener, and going to look with him at his show of greenhouse plants, which were all out now, enjoying the free air.

At this beautiful season, Charlotte was much pleased to receive a visit from an English nobleman, who had made acquaintance with Edward abroad, having met him more than once, and who was now curious to see the laying out of his park, which he had heard so much admired. He brought with him a letter of introduction from the Count, and introduced at the same time a quiet but most agreeable man as his travelling companion. He went about seeing everything, sometimes with Charlotte and Ottilie, sometimes with the gardeners and the foresters, often with his friend, and now and then alone; and they could perceive clearly from his observations that he took an interest in such matters, and understood them well; indeed, that he had himself probably executed many such.

Although he was now advanced in life, he entered warmly into everything which could serve for an ornament to life, or contribute anything to its importance.

In his presence, the ladies came first properly to enjoy what was round them. His practised eye received every effect in its freshness, and he found all the more pleasure in what was before him, as he had not previously known the place, and was scarcely able to distinguish what man had done there from what nature had presented to him ready made.

We may even say that through his remarks the park grew and enriched itself; he was able to anticipate in their fulfilment the promises of the growing plantations. There was not a spot where there was any effect which could be either heightened or produced, but what he observed it.

In one place he pointed to a fountain which, if it was cleaned out, promised to be the most beautiful spot for a picnic party. In another, to a cave which had only to be enlarged and swept clear of rubbish to form a desirable seat. A few trees might be cut down, and a view would be opened from it of some grand masses of rock, towering magnificently against the sky. He wished the owners joy that so much was still remaining for them to do, and he besought them not to be in a hurry about it, but to keep for themselves for years to come the pleasures of shaping and improving.

At the hours which the ladies usually spent alone he was never in the way, for he was occupied the greatest part of the day in catching such views in the park as would make good paintings in a portable camera obscura, and drawing from them, in order to secure some desirable fruits from his travels for himself and others. For many years past he had been in the habit of doing this in all remarkable places which he visited, and had provided himself by it with a most charming and interesting collection. He showed the ladies a large portfolio which he had brought with him, and entertained them with the

pictures and with descriptions. And it was a real delight
to them here in their solitude, to travel so pleasantly over
the world, and see sweep past them, shores and havens,
mountains, lakes, and rivers, cities, castles, and a hundred
other localities which have a name in history.

Each of the two ladies had an especial interest in it —
Charlotte the more general interest in whatever was
historically remarkable ; Ottilie dwelling in preference on
the scenes of which Edward used most to talk, — where
he liked best to stay, and which he would most often re-
visit. Every man has somewhere, far or near, his peculiar localities which attract him ; scenes which, according
to his character, either from first impressions, or from
particular associations, or from habit, have a charm for
him beyond all others.

She, therefore, asked the Earl which, of all these places,
pleased him best, where he would like to settle, and live
for himself, if he might choose. There was more than
one lovely spot which he pointed out, with what had
happened to him there to make him love and value it ;
and the peculiar accentuated French in which he spoke,
made it most pleasant to listen to him.

To the further question, which was his ordinary residence, which he properly considered his home ; he replied, without any hesitation, in a manner quite unexpected by the ladies.

" I have accustomed myself by this time to be at home
everywhere, and I find, after all, that it is much more
agreeable to allow others to plant, and build, and keep
house for me. I have no desire to return to my own
possessions, partly on political grounds, but principally
because my son, for whose sake alone it was any pleasure
to me to remain and work there,— who will, by-and-by,

inherit it, and with whom I hoped to enjoy it, — took no interest in the place at all, but has gone out to India, where, like many other foolish fellows, he fancies he can make a higher use of his life. He is more likely to squander it.

" Assuredly we spend far too much labor and outlay in preparation for life. Instead of beginning at once to make ourselves happy in a moderate condition, we spread ourselves out wider and wider, only to make ourselves more and more uncomfortable. Who is there now to enjoy my mansion, my park, my gardens? Not I, nor any of mine, — strangers, visitors, or curious, restless travellers.

" Even with large means, we are ever but half and half at home, especially in the country, where we miss many things to which we have become accustomed in town. The book for which we are most anxious is not to be had, and just the thing which we most wanted is forgotten. We take to being domestic, only again to go out of ourselves; if we do not go astray of our own will and caprice, circumstances, passions, accidents, necessity, and one does not know what besides, manage it for us."

Little did the Earl imagine how deeply his friend would be touched by these random observations. It is a danger to which we are all of us exposed when we venture on general remarks in a society the circumstances of which we might have supposed were well enough known to us. Such casual wounds, even from well-meaning, kindly-disposed people, were nothing new to Charlotte. She so clearly, so thoroughly knew and understood the world, that it gave her no particular pain if it did happen that through somebody's thoughtlessness or imprudence she had her attention forced into this or that

unpleasant direction. But it was very different with
Ottilie. At her half-conscious age, at which she rather
felt than saw, and at which she was disposed, indeed
was obliged, to turn her eyes away from what she should
not or would not see, Ottilie was thrown by this melancholy conversation into the most pitiable state. It rudely
tore away the pleasant veil from before her eyes, and it
seemed to her as if everything which had been done all
this time for house and court, for park and garden, for all
their wide environs, were utterly in vain, because he to
whom it all belonged could not enjoy it; because he, like
their present visitor, had been driven out to wander up
and down in the world — and, indeed, in the most perilous paths of it — by those who were nearest and dearest
to him. She was accustomed to listen in silence, but on
this occasion she sat on in the most painful condition;
which, indeed, was made rather worse than better by
what the stranger went on to say, as he continued with
his peculiar, humorous gravity:

"I think I am now on the right way. I look upon myself steadily as a traveller, who renounces many things
in order to enjoy more. I am accustomed to change; it
has become, indeed, a necessity to me; just as in the
opera, people are always looking out for new and new
decorations, because there have already been so many.
I know very well what I am to expect from the best
hotels, and what from the worst. It may be as good or
it may be as bad as it will, but I nowhere find anything
to which I am accustomed, and in the end it comes to
much the same thing whether we depend for our enjoyment entirely on the regular order of custom, or entirely
on the caprices of accident. I have never to vex myself
now, because this thing is mislaid, or that thing is lost;

because the room in which I live is uninhabitable, and I must have it repaired; because somebody has broken my favorite cup, and for a long time nothing tastes well out of any other. All this I am happily raised above. If the house catches fire about my ears, my people quietly pack my things up, and we pass away out of the town in search of other quarters. And considering all these advantages, when I reckon carefully, I calculate that, by the end of the year, I have not sacrificed more than it would have cost me to be at home."

In this description Ottilie saw nothing but Edward before her; how he too was now amidst discomfort and hardship, marching along untrodden roads, lying out in the fields in danger and want, and in all this insecurity and hazard growing accustomed to be homeless and friendless, learning to fling away everything that he might have nothing to lose. Fortunately, the party separated for a short time. Ottilie escaped to her room, where she could give way to her tears. No weight of sorrow had ever pressed so heavily upon her as this clear perception (which she tried, as people usually do, to make still clearer to herself,) that men love to dally with and exaggerate the evils which circumstances have once begun to inflict upon them.

The state in which Edward was, came before her in a light so piteous, so miserable, that she made up her mind, let it cost her what it would, that she would do everything in her power to unite him again with Charlotte, and she herself would go and hide her sorrow and her love in some silent scene, and beguile the time with such employment as she could find.

Meanwhile the Earl's companion, a quiet, sensible man and a keen observer, had remarked the mistake in the
11*

conversation, and spoke to his friend about it. The
latter knew nothing of the circumstances of the family;
but the other being one of those persons whose principal
interest in travelling lay in gathering up the strange
occurrences which arose out of the natural or artificial
relations of society, which were produced by the conflict
of the restraint of law with the violence of the will, of
the understanding with the reason, of passion with preju-
dice — had some time before made himself acquainted
with the outline of the story, and since he had been in
the family he had learnt exactly all that had taken place,
and the present position in which things were standing.

The Earl, of course, was very sorry, but it was not a
thing to make him uneasy. A man must hold his tongue
altogether in society if he is never to find himself in such
a position; for not only remarks with meaning in them,
but the most trivial expressions, may happen to clash in
an inharmonious key with the interest of somebody present.

"We will set things right this evening," said he, "and
escape from any general conversation; you shall let them
hear one of the many charming anecdotes with which
your portfolio and your memory have enriched themselves while we have been abroad."

However, with the best intentions, the strangers did
not, on this next occasion, succeed any better in gratifying their friends with unalloyed entertainment. The
Earl's friend told a number of singular stories — some
serious, some amusing, some touching, some terrible —
with which he had roused their attention and strained
their interest to the highest tension, and he thought to
conclude with a strange but softer incident, little dream
ing how nearly it would touch his listeners.

THE TWO STRANGE CHILDREN.

"Two children of neighboring families, a boy and a girl, of an age which would suit well for them at some future time to marry, were brought up together with this agreeable prospect, and the parents on both sides, who were people of some position in the world, looked forward with pleasure to their future union.

"It was too soon observed, however, that the purpose seemed likely to fail; the dispositions of both children promised everything which was good, but there was an unaccountable antipathy between them. Perhaps they were too much like each other. Both were thoughtful, clear in their wills, and firm in their purposes. Each separately was beloved and respected by his or her companions, but whenever they were together they were always antagonists. Forming separate plans for themselves, they only met mutually to cross and thwart one another; never emulating each other in pursuit of one aim, but always fighting for a single object. Good-natured and amiable everywhere else, they were spiteful and even malicious whenever they came in contact.

"This singular relation first showed itself in their childish games, and it continued with their advancing years. The boys used to play at soldiers, divide into parties, and give each other battle, and the fierce haughty young lady set herself at once at the head of one of the armies, and fought against the other with such animosity and bitterness that the latter would have been put to a shameful flight, except for the desperate bravery of her own particular rival, who at last disarmed his antagonist and took her prisoner; and even then she defended herself with so much fury that to save his eyes from being torn out, and at the same time not to injure his enemy, he had been obliged to take off his silk handkerchief and tie her hands with it behind her back.

"This she never forgave him: she made so many attempts, she laid so many plans to injure him, that the parents, who had been long watching these singular passions, came to an understanding together and resolved to separate these two hostile creatures, and sacrifice their favorite hopes.

"The boy shot rapidly forward in the new situation in which he was placed. He mastered every subject which he was taught. His friends and his own inclination chose the army for his profession, and everywhere, let him be where he would, he was looked up to and beloved. His disposition seemed formed to labor for the well-being and the pleasure of others; and he himself, without being clearly conscious of it, was in himself happy at having got rid of the only antagonist which nature had assigned to him.

"The girl, on the other hand, became at once an altered creature. Her growing age, the progress of her education, above all, her own inward feelings, drew her away from the boisterous games with boys in which she had hitherto delighted. Altogether she seemed to want something; there was nothing anywhere about her which could deserve to excite her hatred, and she had never found any one whom she could think worthy of her love.

"A young man, somewhat older than her previous neighbor-antagonist, of rank, property, and consequence, beloved in society, and much sought after by women, bestowed his affections upon her. It was the first time that friend, lover, or servant had displayed any interest in her. The preference which he showed for her above others who were older, more cultivated, and of more brilliant pretensions than herself, was naturally gratifying; the constancy of his attention, which was never obtrusive, his standing by her faithfully through a number of unpleasant incidents, his quiet suit, which was declared indeed to her parents, but which as she was still very young he did not press, only asking to be allowed to hope; all this engaged him to her, and custom and the assumption in the world that the thing was already settled, carried her along with it. She had so often been called his bride that at last she began to consider herself so, and neither she nor any one else ever thought any further trial could be necessary before she exchanged rings with the person who for so long a time had passed for her bridegroom.

"The peaceful course which the affair had all along followed was not at all precipitated by the betrothal. Things were allowed to go on both sides just as they were; they were happy in being together, and they could enjoy to the end the fair season of the year as the spring of their future more serious life.

"The absent youth had meanwhile grown up into everything which was most admirable. He had obtained a well-deserved rank in his profession, and came home on leave to visit his family. Towards his fair neighbor he found himself again in a natural but singular position. For some time past she had been nourishing in herself such affectionate family feelings as suited her position as a bride; she was in harmony with everything about her; she believed that she was happy, and in a certain sense she was so. Now first for a long time something again stood in her way. It was not to be hated — she had become incapable of hatred. Indeed the childish hatred, which had in fact been nothing more than an obscure

recognition of inward worth, expressed itself now in a
happy astonishment, in pleasure at meeting, in ready
acknowledgments, in a half willing, half unwilling, and
yet irresistible attraction; and all this was mutual. Their
long separation gave occasion for longer conversations;
even their old childish foolishness served, now that they
had grown wiser, to amuse them as they looked back;
and they felt as if at least they were bound to make
good their petulant hatred by friendliness and attention
to each other — as if their first violent injustice to each
other ought not to be left without open acknowledgment.

On his side it all remained in a sensible, desirable
moderation. His position, his circumstances, his efforts,
his ambition, found him so abundant an occupation, that
the friendliness of this pretty bride he received as a very
thankworthy present; but without, therefore, even so
much as thinking of her in connection with himself, or
entertaining the slightest jealousy of the bridegroom,
with whom he stood on the best possible terms.

With her, however, it was altogether different. She
seemed to herself as if she had awakened out of a dream.
Her fightings with her young neighbor had been the
beginnings of an affection; and this violent antagonism
was no more than an equally violent innate passion for
him, first showing under the form of opposition. She
could remember nothing else than that she had always
loved him. She laughed over her martial encounter
with him with weapons in her hand; she dwelt upon the
delight of her feelings when he disarmed her. She
imagined that it had given her the greatest happiness
when he bound her; and whatever she had done afterwards to injure him, or to vex him, presented itself to

her as only an innocent means of attracting his attention.
She cursed their separation. She bewailed the sleepy
state into which she had fallen. She execrated the
insidious lazy routine which had betrayed her into accept-
ing so insignificant a bridegroom. She was transformed
— doubly transformed, forwards or backwards, which
ever way we like to take it.

"She kept her feelings entirely to herself; but if any
one could have divined them and shared them with her,
he could not have blamed her; for indeed the bridegroom
could not sustain a comparison with the other as soon as
they were seen together. If a sort of regard to the one
could not be refused, the other excited the fullest trust
and confidence. If one made an agreeable acquaintance,
the other we should desire for a companion; and in extraordinary cases, where higher demands might have to
be made on them, the bridegroom was a person to be
utterly despaired of, while the other would give the feeling of perfect security.

"There is a peculiar innate tact in women which dis-
covers to them differences of this kind; and they have
cause as well as occasion to cultivate it.

"The more the fair bride was nourishing all these feelings in secret, the less opportunity there was for any one
to speak a word which could tell in favor of her bridegroom, to remind her of what her duty and their relative
position advised and commanded — indeed, what an
unalterable necessity seemed now irrevocably to require;
the poor heart gave itself up entirely to its passion.

"On one side she was bound inextricably to the bridegroom by the world, by her family, and by her own
promise; on the other, the ambitious young man made
no secret of what he was thinking and planning for him-

self, conducting himself, towards her no more than a kind
but not at all a tender brother, and speaking of his departure as immediately impending; and now it seemed
as if her early childish spirit woke up again in her with
all its spleen and violence, and was preparing itself in its
distemper, on this higher stage of life, to work more
effectively and destructively. She determined that she
would die to punish the once hated, and now so passionately loved, youth for his want of interest in her; and as
she could not possess himself, at least she would wed herself for ever to his imagination and to his repentance.
Her dead image should cling to him, and he should never
be free from it. He should never cease to reproach himself for not having understood, not examined, not valued
her feelings toward him.

"This singular insanity accompanied her wherever she
went. She kept it concealed under all sorts of forms;
and although people thought her very odd, no one was
observant enough or clever enough to discover the real
inward reason.

"In the mean time, friends, relations, acquaintances had
exhausted themselves in contrivances for pleasure parties.
Scarcely a day had passed, but something new and unexpected was set on foot. There was hardly a pretty spot
in the country round which had not been decked out and
prepared for the reception of some merry party. And
now our young visitor before departing wished to do his
part as well, and invited the young couple, with a small
family circle, to an expedition on the water. They went
on board a large beautiful vessel dressed out in all its
colors, — one of the yachts which had a small saloon and
a cabin or two besides, and are intended to carry with
them upon the water the comfort and conveniences of
land.

"They set out upon the broad river with music playing. The party had collected in the cabin, below deck, during the heat of the day, and were amusing themselves with games. Their young host, who could never remain without doing something, had taken charge of the helm, to relieve the old master of the vessel, and the latter had lain down and was fast asleep. It was a moment when the steerer required all his circumspectness, as the vessel was nearing a spot where two islands narrowed the channel of the river, while shallow banks of shingle stretching off, first on one side and then on the other, made the navigation difficult and dangerous. Prudent and sharpsighted as he was, he thought for a moment that it would be better to wake the master; but he felt confident in himself, and he thought he would venture and make straight for the narrows. At this moment his fair enemy appeared upon deck with a wreath of flowers in her hair. 'Take this to remember me by,' she cried out. She took it off and threw it to the steerer. 'Don't disturb me,' he answered quickly, as he caught the wreath; 'I require all my powers and all my attention now.' 'You will never be disturbed by me any more,' she cried; 'you will never see me again.' As she spoke, she rushed to the forward part of the vessel, and from thence she sprang into the water. Voice upon voice called out, 'Save her, save her, she is sinking!' He was in the most terrible difficulty. In the confusion the old ship-master woke, and tried to catch the rudder, which the young man bid him take. But there was no time to change hands. The vessel stranded; and at the same moment, flinging off the heaviest of his upper garments, he sprang into the water and swam towards his beautiful enemy. The water is a friendly element to a man who is at home in it, and who

knows how to deal with it; it buoyed him up, and
acknowledged the strong swimmer as its master. He
soon overtook the beautiful girl, who had been swept
away before him; he caught hold of her, raised her and
supported her, and both of them were carried violently
down by the current, till the shoals and islands were left
far behind, and the river was again open and running
smoothly. He now began to collect himself; they had
past the first immediate danger, in which he had been
obliged to act mechanically without time to think; he
raised his head as high as he could to look about him;
and then swam with all his might to a low bushy point,
which ran out conveniently into the stream. There he
brought his fair burden to dry land, but he could find no
signs of life in her; he was in despair, when he caught
sight of a trodden path leading among the bushes. Again
he caught her up in his arms, hurried forward, and presently
reached a solitary cottage. There he found kind, good
people — a young married couple; the misfortunes and
the dangers explained themselves instantly; every remedy he could think of was instantly applied; a bright fire
blazed up: woollen blankets were spread on a bed, coun-
terpane, cloaks, skins, whatever there was at hand which
would serve for warmth, were heaped over her as fast as
possible. The desire to save life overpowered, for the
present, every other consideration. Nothing was left
undone to bring back to life the beautiful half-torpid,
naked body. It succeeded; she opened her eyes! her
friend was before her; she threw her heavenly arms about
his neck. In this position she remained for a time; and
then a stream of tears burst out and completed her recovery. 'Will you forsake me,' she cried, 'now when I find
you again thus?' 'Never,' he answered, 'never:'

hardly knowing what he said or did. 'Only consider yourself,' she added; 'take care of yourself, for your sake and for mine.'

"She now began to collect herself, and for the first time recollected the state in which she was; she could not be ashamed before her darling, before her preserver; but she gladly allowed him to go, that he might take care of himself; for the clothes which he still wore were wet and dripping."

"Their young hosts considered what could be done. The husband offered the young man, and the wife offered the fair lady, the dresses in which they had been married, which were hanging up in full perfection, and sufficient for a complete suit, inside and out, for two people. In a short time our pair of adventurers were not only equipped, but in full costume. They looked most charming, gazed at one another, when they met, with admiration, and then with infinite affection, half laughing at the same time at the quaintness of their appearance, they fell into each other's arms.

"The power of youth and the quickening spirit of love in a few moments completely restored them; and there was nothing wanted but music to have set them both off dancing.

" To have found themselves brought from the water on dry land, from death into life, from the circle of their families into a wilderness, from despair into rapture, from indifference to affection and to love, all in a moment: the head was not strong enough to bear it; it must either burst, or go distracted; or if so distressing an alternative were to be escaped, the heart must put out all its efforts.

" Lost wholly in each other, it was long before they recollected the alarm and anxiety of those who had been left behind; and they themselves, indeed, could not well think, without alarm and anxiety, how they were again to encounter them. 'Shall we run away? shall we hide ourselves?' said the young man. 'We will remain together,' she said, as she clung about his neck.

"The peasant having heard them say that a party was aground on the shoal, had hurried down, without stopping to ask another question, to the shore. When he arrived there, he saw the vessel coming safely down the stream. After much labor it had been got off; and they were now going on in uncertainty, hoping to find their lost ones again somewhere. The peasant shouted and made signs to them, and at last caught the attention of those on board; then he ran to a spot where there was a convenient place for landing, and went on signalling and shouting till the vessel's head was turned toward the shore; and what a scene there was for them when they landed. The parents of the two betrothed first pressed on the banks; the poor loving bridegroom had almost lost his senses. They had scarcely learnt that their dear children had been saved, when in their strange disguise the latter came forward out of the bushes to meet them. No one recognized them till they were come quite close. 'Who do I see?' cried the mothers. 'What do I see?' cried the fathers. The preserved ones flung themselves on the ground before them. 'Your children,' they called out; 'a pair.' 'Forgive us!' cried the maiden. 'Give us your blessing!' cried the young man. 'Give us your blessing!' they cried both, as all the world stood still in wonder. Your blessing! was repeated the third time; and who would have been able to refuse it?"

CHAPTER XI.

THE narrator made a pause, or rather he had already finished his story, before he observed the emotion into which Charlotte had been thrown by it. She got up, uttered some sort of an apology, and left the room. To her it was a well-known history. The principal incident in it had really taken place with the Captain and a neighbor of her own ; not exactly, indeed, as the Englishman had related it. • But the main features of it were the same. It had only been more finished off and elaborated in its details, as stories of that kind always are, when they have passed first through the lips of the multitude, and then through the fancy of a clever and imaginative narrator; the result of the process being usually to leave everything and nothing as it was. Ottilie followed Charlotte, as the two friends begged her to do; and then it was the Earl's turn to remark that perhaps they had made a second mistake, and that the subject of the story had been well known to or was in some way connected with the family. " We must take care," he added, " that we do no more mischief here ; we seem to bring little good to our entertainers for all the kindness and hospitality which they have shown us; we will make some excuse for ourselves, and then take our leave."

" I must confess," answered his companion, " that there is something else which still holds me here, which I should be very sorry to leave the house without seeing cleared up or in some way explained. You were too busy yourself yesterday when we were in the park with the camera, in looking for spots where you could make your

sketches, to have observed anything else which was passing. You left the broad walk, you remember, and went
to a sequestered place on the side of the lake. There
was a fine view of the opposite shore which you wished
to take. Well, Ottilie, who was with us, got up to follow; and then proposed that she and I should find our
way to you in the boat. I got in with her, and was
delighted with the skill of my fair conductress. I assured
her that never since I had been in Switzerland, where
the young ladies so often fill the place of the boatmen,
had I been so pleasantly ferried over the water. At the
same time I could not help asking her, why she had shown
such an objection to going the way which you had gone,
along the little bye-path. I had observed her shrink from
it with a sort of painful uneasiness. She was not at all
offended. 'If you will promise not to laugh at me,' she
answered, 'I will tell you as much as I know about it;
but to myself it is a mystery which I cannot explain.
There is a particular spot in that path which I never pass
without a strange shiver passing over me, which I do not
remember ever feeling anywhere else, and which I cannot
the least understand. But I shrink from exposing myself
to the sensation, because it is followed immediately after
by a pain on the left side of my head, from which at other
times I suffer severely.' We landed. Ottilie was engaged
with you, and I took the opportunity of examining the
spot, which she pointed out to me as we went by on the
water. I was not a little surprised to find there distinct
traces of coal, in sufficient quantities to convince me that
at a short distance below the surface there must be a considerable bed of it.

"Pardon me, my Lord, I see you smile; and I know
very well that you have no faith in these things about

which I am so eager, and that it is only your sense and
your kindness which enable you to tolerate me. However, it is impossible for me to leave this place without
trying on that beautiful creature an experiment with the
pendulum."

The Earl, whenever these matters came to be spoken
of, never failed to repeat the same objections to them
over and over again; and his friend endured them all
quietly and patiently, remaining firm, nevertheless, to his
own opinion, and holding to his own wishes. He, too,
again repeated, that there was no reason, because the
experiment did not succeed with every one, that they
should give them up, as if there was nothing in them but
fancy. They should be examined into all the more
earnestly and scrupulously; and there was no doubt that
the result would be the discovery of a number of affinities
of inorganic creatures for one another, and of organic
creatures for them, and again for each other, which at
present were unknown to us.

He had already spread out his apparatus of gold rings,
markasites, and other metallic substances, a pretty little
box of which he always carried about with himself: and
he suspended a piece of metal by a string over another
piece, which he placed upon the table. "Now, my Lord,"
he said, "you may take what pleasure you please (I can
see in your face what you are feeling,) at perceiving that
nothing will set itself in motion with me, or for me. But
my operation is no more than a pretence; when the
ladies come back, they will be curious to know what
strange work we are about."

The ladies returned. Charlotte understood at once
what was going on. "I have heard much of these
things," she said; "but I never saw the effect myself

You have everything ready there. Let me try whether I can succeed in producing anything."

She took the thread in her hand, and as she was perfectly serious, she held it steady, and without any agitation. Not the slightest motion, however, could be detected. Ottilie was then called upon to try. She held the pendulum still more quietly and unconsciously over the plate on the table. But in a moment the swinging piece of metal began to stir with a distinct rotatory action, and turned as they moved the position of the plate, first to one side and then to the other; now in circles, now in ellipses; or else describing a series of straight lines; doing all the Earl's friend could expect, and far exceeding, indeed, all his expectations.

The Earl himself was a little staggered; but the other could never be satisfied, from delight and curiosity, and begged for the experiment again and again with all sorts of variations. Ottilie was good-natured enough to gratify him; till at last she was obliged to desire to be allowed to go, as her headache had come on again. In further admiration and even rapture, he assured her with enthusiasm that he would cure her for ever of her disorder, if she would only trust herself to his remedies. For a moment they did not know what he meant; but Charlotte, who comprehended immediately after, declined his well-meant offer, not liking to have introduced and practised about her a thing of which she had always had the strongest apprehensions.

The strangers were gone, and notwithstanding their having been the inadvertent cause of strange and painful emotions left the wish behind them, that this meeting might not be the last. Charlotte now made use of the beautiful weather to return visits in the neighborhood, which, indeed, gave her work enough to do; seeing that the whole country round, some from a real interest, some merely from custom, had been most attentive in calling to inquire after her. At home her delight was the sight of the child, and really it well deserved all love and interest. People saw in it a wonderful, indeed a miraculous child; the brightest, sunniest little face; a fine, well-proportioned body, strong and healthy; and what surprised them more, the double resemblance, which became more and more conspicuous. In figure and in the features of the face, it was like the Captain; the eyes every day it was less easy to distinguish from the eyes of Ottilie.

Ottilie herself, partly from this remarkable affinity, perhaps still more under the influence of that sweet woman's feeling which makes them regard with the most tender affection the offspring, even by another, of the man they love, was as good as a mother to the little creature as it grew, or rather, she was a second mother of another kind. If Charlotte was absent, Ottilie remained alone with the child and the nurse. Nanny had for some time past been jealous of the boy for monopolizing the entire affections of her mistress; she had left her in a fit of crossness, and gone back to her mother. Ottilie would carry the child about in the open air, and by degrees took longer and longer walks with it. She took her bottle of milk to give the child its food when it wanted any. Generally, too, she took a book with her: and so with the child in her arms, reading and wandering, she made a very pretty Penserosa.

12

CHAPTER XII.

THE object of the campaign was attained, and Edward, with crosses and decorations, was honorably dismissed. He betook himself at once to the same little estate, where he found exact accounts of his family waiting for him, on whom all this time, without their having observed it or known of it, a sharp watch had been kept under his orders. His quiet residence looked most sweet and pleasant when he reached it. In accordance with his orders, various improvements had been made in his absence, and what was wanting to the establishment in extent, was compensated by its internal comforts and conveniences. Edward, accustomed by his more active habits of life, to take decided steps, determined to execute a project, which he long had sufficient time to think over. First of all, he invited the Major to come to him. This pleasure in meeting again was very great to both of them. The friendships of boyhood, like relationship of blood, possess this important advantage, that mistakes and misunderstandings never produce irreparable injury; and the old regard after a time will always re-establish itself.

Edward began with inquiring about the situation of his friend, and learnt that fortune had favored him exactly as he most could have wished. He then half-seriously asked whether there was not something going forward about a marriage; to which he received a most decided and positive denial.

" I cannot and will not have any reserve with you," he proceeded. " I will tell you at once what my own feelings are, and what I intend to do. You know my passion for Ottilie; you must long have comprehended that it was this which drove me into the campaign. I do not deny that I desired to be rid of a life which, without her, would be of no further value to me. At the same time, however, I acknowledge that I could never bring myself utterly to despair. The prospect of happiness with her was so beautiful, so infinitely charming, that it was not possible for me entirely to renounce it. Feelings, too, which I cannot explain, and a number of happy omens, have combined to strengthen me in the belief, in the assurance, that Ottilie will one day be mine. The glass with our initials cut upon it, which was thrown into the air when the foundation-stone was laid, did not go to pieces; it was caught, and I have it again in my possession. After many miserable hours of uncertainty, spent in this place, I said to myself, 'I will put myself in the place of this glass, and it shall be an omen whether our union be possible or not. I will go; I will seek for death; not like a madman, but like a man who still hopes that he may live. Ottilie shall be the prize for which I fight. Ottilie shall be behind the ranks of the enemy; in every entrenchment, in every beleagued fortress, I shall hope to find her, and to win her. I will do wonders, with the wish to survive them; with the hope to gain Ottilie, not to lose her.' These feelings have led me on; they have stood by me through all dangers; and now I find myself like one who has arrived at his goal, who has overcome every difficulty and who has nothing more left in his way. Ottilie is mine, and whatever lies between the thought and the execution of it, I can only regard as unimportant."

"With a few strokes you blot out," replied the Major, "all the objections that we can or ought to urge upon you, and yet they must be repeated. I must leave it to yourself to recall the full value of your relation with your wife; but you owe it to her, and you owe it to yourself, not to close your eyes to it. How can I so much as recollect that you have had a son given to you, without acknowledging at once that you two belong to one another forever, that you are bound, for this little creature's sake, to live united, that united you may educate it, and provide for its future welfare?"

"It is no more than the blindness of parents," answered Edward, "when they imagine their existence to be of so much importance to their children. Whatever lives, finds nourishment and finds assistance; and if the son who has early lost his father does not spend so easy, so favored a youth, he profits, perhaps, for that very reason, in being trained sooner for the world, and comes to a timely knowledge that he must accommodate himself to others, a thing which sooner or later we are all forced to learn. Here, however, even these considerations are irrelevant; we are sufficiently well off to be able to provide for more children than one, and it is neither right nor kind to accumulate so large a property on a single head."

The Major attempted to say something of Charlotte's worth, and Edward's long-standing attachment to her; but the latter hastily interrupted him. "We committed ourselves to a foolish thing, that I see all too clearly. Whoever, in middle age, attempts to realize the wishes and hopes of his early youth, invariably deceives himself. Each ten years of a man's life has its own fortunes, its own hopes, its own desires. Woe to him, who, either by circumstances or by his own infatuation, is induced to grasp at anything before him or behind him. We have done a foolish thing. Are we to abide by it all our

lives? Are we, from some respect of prudence, to refuse
to ourselves what the customs of the age do not forbid?
In how many matters do men recall their intentions and
their actions; and shall it not be allowed to them here,
here, where the question is not of this thing or of that,
but of everything; not of our single condition of life,
but of the whole complex life itself?"

Again the Major powerfully and impressively urged on
Edward to consider what he owed to his wife, what was
due to his family, to the world, and to his own position;
but he could not succeed in producing the slightest
impression.

"All these questions, my friend," he returned, "I have
considered already again and again. They have passed
before me in the storm of battle, when the earth was
shaking with the thunder of the cannon, with the balls
singing and whistling round me, with my comrades falling right and left, my horse shot under me, my hat
pierced with bullets. They have floated before me by
the still watch-fire under the starry vault of the sky. I
have thought them all through, felt them all through.
I have weighed them, and I have satisfied myself about
them again and again, and now for ever. At such
moments why should I not acknowledge it to you? you
too were in my thoughts, you too belonged to my circle;
as, indeed, you and I have long belonged to one another.
If I have ever been in your debt I am now in a position
to repay it with interest; if you have been in mine you
have now the means to make it good to me. I know
that you love Charlotte, and she deserves it. I know
that you are not indifferent to her, and why should she
not feel your worth? Take her at my hand and give

Ottilie to me, and we shall be the happiest beings upon the earth."

"If you choose to assign me so high a character," replied the Major, "it is the more reason for me to be firm and prudent. Whatever there may be in this proposal to make it attractive to me, instead of simplifying the problem, it only increases the difficulty of it. The question is now of me as well as of you. The fortunes, the good name, the honor of two men, hitherto unsullied with a breath, will be exposed to hazard by so strange a proceeding, to call it by no harsher name, and we shall appear before the world in a highly questionable light."

"Our very characters being what they are," replied Edward, "give us a right to take this single liberty. A man who has borne himself honorably through a whole life, makes an action honorable which might appear ambiguous in others. As concerns myself, after these last trials which I have taken upon myself, after the difficult and dangerous actions which I have accomplished for others, I feel entitled now to do something for myself. For you and Charlotte, that part of the business may, if you like it, be given up; but neither you nor any one shall keep me from doing what I have determined. If I may look for help and furtherance, I shall be ready to do everything which can be wished; but if I am to be left to myself, or if obstacles are to be thrown in my way, some extremity or other is sure to follow."

The Major thought it his duty to combat Edward's purposes as long as it was possible; and now he changed the mode of his attack and tried a diversion. He seemed to give way, and only spoke of the form of what they would have to do to bring about this separation, and these new unions; and so mentioned a number of ugly,

undesirable matters, which threw Edward into the worst
of tempers.

"I see plainly," he cried at last, "that what we desire
can only be carried by storm, whether it be from our
enemies or from our friends. I keep clearly before my
own eyes what I demand, what, one way or another, I
must have; and I will seize it promptly and surely.
Connections like ours, I know very well, cannot be
broken up and reconstructed again without much being
thrown down which is standing, and much having to
give way which would be glad enough to continue. We
shall come to no conclusion by thinking about it. All
rights are alike to the understanding, and it is always
easy to throw extra weight into the ascending scale. Do
you make up your mind, my friend, to act, and act
promptly, for me and for yourself. Disentangle and
untie the knots, and tie them up again. Do not be deterred from it by nice respects. We have already given
the world something to say about us. It will talk about
us once more; and when we have ceased to be a nine
days' wonder, it will forget us as it forgets everything
else, and allow us to follow our own way without further
concern with us." The Major had nothing further to say
and was at last obliged to sit silent; while Edward
treated the affair as now conclusively settled, talked
through in detail all that had to be done, and pictured
the future in every most cheerful color, and then he went
on again seriously and thoughtfully: "If we think to
leave ourselves to the hope, to the expectation, that all
will go right again of itself, that accident will lead us
straight, and take care of us, it will be a most culpable
self-deception. In such a way it would be impossible for
us to save ourselves, or reestablish our peace again. I

who have been the innocent cause of it all, how am I ever
to console myself?   By my own importunity I prevailed
on Charlotte to write to you to stay with us; and Ottilie
followed in consequence.   We have had no more control
over what ensued out of this, but we have the power to
make it innocuous; to guide the new circumstances to
our own happiness.   Can you turn away your eyes from
the fair and beautiful prospects which I open to us?   Can
you insist to me, can you insist to us all, on a wretched
renunciation of them?   Do you think it possible?   Is it
possible?   Will there be no vexations, no bitterness, no
inconvenience to overcome, if we resolve to fall back into
our old state? and will any good, any happiness whatever, arise out of it?   Will your own rank, will the high
position which you have earned, be any pleasure to you,
if you are to be prevented from visiting me, or from living with me?   And after what has passed, it would
not be anything but painful.   Charlotte and I, with all
our property, would only find ourselves in a melancholy
state.   And if, like other men of the world, you can
persuade yourself that years and separation will eradi-
cate our feelings; will obliterate impressions so deeply
engraved; why, then the question is of these very years,
which it would be better to spend in happiness and comfort than in pain and misery.   But the last and most
important point of all which I have to urge is this: supposing that we, our outward and inward condition being
what it is, could nevertheless make up our minds to wait
at all hazards, and bear what is laid upon us, what is
to become of Ottilie?   She must leave our family: she
must go into society where we shall not be to care for
her, and she will be driven wretchedly to and fro in a
hard, cold world.   Describe to me any situation in

which Ottilie, without me, without us, could be happy, and you will then have employed an argument which will be stronger than every other; and if I will not promise to yield to it, if I will not undertake at once to give up all my own hopes, I will at least reconsider the question, and see how what you have said will affect it."

This problem was not so easy to solve; at least, no satisfactory answer to it suggested itself to his friend, and nothing was left to him except to insist again and again, how grave and serious, and in many senses how dangerous, the whole undertaking was; and at least that they ought maturely to consider how they had better enter upon it. Edward agreed to this, and consented to wait before he took any steps, but only under the condition that his friend should not leave him until they had come to a perfect understanding about it, and until the first measures had been taken.

CHAPTER XIII.

MEN who are complete strangers, and wholly indifferent to one another, if they live a long time together, are sure both of them to expose something of their inner nature, and thus a kind of intimacy will arise between them. All the more was it to be expected that there would soon be no secrets between our two friends, now that they were again under the same roof together, and in daily and hourly intercourse. They went over again the earlier stages of their history, and the Major

12*

confessed to Edward that Charlotte had intended Ottilie
for him at the time at which he returned from abroad,
and hoped that some time or other he might marry her.
Edward was in ecstacies at this discovery, he spoke without reserve of the mutual affection of Charlotte and the
Major, which, because it happened to fall in so conveniently with his own wishes, he painted in very lively
colors.

Deny it altogether, the Major could not; at the same
time, he could not altogether acknowledge it. But
Edward only insisted on it the more. He had pictured
the whole thing to himself not as possible, but as already
concluded; all parties had only to resolve on what they
all wished; there would be no difficulty in obtaining a
separation; the marriages should follow as soon after as
possible, and Edward could travel with Ottilie.

Of all the pleasant things which imagination pictures
to us, perhaps there is none more charming than when
lovers and young married people look forward to enjoying their new relation to each other in a fresh, new
world, and test the endurance of the bond between
them in so many changing circumstances. The Major
and Charlotte were in the meantime to have unrestricted
powers to settle all questions of money, property, and
other such important worldly matters; and to do whatever was right and proper for the satisfaction of all parties. What Edward dwelt the most upon, however, what
he seemed to promise himself the most advantage from
was this:—as the child would have to remain with the
mother, the Major would charge himself with the education of it; he would train the boy according to his own
views, and develop what capacities there might be in
him. It was not for nothing that he had received in his

baptism the name of Otto, which belonged to them both.

Edward had so completely arranged everything for himself, that he could not wait another day to carry it into execution. On their way to the castle, they arrived at a small town, where Edward had a house, and where he was to stay to await the return of the Major. He could not, however, prevail upon himself to alight there at once, and accompanied his friend through the place. They were both on horseback, and falling into some interesting conversation, rode on further together.

On a sudden they saw, in the distance, the new house on the height, with its red tiles shining in the sun. An irresistible longing came over Edward; he would have it all settled that very evening; he would remain concealed in a village close by. The Major was to urge the business on Charlotte with all his power; he would take her prudence by surprise; and oblige her by the unexpectedness of his proposal to make a free acknowledgment of her feelings. Edward had transferred his own wishes to her; he felt certain that he was only meeting her halfway, and that her inclinations were as decided as his own; and he looked for an immediate consent from her, because he himself could think of nothing else.

Joyfully he saw the prosperous issue before his eyes; and that it might be communicated to him as swiftly as possible, a few cannon shots were to be fired off, and if it was dark, a rocket or two sent up.

The Major rode to the castle. He did not find Charlotte there; he learnt that for the present she was staying at the new house; at that particular time, however, she was paying a visit in the neighborhood, and she probably would not have returned till late that evening.

He walked back to the hotel, to which he had previously
sent his horse.

Edward, in the meantime, unable to sit still from restlessness and impatience, stole away out of his concealment along solitary paths only known to foresters and
fishermen, into his park; and he found himself towards
evening in the copse close to the lake, the broad mirror
of which he now for the first time saw spread out in its
perfectness before him.

Ottilie had gone out that afternoon for a walk along
the shore. She had the child with her, and read as she
usually did while she went along. She had gone as far
as the oak tree by the ferry. The boy had fallen asleep;
she sat down; laid it on the ground at her side, and continued reading. The book was one of those which attract
persons of delicate feeling, and afterwards will not let
them go again. She forgot the time and the hours; she
never thought what a long way round it was by land to the
new house; but she sat lost in her book and in herself, so
beautiful to look at, that the trees and the bushes round her
ought to have been alive, and to have had eyes given
them to gaze upon her and admire her. The sun was
sinking; a ruddy streak of light fell upon her from behind,
tinging with gold her cheek and shoulder. Edward, who
had made his way to the lake without being seen, finding his park desolate, and no trace of human creature to
be seen anywhere, went on and on. At last he broke
through the copse behind the oak tree, and saw her.
At the same moment she saw him. He flew to her, and
threw himself at her feet. After a long, silent pause, in
which they both endeavored to collect themselves, he
explained in a few words why and how he had come
there. He had sent the Major to Charlotte; and perhaps

at that moment their common destiny was being decided. Never had he doubted her affection, and she assuredly had never doubted his. He begged for her consent; she hesitated; he implored her. He offered to resume his old privilege, and throw his arms around her, and embrace her; she pointed down to the child.

Edward looked at it and was amazed. "Great God!" he cried; "if I had cause to doubt my wife and my friend, this face would witness fearfully against them. Is not this the very image of the Major? I never saw such a likeness."

"Indeed!" replied Ottilie; "all the world say it is like me."

"Is it possible?" Edward answered; and at the moment the child opened its eyes — two large, black, piercing eyes, deep and full of love; already the little face was full of intelligence. He seemed as if he knew both the figures which he saw standing before him. Edward threw himself down beside the child, and then knelt a second time before Ottilie. "It is you," he cried: "the eyes are yours! ah, but let me look into yours; let me throw a veil over that ill-starred hour which gave its being to this little creature. Shall I shock your pure spirit with the fearful thought, that man and wife who are estranged from each other, can yet press each other to their heart, and profane the bonds by which the law unites them by other eager wishes? Oh yes! As I have said so much; as my connection with Charlotte must now be severed; as you will be mine, why should I not speak out the words to you? This child is the offspring of a double adultery; it should have been a tie between my wife and myself; but it severs her from me, and me from her. Let it witness, then, against me. Let these fair eyes say to yours, that in the arms of another I belong to you. You must feel, Ottilie, oh! you must feel, that my fault, my crime, I can only expiate in your arms."

"Hark!" he called out, as he sprang up and listened. He thought that he had heard a shot, and that it was the sign which the Major was to give. It was the gun of a forester on the adjoining hill. Nothing followed. Edward grew impatient.

Ottilie now first observed that the sun was down behind the mountains; its last rays were shining on the windows of the house above. "Leave me, Edward," she cried; "go. Long as we have been parted, much as we have borne, yet remember what we both owe to Charlotte. She must decide our fate; do not let us anticipate her judgment. I am yours if she will permit it to be so. If she will not I must renounce you. As you think it is now so near an issue, let us wait. Go back to the village, where the Major supposes you to be. Is it likely that a rude cannon-shot will inform you of the results of such an interview? Perhaps at this moment he is seeking for you. He will not have found Charlotte at home; of that I am certain. He may have gone to meet her; for they knew at the castle where she was. How many things may have happened! Leave me! she must be at home by this time; she is expecting me with the baby above."

Ottilie spoke hurriedly; she called together all the possibilities. It was too delightful to be with Edward; but she felt that he must now leave her. "I beseech, I implore you, my beloved," she cried out; "go back and wait for the Major."

"I obey your commands," cried Edward. He gazed at her for a moment with rapturous love, and then caught her close in his arms. She wound her own about him, and pressed him tenderly to her breast. Hope streamed away, like a star shooting in the sky, above their heads. They thought then, they believed, that they did indeed belong to one another. For the first time they exchanged free, genuine kisses, and separated with pain and effort.

The sun had gone down. It was twilight, and a damp mist was rising about the lake. Ottilie stood confused and agitated. She looked across to the house on the hill, and she thought she saw Charlotte's white dress on the balcony. It was a long way round by the end of the lake; and she knew how impatiently Charlotte would be waiting for the child. She saw the plane-trees just opposite her, and only a narrow interval of water divided her from the path which led straight up to the house. Her nervousness about venturing on the water with the child vanished in her present embarrassment. She hastened to the boat; she did not feel that her heart was beating: that her feet were tottering; that her senses were threatening to fail her.

She sprang in, seized the oar, and pushed off. She had to use force; she pushed again. The boat shot off, and glided, swaying and rocking into the open water. With the child in her left arm, the book in her left hand, and the oar in her right, she lost her footing, and fell over the seat; the oar slipped from her on one side, and as she tried to recover herself, the child and book slipped on the other, all into the water. She caught the floating dress, but lying entangled as she was herself, she was unable to rise. Her right hand was free, but she could not reach round to help herself up with it; at last she succeeded. She drew the child out of the water; but its eyes were closed, and it had ceased to breathe.

In a moment she recovered all her self-possession; but so much the greater was her agony; the boat was driving fast into the middle of the lake; the oar was swimming far away from her. She saw no one on the shore; and, indeed, if she had, it would have been of no service to her. Cut off from all assistance, she was floating on the faithless, unstable element.

She sought for help from herself; she had often heard of the recovery of the drowned; she had herself witnessed an instance of it on the evening of her birthday; she took off the child's clothes, and dried it with her muslin dress; she threw open her bosom, laying it bare for the first time to the free heaven. For the first time she pressed a living being to her pure, naked breast. Alas! and it was not a living being. The cold limbs of the ill-starred little creature chilled her to the heart. Streams of tears gushed from her eyes, and lent a show of life and warmth to the outside of the torpid limbs. She persevered with her efforts; she wrapped it in her shawl, she drew it close to herself, stroked it, breathed upon it, and with tears and kisses labored to supply the help which, cut off as she was, she was unable to find.

It was all in vain; the child lay motionless in her arms; motionless the boat floated on the glassy water. But even here her beautiful spirit did not leave her forsaken. She turned to the Power above. She sank down upon her knees in the boat, and with both arms raised the unmoving child above her innocent breast, like marble in its whiteness; alas, too, like marble cold; with moist eyes she looked up and cried for help, where a tender heart hopes to find it in its fulness, when all other help has failed. The stars were beginning one by one to glimmer down upon her; she turned to them and not in vain; a soft air stole over the surface, and wafted the boat under the plane-trees.

CHAPTER XIV.

SHE hurried to the new house, and called the surgeon and gave the child into his hands. It was carried at once to Charlotte's sleeping-room. Cool and collected from a wide experience, he submitted the tender body to the usual process. Ottilie stood by him, through it all. She prepared everything, she fetched everything, but as if she were moving in another world; for the height of misfortune, like the height of happiness, alters the aspect of every object. And it was only when after every resource had been exhausted, the good man shook his head, and to her questions, whether there was hope, first was silent, and then answered with a gentle No! that she left the apartment, and had scarcely entered the sitting-room, when she fell fainting, with her face upon the carpet, unable to reach the sofa.

At that moment Charlotte was heard driving up. The surgeon implored the servants to keep back, and allow him to go to meet her and prepare her. But he was too late; while he was speaking she had entered the drawing-room. She found Ottilie on the ground, and one of the girls of the house came running and screaming to her open-mouthed. The surgeon entered at the same moment, and she was informed of everything. She could not at once, however, give up all hope. She was flying up stairs to the child, but the physician besought her to remain where she was. He went himself, to deceive her with a show of fresh exertions, and she sat down upon the sofa. Ottilie was still lying on the ground; Charlotte raised her, and supported her against herself, and her beautiful head sank down upon her knee. The kind medical man went backwards and forwards; he appeared to be busy about the child; his real care was for the ladies; and so came on midnight, and the stillness grew more and more deathly. Charlotte did not try to conceal from herself any longer that her child would never return to life again. She desired to see it now. It had been wrapped up in warm woollen coverings. And it was brought down as it was, lying in its cot which was placed at her side on the sofa. The little face was uncovered; and there it lay in its calm sweet beauty.

The report of the accident soon spread through the village; every one was roused, and the story reached the hotel. The Major hurried up the well-known road; he went round and round the house; at last he met a servant who was going to one of the out-buildings to fetch something. He learnt from him in what state things were, and desired him to tell the surgeon that he was there. The latter came out, not a little surprised at the appearance of his old patron. He told him exactly what had happened, and undertook to prepare Charlotte to see him. He then went in, began some conversation to distract her attention, and led her imagination from one object to another, till at last he brought it to rest upon her friend, and the depth of feeling and of sympathy which would surely be called out in him. From the imaginative she was brought at once to the real. Enough! she was

informed that he was at the door, that he knew everything and desired to be admitted.

The Major entered. Charlotte received him with a
miserable smile. He stood before her; she lifted off the
green silk covering under which the body was lying;
and by the dim light of a taper, he saw before him, not
without a secret shudder, the stiffened image of himself.
Charlotte pointed to a chair, and there they sat opposite
to one another, without speaking, through the night.
Ottilie was still lying motionless on Charlotte's knee; she
breathed softly, and slept or seemed to sleep.

The morning dawned, the lights went out; the two
friends appeared to awake out of a heavy dream. Charlotte looked towards the Major, and said quietly: " Tell
me through what circumstances you have been brought
hither, to take part in this mourning scene."

" The present is not a time," the Major answered, in
the same low tone as that in which Charlotte had spoken,
for fear lest she might disturb Ottilie; " this is not a time
and this is not a place for reserve. The condition in
which I find you is so fearful that even the earnest matter on which I am here, loses its importance by the side
of it." He then informed her, quite calmly and simply,
of the object of his mission, in so far as he was the am-
bassador of Edward; of the object of his coming, in so
far as his own free will and his own interests were concerned in it. He laid both before her, delicately but
uprightly; Charlotte listened quietly, and showed neither
surprise nor unwillingness.

As soon as the Major had finished, she replied, in a
voice so light that to catch her words he was obliged to
draw his chair closer to her: " In such a case as this I
have never before found myself; but in similar cases I

have always said to myself, how will it be to-morrow?
I feel very clearly that the fate of many persons is now
in my hands, and what I have to do is soon said without
scruple or hesitation. I consent to the separation; I
ought to have made up my mind to it before; by my
unwillingness and reluctance I have destroyed my child.
There are certain things on which destiny obstinately
insists. In vain may reason, may virtue, may duty, may
all holy feelings place themselves in its way. Something
shall be done which to it seems good, and which to us
seems not good; and it forces its own way through at
last, let us conduct ourselves as we will.

"And, indeed, what am I saying? It is but my own
desire, my own purpose, against which I acted so unthinkingly, which destiny is again bringing in my way? Did
I not long ago, in my thoughts, design Edward and
Ottilie for one another? Did I not myself labor to
bring them together? And you, my friend, you yourself
were an accomplice in my plot. Why, why, could I not
distinguish mere man's obstinacy from real love? Why
did I accept his hand, when I could have made him
happy as a friend, and when another could have made
him happy as a wife? And now, look here on this unhappy slumberer. I tremble for the moment when she
will recover out of this half death sleep into consciousness. How can she endure to live? How shall she ever
console herself, if she may not hope to make good that
to Edward, of which, as the instrument of the most wonderful destiny, she has deprived him? And she can
make it all good again by the passion, by the devotion
with which she loves him. If love be able to bear all
things, it is able to do yet more; it can restore all things:
of myself at such a moment I may not think.

"Do you go quietly away, my dear Major; say to Edward that I consent to the separation; that I leave it to him, to you, and to Mittler, to settle whatever is to be done. I have no anxiety for my own future condition; it may be what it will; it is nothing to me. I will subscribe whatever paper is submitted to me, only he must not require me to join actively. I cannot have to think about it, or give advice."

The Major rose to go. She stretched out her hand to him across Ottilie. He pressed it to his lips, and whispered gently: "And for myself, may I hope anything?"

"Do not ask me now!" replied Charlotte. "I will tell you another time. We have not deserved to be miserable; but neither can we say that we have deserved to be happy together."

"The Major left her, and went, feeling for Charlotte to the bottom of his heart, but not being able to be sorry for the fate of the poor child. Such an offering seemed necessary to him for their general happiness. He pictured Ottilie to himself with a child of her own in her arms as the most perfect compensation for the one of which she had deprived Edward. He pictured himself with his own son on his knee, who should have better right to resemble him than the one which was departed.

With such flattering hopes and fancies passing through his mind, he returned to the hotel, and on his way back he met Edward, who had been waiting for him the whole night through in the open air, since neither rocket nor report of cannon would bring him news of the successful issue of his undertaking. He had already heard of the misfortune; and he too, instead of being sorry for the poor creature, regarded what had befallen it, without being exactly ready to confess it to himself, as a conven-

ient accident, through which the only inpediment in the
way of his happiness was at once removed.

The Major at once informed him of his wife's resolution, and he therefore easily allowed himself to be prevailed upon to return again with him to the village, and
from thence to go for a while to' the little town, where
they would consider what was next to be done, and
make their arrangements.

After the Major had left her, Charlotte sat on, buried
in her own reflections; but it was only for a few minutes.
Ottilie suddenly raised herself from her lap, and looked
full with her large eyes in her friend's face. Then she
got up from off the ground, and stood upright before
her.

"This is the second time," began the noble girl, with
an irresistible solemnity of manner, "this is the second
time that the same thing has happened to me. You once
said to me that similar things often befall people more
than once in their lives in a similar way, and if they do,
it is always at important moments. I now find that
what you said is true, and I have to make a confession to
you. Shortly after my mother's death, when I was a
very little child, I was sitting one day on a footstool
close to you. You were on the sofa, as you are at this
moment, and my head rested on your knees. I was not
asleep, I was not awake: I was in a trance. I knew
everything which was passing about me. I heard every
word which was said with the greatest distinctness, and
yet I could not stir, I could not speak; and if I had
wished it, I could not have given a hint that I was
conscious. On that occasion you were speaking about
me to one of your friends; you were commiserating my
fate, left as I was a poor orphan in the world. You

described my dependant position, and how unfortunate
a future was before me, unless some very happy star
watched over me. I understood well what you said. I
saw, perhaps too clearly, what you appeared to hope of
me, and what you thought I ought to do. I made rules
to myself, according to such limited insight as I had, and
by these I have long lived; by these, at the time when
you so kindly took charge of me, and had me with you
in your home, I regulated whatever I did, and whatever
I left undone.

" But I have wandered out of my course; I have
broken my rules; I have lost the very power of feeling
them. And now, after a dreadful occurrence, you have
again made clear to me my situation, which is more pitiable than the first. While lying in a half torpor on your
lap, I have again, as if out of another world, heard every
syllable which you uttered. I know from you how all is
with me. I shudder at the thought of myself; but again,
as I did then, in my half sleep of death, I have marked
out my new path for myself.

" I am determined, as I was before, and what I have
determined I must tell you at once. I will never be
Edward's wife. In a terrible manner God has opened my
eyes to see the sin in which I was entangled. I will
atone for it, and let no one think to move me from my
purpose. It is by this, my dearest, kindest friend, that
you must govern your own conduct. Send for the Major
to come back to you. Write to him that no steps must
be taken. It made me miserable that I could not stir or
speak when he went; — I tried to rise, — I tried to cry
out. Oh, why did you let him leave you with such un-
lawful hopes ! "

Charlotte saw Ottilie's condition, and she felt for it;

but she hoped that by time and persuasion she might be
able to prevail upon her. On her uttering a few words,
however, which pointed to a future, — to a time when her
sufferings would be alleviated, and when there might be
better room for hope, "No!" Ottilie cried with vehemence, "do not endeavor to move me; do not seek to
deceive me. At the moment at which I learn that you
have consented to the separation, in that same lake I will
expiate my errors and my crimes."

CHAPTER XV.

FRIENDS and relations, and all persons living in the
same house together, are apt, when life is going
smoothly and peacefully with them, to make what they
are doing, or what they are going to do, even more than
is right or necessary, a subject of constant conversation.
They talk to each other of their plans and their occupations, and, without exactly taking one another's advice,
consider and discuss together the entire progress of their
lives. But this is far from being the case in serious moments; just when it would seem men most require the
assistance and support of others, they all draw singly
within themselves every one to act for himself, every one
to work in his own fashion; they conceal from one another
the particular means which they employ, and only the
result, the object, the thing which they realize, is again
made common property.

After so many strange and unfortunate incidents, a

sort of silent seriousness had passed over the two ladies, which showed itself in a sweet mutual effort to spare each other's feelings. The child had been buried privately in the chapel. It rested there as the first offering to a destiny full of ominous foreshadowings.

Charlotte, as soon as ever she could, turned back to life and occupation, and here she first found Ottilie standing in need of her assistance. She occupied herself almost entirely with her, without letting it be observed. She knew how deeply the noble girl loved Edward. She had discovered by degrees the scene which had preceded the accident, and had gathered every circumstance of it, partly from Ottilie herself, partly from the letters of the Major.

Ottilie, on her side, made Charlotte's immediate life much more easy for her. She was open, and even talkative, but she never spoke of the present, or of what had lately past. She had been a close and thoughtful observer. She knew much, and now it all came to the surface. She entertained, she amused Charlotte, and the latter still nourished a hope in secret to see her married to Edward after all.

But something very different was passing in Ottilie. She had disclosed the secret of the course of her life to her friend, and she showed no more of her previous restraint and submissiveness. By her repentance and her resolution she felt herself freed from the burden of her fault and her misfortune. She had no more violence to do to herself. In the bottom of her heart she had forgiven herself solely under condition of the fullest renunciation, and it was a condition which would remain binding for all time to come.

So passed away some time, and Charlotte now felt how

13

deeply house and park, and lake and rocks and trees,
served to keep alive in them all their most painful reminiscences.   They wanted change of scene, both of them,
it was plain enough; but how it was to be effected was
not so easy to decide.

Were the two ladies to remain together?   Edward's
previously-expressed will appeared to enjoin it, — his
declarations and his threats appeared to make it necessary; only it could not be now mistaken that Charlotte
and Ottilie, with all their good-will, with all their sense,
with all their efforts to conceal it, could not avoid finding
themselves in a painful situation towards one another.
In their conversation there was a constant endeavor to
avoid doubtful subjects.   They were often obliged only
half to understand some allusion; more often, expressions were misinterpreted, if not by their understandings,
at any rate by their feelings.   They were afraid to give
pain to one another, and this very fear itself produced
the evil which they were seeking to avoid.

If they were to try change of scene, and at the same
time (at any rate for awhile) to part, the old question
came up again, where Ottilie was to go?   There was the
grand, rich family, who still wanted a desirable companion for their daughter, their attempts to find a person
whom they could trust having hitherto proved ineffectual.   The last time the Baroness had been at the castle,
she had urged Charlotte to send Ottilie there, and she
had been lately pressing it again and again in her letters.
Charlotte now a second time proposed it; but Ottilie
expressly declined going anywhere, where she would be
thrown into what is called the great world.

"Do not think me foolish or self-willed, my dear aunt,"
she said; "I had better tell you what I feel, for fear you

should judge hardly of me; although in any other case it would be my duty to be silent. A person who has fallen into uncommon misfortunes, however guiltless he may be, carries a frightful mark upon him. His presence, in every one who sees him and is aware of his history, excites a kind of horror. People see in him the terrible fate which has been laid upon him, and he is the object of a diseased and nervous curiosity. It is so with a house, it is so with a town, where any terrible action has been done; people enter them with awe; the light of day shines less brightly there, and the stars seem to lose their lustre.

"Perhaps we ought to excuse it, but how extreme is the indiscretion with which people behave towards such unfortunates, with their foolish importunities and awkward kindness! You must forgive me for speaking in this way, but that poor girl whom Luciana tempted out of her retirement, and with such mistaken good nature tried to force into society and amusement, has haunted me and made me miserable. The poor creature, when she was so frightened and tried to escape, and then sank and swooned away, and I caught her in my arms, and the party came all crowding round in terror and curiosity! little did I think, then, that the same fate was in store for me. But my feeling for her is as deep and warm and fresh as ever it was; and now I may direct my compassion upon myself, and secure myself from being the object of any similar exposure."

"But, my dear child," answered Charlotte, "you will never be able to withdraw yourself where no one can see you; we have no cloisters now: otherwise, there, with your present feelings, would be your resource."

"Solitude would not give me the resource for which I

wish, my dear aunt," answered Ottilie. "The one true
and valuable resource is to be looked for where we can
be active and useful; all the self-denials and all the pen-
ances on earth will fail to deliver us from an evil-omened
destiny, if it be determined to persecute us. Let me sit
still in idleness and serve as a spectacle for the world,
and it will overpower me and crush me. But find me
some peaceful employment, where I can go steadily and
unweariedly on doing my duty, and I shall be able to
bear the eyes of men, when I need not shrink under the
eyes of God."

"Unless I am much mistaken," replied Charlotte,
"your inclination is to return to the school."

"Yes," Ottilie answered; "I do not deny it. I think
it a happy destination to train up others in the beaten
way, after having been trained in the strangest myself.
And do we not see the same great fact in history? some
moral calamity drives men out into the wilderness, but
they are not allowed to remain as they had hoped in
their concealment there. They are summoned back into
the world, to lead the wanderers into the right way; and
who are fitter for such a service, than those who have
been initiated into the labyrinths of life? They are
commanded to be the support of the unfortunate; and
who can better fulfil that command than those who have
no more misfortunes to fear upon earth?"

"You are selecting an uncommon profession for yourself," replied Charlotte. "I shall not oppose you, however. Let it be as you wish; only I hope it will be but
for a short time."

"Most warmly I thank you," said Ottilie, "for giving
me leave at least to try, to make the experiment. If I
am not flattering myself too highly, I am sure I shall

succeed: wherever I am, I shall remember the many trials which I went through myself, and how small, how infinitely small they were compared to those which I afterwards had to undergo. It will be my happiness to watch the embarrassments of the little creatures as they grow; to cheer them in their childish sorrows, and guide them back with a light hand out of their little aberrations. The fortunate is not the person to be of help to the fortunate; it is in the nature of man to require ever more and more of himself and others, the more he has received. The unfortunate who has himself recovered, knows best how to nourish, in himself and them, the feeling that every moderate good ought to be enjoyed with rapture."

"I have but one objection to make to what you propose," said Charlotte, after some thought, "although that one seems to me of great importance. I am not thinking of you, but of another person: you are aware of the feelings towards you of that good, right-minded, excellent assistant. In the way in which you desire to proceed, you will become every day more valuable and more indispensable to him. Already he himself believes that he can never live happily without you, and hereafter, when he has become accustomed. to have you to work with him, he will be unable to carry on his business if he loses you; you will have assisted him at the begin-ning only to injure him in the end."

"Destiny has not dealt with me with too gentle a hand," replied Ottilie; "and whoever loves me has perhaps not much better to expect. Our friend is so good and so sensible, that I hope he will be able to reconcile himself to remaining in a simple relation with me; he will learn to see in me a consecrated person, lying under the shadow of an awful calamity, and only able to support

herself and bear up against it by devoting herself to that
Holy Being who is invisibly around us, and alone is able
to shield us from the dark powers which threaten to
overwhelm us."

All this, which the dear girl poured out so warmly,
Charlotte privately reflected over; on many different
occasions, although only in the gentlest manner, she had
hinted at the possibility of Ottilie's being brought again
in contact with Edward; but the slightest mention of it,
the faintest hope, the least suspicion, seemed to wound
Ottilie to the quick. One day when she could not evade
it, she expressed herself to Charlotte clearly and per-
emptorily on the subject.

"If your resolution to renounce Edward," returned
Charlotte, "is so firm and unalterable, then you had
better avoid the danger of seeing him again. At a distance from the object of our love, the warmer our affection, the stronger is the control which we fancy that we
can exercise on ourselves; because the whole force of the
passion, diverted from its outward objects, turns inwards
on ourselves. But how soon, how swiftly is our mistake
made clear to us, when the thing which we thought that
we could renounce, stands again before our eyes as
indispensable to us! You must now do what you
consider best suited to your circumstances. Look well
into yourself; change, if you prefer it, the resolution
which you have just expressed. But do it of yourself,
with a free consenting heart. Do not allow yourself to
be drawn in by an accident; do not let yourself be
surprised into your former position. It will place you at
issue with yourself and will be intolerable to you. As I
said, before you take this step, before you remove from
me, and enter upon a new life, which will lead you no

one knows in what direction, consider once more whether really, indeed, you can renounce Edward for the whole time to come. If you have faithfully made up your mind that you will do this, then will you enter into an engagement with me, that you will never admit him into your presence; and if he seeks you out and forces himself upon you, that you will not exchange words with him ? "

Ottilie did not hesitate a moment; she gave Charlotte the promise, which she had already made to herself.

Now, however, Charlotte began to be haunted with Edward's threat, that he would only consent to renounce Ottilie, as long as she was not parted from Charlotte. Since that time, indeed, circumstances were so altered, so many things had happened, that an engagement which was wrung from him in a moment of excitement might well be supposed to have been cancelled. She was unwilling, however, in the remotest sense to venture anything or to undertake anything which might displease him, and Mittler was therefore to find Edward, and inquire what, as things now were, he wished to be done.

Since the death of the child, Mittler had often been at the castle to see Charlotte, although only for a few moments at a time. The unhappy accident which had made her reconciliation with her husband in the highest degree improbable, had produced a most painful effect upon him. But ever, as his nature was, hoping and striving, he rejoiced secretly at the resolution of Ottilie. He trusted to the softening influence of passing time; he hoped that it might still be possible to keep the husband and the wife from separating; and he tried to regard these convulsions of passion only as trials of wedded love and fidelity.

Charlotte, at the very first, had informed the Major by letter of Ottilie's declaration. She had entreated him most earnestly to prevail on Edward to take no further steps for the present. They should keep quiet and wait, and see whether the poor girl's spirits would recover. She had let him know from time to time whatever was necessary of what had more lately fallen from her. And now Mittler had to undertake the really difficult commission of preparing Edward for an alteration in her situation. Mittler, however, well knowing that men can be brought more easily to submit to what is already done, than to give their consent to what is yet to be done, persuaded Charlotte that it would be better to send Ottilie off at once to the school.

Consequently as soon as Mittler was gone, preparations were at once made for the journey. Ottilie put her things together; and Charlotte observed that neither the beautiful box, nor anything out of it, was to go with her. Ottilie had said nothing to her on the subject; and she took no notice, but let her alone. The day of the departure came; Charlotte's carriage was to take Ottilie the first day as far as a place where they were well known, where she was to pass the night, and on the second she would go on in it to the school. It was settled that Nanny was to accompany her, and remain as her attendant.

This capricious little creature had found her way back to her mistress after the death of the child, and now hung about her as warmly and passionately as ever; indeed she seemed, with her loquacity and attentiveness, as if she wished to make good her past neglect, and henceforth devote herself entirely to Ottilie's service. She was quite beside herself now for joy at the thought of travelling with her, and of seeing strange places, when she had hitherto never been away from the scene of her birth ; and she ran from the castle to the village to carry the news of her good fortune to her parents and her relations, and to take leave. Unluckily for herself, she went among other places into a room where a person was who had the measles, and caught the infection, which came out upon her at once. The journey could not be postponed. Ottilie herself was urgent to go. She had travelled once already the same road. She knew the people of the hotel where she was to sleep. The coachman from the castle was going with her. There could be nothing to fear.

Charlotte made no opposition. She, too, in thought, was making haste to be clear of present embarrassments. The rooms which Ottilie had occupied at the castle she would have prepared for Edward as soon as possible, and restored to the old state in which they had been before the arrival of the Captain. The hope of bringing back old happy days burns up again and again in us, as if it never could be extinguished. And Charlotte was quite right; there was nothing else for her except to hope as she did.

CHAPTER XVI.

WHEN Mittler was come to talk the matter over with Edward, he found him sitting by himself, with his head supported on his right hand, and his arm resting on the table. He appeared in great suffering.

"Is your headache troubling you again?" asked Mittler.

13*

"It is troubling me," answered he; "and yet I cannot wish it were not so, for it reminds me of Ottilie. She too, I say to myself is also suffering in the same way at this same moment, and suffering more perhaps than I; and why cannot I bear it as well as she? These pains are good for me. I might almost say that they were welcome; for they serve to bring out before me with the greater vividness her patience and all her other graces. It is only when we suffer ourselves, that we feel really the true nature of all the high qualities which are required to bear suffering."

Mittler, finding his friend so far resigned, did not hesitate to communicate the message with which he had been sent. He brought it out piecemeal, however; in order of time, as the idea had itself arisen between the ladies, and had gradually ripened into a purpose. Edward scarcely made an objection. From the little which he said, it appeared as if he was willing to leave everything to them; the pain which he was suffering at the moment making him indifferent to all besides.

Scarcely, however, was he again alone, than he got up, and walked rapidly up and down the room; he forgot his pain, his attention now turning to what was external to himself. Mittler's story had stirred the embers of his love, and awakened his imagination in all its vividness. He saw Ottilie by herself, or as good as by herself, travelling on a road which was well known to him — in a hotel with every room of which he was familiar. He thought, he considered, or rather he neither thought nor considered; he only wished — he only desired. He would see her; he would speak to her. Why, or for what good end that was to come of it, he did not care to ask himself; but he made up his mind at once. He must do it.

He summoned his valet into his council, and through him he made himself acquainted with the day and hour when Ottilie was to set out. The morning broke. Without taking any person with him, Edward mounted his horse, and rode off to the place where she was to pass the night. He was there too soon. The hostess was overjoyed at the sight of him; she was under heavy obligations to him for a service which he had been able to do for her. Her son had been in the army, where he had conducted himself with remarkable gallantry. He had performed one particular action of which no one had been a witness but Edward; and the latter had spoken of it to the commander-in-chief in terms of such high praise, that notwithstanding the opposition of various ill-wishers, he had obtained a decoration for him. The mother, therefore, could never do enough for Edward. She got ready her best room for him, which indeed was her own wardrobe and store-room, with all possible speed. He informed her, however, that a young lady was coming to pass the night there, and he ordered an apartment for her at the back, at the end of the gallery. It sounded a mysterious sort of affair; but the hostess was ready to do anything to please her patron, who appeared so interested and so busy about it. And he, what were his sensations as he watched through the long, weary hours till evening? He examined the room round and round in which he was to see her; with all its strangeness and homeliness it seemed to him to be an abode for angels. He thought over and over what he had better do; whether he should take her by surprise, or whether he should prepare her for meeting him. At last the second course seemed the preferable one. He sat down and wrote a letter, which she was to read:

EDWARD TO OTTILIE.

"While you read this letter, my best beloved, I am close to you. Do not agitate yourself; do not be alarmed; you have nothing to fear from me. I will not force myself upon you. I will see you or not, as you yourself shall choose.

"Consider, oh! consider your condition and mine. How must I not thank you, that you have taken no decisive step! But the step which you have taken is significant enough. Do not persist in it. Here as it were, at a parting of the ways, reflect once again. Can you be mine? — will you be mine? Oh, you will be showing mercy on us all if you will; and on me infinite mercy.

"Let me see you again! — happily, joyfully see you once more! Let me make my request to you with my own lips; and do you give me your answer your own beautiful self, on my breast, Ottilie! where you have so often rested, and which belongs to you for ever!"

As he was writing, the feeling rushed over him that what he was longing for was coming — was close — would be there almost immediately. By that door she would come in; she would read that letter; she in her own person would stand there before him as she used to stand; she for whose appearance he had thirsted so long. Would she be the same as she was? — was her form, were her feelings changed? He still held the pen in his hand; he was going to write as he thought, when the carriage rolled into the court. With a few hurried strokes he added: "I hear you coming. For a moment, farewell!"

He folded the letter, and directed it. He had no time for sealing. He darted into the room through which there was a second outlet into the gallery, when the next moment he recollected that he had left his watch and seals lying on the table. She must not see these first. He ran back and brought them away with him. At the same instant he heard the hostess in the antechamber showing Ottilie the way to her apartments. He sprang to the bedroom door. It was shut. In his haste, as he had come back for his watch, he had forgotten to take out the key, which had fallen out, and lay the other side. The door had closed with a spring, and he could not open it. He pushed at it with all his might, but it would not yield. Oh, how gladly would he have been a spirit, to escape through its cracks! In vain. He hid his face against the panels. Ottilie entered, and the hostess, seeing him, retired. From Ottilie herself, too, he could not remain concealed for a moment. He turned towards her; and there stood the lovers once more, in such strange fashion, in one another's presence. She looked at him calmly and earnestly, without advancing or retiring. He made a movement to approach her, and she withdrew a few steps towards the table. He stepped back again. "Ottilie!" he cried aloud, "Ottilie! let me break this frightful silence! Are we shadows, that we stand thus gazing at each other? Only listen to me; listen to this at least. It is an accident that you find me here thus. There is a letter on the table, at your side there, which was to · have prepared you. Read it, I implore you — read it — and then determine as you will!"

She looked down at the letter; and after thinking a few seconds, she took it up, opened it, and read it: she

finished it without a change of expression; and she laid
it lightly down; then joining the palms of her hands
together, turning them upwards, and drawing them
against her breast, she leant her body a little forward,
and regarded Edward with such a look, that, eager as he
was, he was compelled to renounce everything he wished
or desired of her. Such an attitude cut him to the
heart; he could not bear it. It seemed exactly as if she
would fall upon her knees before him, if he persisted.
He hurried in despair out of the room, and leaving her
alone, sent the hostess in to her.

He walked up and down the antechamber. Night
had come on, and there was no sound in the room. At
last the hostess came out and drew the key out of the
lock. The good woman was embarrassed and agitated,
not knowing what it would be proper for her to do. At
last as she turned to go, she offered the key to Edward,
who refused it; and putting down the candle, she went
away.

In misery and wretchedness, Edward flung himself
down on the threshold of the door which divided him
from Ottilie, moistening it with his tears as he lay. A
more unhappy night had been seldom passed by two
lovers in such close neighborhood!

Day came at last. The coachman brought round the
carriage, and the hostess unlocked the door and went in
Ottilie was asleep in her clothes; she went back and
beckoned to Edward with a significant smile. They
both entered and stood before her as she lay; but the
sight was too much for Edward. He could not bear it.
She was sleeping so quietly that the hostess did not like
to disturb her, but sat down opposite her, waiting till she
woke. At last Ottilie opened her beautiful eyes, and

raised herself on her feet. She declined taking any breakfast, and then Edward went in again and stood before her. He entreated her to speak but one word to him; to tell him what she desired. He would do it, be it what it would, he swore to her; but she remained silent. He asked her once more, passionately and tenderly, whether she would be his. With downcast eyes, and with the deepest tenderness of manner she shook her head to a gentle *No*. He asked if she still desired to go to the school. Without any show of feeling she declined. Would she then go back to Charlotte? She inclined her head in token of assent, with a look of comfort and relief. He went to the window to give directions to the coachman, and when his back was turned she darted like lightning out of the room, and was down the stairs and in the carriage in an instant. The coachman drove back along the road which he had come the day before, and Edward followed at some distance on horseback.

CHAPTER XVII.

IT was with the utmost surprise that Charlotte saw the carriage drive up with Ottilie, and Edward at the same moment ride into the court-yard of the castle. She ran down to the hall. Ottilie alighted, and approached her and Edward. Violently and eagerly she caught the hands of the wife and husband, pressed them together, and hurried off to her own room. Edward threw himself on Charlotte's neck and burst into tears. He could not give her any explanation; he besought her to have patience with him, and to go at once to see Ottilie. Charlotte followed her to her room, and she could not enter it without a shudder. It had been all cleared out. There was nothing to be seen but the empty walls, which stood there looking cheerless, vacant, and miserable. Everything had been carried away except the little box, which from an uncertainty what was to be done with it, had been left in the middle of the room. Ottilie was lying stretched upon the ground, her arm and head leaning across the cover. Charlotte bent anxiously over her, and asked what had happened; but she received no answer.

Her maid had come with restoratives. Charlotte left her with Ottilie, and herself hastened back to Edward. She found him in the saloon, but he could tell her nothing. He threw himself down before her; he bathed her hands with tears; he flew to his own room, and she was going to follow him thither when she met his valet. From this man she gathered as much as he was able to tell. The rest she put together in her own thoughts as well as she could, and then at once set herself resolutely to do what the exigencies of the moment required. Ottilie's room was put to rights again as quickly as possible. Edward found his, to the last paper, exactly as he had left it.

The three appeared again to fall into some sort of relation with one another. But Ottilie persevered in her silence, and Edward could do nothing except entreat his wife to exert a patience which seemed wanting to himself. Charlotte sent messengers to Mittler and to the Major. The first was absent from home and could not be found. The latter came. To him Edward poured out all his heart, confessing every most trifling circumstance to him, and thus Charlotte learnt fully what had passed; what it had been which had produced such violent excitement, and how so strange an alteration of their mutual position had been brought about.

She spoke with the utmost tenderness to her husband. She had nothing to ask of him, except that for the present he would leave the poor girl to herself. Edward was not insensible to the worth, the affection, the strong sense of his wife; but his passion absorbed him exclusively. Charlotte tried to cheer him with hopes. She promised that she herself would make no difficulties about the separation; but it had small effect with him. He was so much shaken that hope and faith alternately forsook him. A species of insanity appeared to have taken possession of him. He urged Charlotte to promise to give her hand to the Major. To satisfy him and to humor him, she did what he required. She engaged to become herself the wife of the Major, in the event of Ottilie consenting to the marriage with .Edward; with this express condition, however, that for the present the two gentlemen should go abroad together. The Major had a foreign appointment from the court, and it was settled that Edward should accompany him. They arranged it all together, and in doing so found a sort of comfort for themselves in the sense that at least something was being done.

In the meantime they had to remark that Ottilie took scarcely anything to eat or drink. She still persisted in refusing to speak. They at first used to talk to her, but it appeared to distress her, and they left it off. We are not, universally at least, so weak as to persist in torturing people for their good. Charlotte thought over what could possibly be done. At last she fancied it might be well to ask the Assistant of the school to come to them. He had much influence with Ottilie, and had been writing with much anxiety to inquire the cause of her not having arrived at the time he had been expecting her; but as yet she had not sent him any answer.

In order not to take Ottilie by surprise, they spoke of their intention of sending this invitation in her presence. It did not seem to please her; she thought for some little time; at last she appeared to have formed some resolution. She retired to her own room, and before the evening sent the following letter to the assembled party:

OTTILIE TO HER FRIENDS.

" Why need I express in words, my dear friends, what is in itself so plain? I have stepped out of my course, and I cannot recover it again. A malignant spirit which has gained power over me seems to hinder me from without, even if within I could again become at peace with myself.

"My purpose was entirely firm to renounce Edward, and to separate myself from him for ever. I had hoped that we might never meet again; it has turned out otherwise. Against his own will he stood before me. Too literally, perhaps, I have observed my promise never to admit him into conversation with me. My conscience and the feelings of the moment kept me silent towards him at the time, and now I have nothing more to say. I have taken upon myself, under the accidental impulse of the moment, a difficult vow, which if it had been formed deliberately, might perhaps be painful and distressing. Let me now persist in the observance of it so long as my heart shall enjoin it to me. Do not call in any one to mediate; do not insist upon my speaking; do not urge me to eat or to drink more than I absolutely must. Bear with me and let me alone, and so help me on through the time; I am young, and youth has many unexpected means of restoring itself. Endure my presence among you; cheer me with your love; make me wiser and better with what you say to one another: but leave me to my own inward self."

The two friends had made all preparation for their journey, but their departure was still delayed by the formalities of the foreign appointment of the Major, a delay most welcome to Edward. Ottilie's letter had roused all his eagerness again; he had gathered hope and comfort from her words, and now felt himself encouraged and justified in remaining and waiting. He declared, therefore, that he would not go; it would be folly, indeed, he cried, of his own accord to throw away, by over precipitateness, what was most valuable and most necessary to him, when although there was a danger of losing it, there was nevertheless a chance that it might be preserved. "What is the right name of conduct such as that?" he said. "It is only that we desire to show that we are able to will and to choose. I myself, under the influences of the same ridiculous folly, have torn myself away, days before there was any necessity for it, from my friends, merely that I might not be forced to go by the definite expiration of my term. This time I will stay: what reason is there for my going; is she not already removed far enough from me? I am not likely now to catch her hand or press her to my heart; I could not even think of it without a shudder. She has not separated herself from me; she has raised herself far above me."

And so he remained as he desired, as he was obliged;
but he was never easy except when he found himself
with Ottilie. She, too, had the same feeling with him;
she.could not tear herself away from the same happy
necessity. On all sides they exerted an indescribable,
almost magical attraction over one another. Living, as
they were, under one roof, without even so much as
thinking of each other, although they might be occupied
with other things, or diverted this way or that way by
the other members of the party, they always drew together. If they were in the same room, in a short time
they were sure to be either standing or sitting near each
other; they were only easy when as close together as
they could be, but they were then completely easy. To
be near was enough; there was no need for them either
to look or to speak: they did not seek to touch one
another, or make sign or gesture, but merely to be together. Then there were not two persons, there was but
one person in unconscious and perfect content, at peace
with itself and with the world. So it was that if either
of them had been imprisoned at the further end of the
house, the other would by degrees, without intending it,
have moved towards its fellow till it found it; life to
them was a riddle the solution of which they could only
find in union.

Ottilie was throughout so cheerful and quiet that they
were able to feel perfectly easy about her; she was seldom absent from the society of her friends; all that she
had desired was that she might be allowed to eat alone,
with no one to attend upon her but Nanny.

What habitually befalls any person repeats itself more
often than one is apt to suppose, because his own nature
gives the immediate occasion for it. Character, individ-

uality, inclination, tendency, locality, circumstance, and habits, form together a whole, in which every man moves as in an atmosphere, and where only he feels himself at ease in his proper element. And so we find men, of whose changeableness so many complaints are made, after many years to our surprise, unchanged, and in all their infinite tendencies, outward and inward, unchangeable.

Thus in the daily life of our friends, almost everything glided on again in its old smooth track. Ottilie still displayed by many silent attentions her obliging nature, and the others like her continued each themselves; and then the domestic circle exhibited an image of their former life, so like it, that they might be pardoned if at any time they dreamt that it might all be again as it was.

The autumn days, which were of the same length with those old spring days, brought the party back into the house out of the air about the same hour. The gay fruits and flowers which belonged to the season, might have made them fancy it was now the autumn of that first spring, and the interval dropped out and forgotten; for the flowers which now were blooming, were the same as those which then they had sown, and the fruits which were now ripening on the trees, were those which at that time they had seen in blossom.

The Major went backwards and forwards, and Mittler came frequently. The evenings were generally spent in exactly the same way. Edward usually read aloud, with more life and feeling than before; much better, and even it may be said with more cheerfulness. It appeared as if he was endeavoring, by light-heartedness as much as by devotion, to quicken Ottilie's torpor into life, and dissolve her silence. He seated himself in the same position as he used to do, that she might look over his book; he was uneasy and distracted unless she was doing so, unless he was sure that she was following his words with her eyes.

Every trace had vanished of the unpleasant, ungracious feelings of the intervening time. No one had any secret complaint against another; there were no cross purposes, no bitterness. The Major accompanied Charlotte's playing with his violin, and Edward's flute sounded again, as formerly, in harmony with Ottilie's piano. Thus they were now approaching Edward's birthday, which the year before they had missed celebrating. This time they were to keep it without any outward festivities, in quiet enjoyment among themselves. They had so settled it together, half expressly, half from a tacit agreement. As they approached nearer to this epoch, however, an anxiety about it, which had hitherto been more felt than observed, became more, noticeable in Ottilie's manner. She was to be seen often in the garden examining the flowers; she had signified to the gardener that he was to save as many as he could of every sort, and that she had been especially occupied with the asters, which this year were blooming in immense profusion.

CHAPTER XVIII.

THE most remarkable feature, however, which was observed about Ottilie was that, for the first time, she had now unpacked the box, and had selected a variety

of things out of it, which she had cut up, and which were
intended evidently to make one complete suit for her.
The rest, with Nanny's assistance, she had endeavored to
replace again, and she had been hardly able to get it
done, the space being over full, although a portion had
been taken out.   The covetous little Nanny could never
satisfy herself with looking at all the pretty things, especially as she found provision made there for every article
of dress which could be wanted, even the smallest. Numbers of shoes and stockings, garters with devices on them,
gloves, and various other things were left, and she begged
Ottilie just to give her one or two of them. Ottilie
refused to do that, but opened a drawer in her wardrobe,
and told the girl to take what she liked. The latter
hastily and awkwardly dashed in her hand and seized
what she could, running off at once with her booty, to
show it off and display her good fortune among the rest
of the servants.

At last Ottilie succeeded in packing everything carefully into its place. She then opened a secret compart-
ment, which was contrived in the lid, where she kept a
number of notes and letters from Edward, many dried
flowers, the mementos of their early walks together, a
lock of his hair, and various other little matters. She
now added one more to them, her father's portrait, and
then locked it all up, and hung the delicate key by a gold
chain about her neck, against her heart.

In the mean time, her friends had now in their hearts
begun to entertain the best hopes for her. Charlotte was
convinced that she would one day begin to speak again.
She had latterly seen signs about her which implied that
she was engaged in secret about something; a look of
cheerful self-satisfaction, a smile like that which hangs

about the face of persons who have something pleasant and delightful, which they are keeping concealed from those whom they love. No one knew that she spent many hours in extreme exhaustion, and that only at rare intervals, when she appeared in public through the power of her will, she was able to rouse herself.

Mittler had latterly been a frequent visitor, and when he came he staid longer than he usually did at other times. This strong-willed, resolute person was only too well aware that there is a certain moment in which alone it will answer to smite the iron. Ottilie's silence and reserve he interpreted according to his own wishes; no steps had as yet been taken towards a separation of the husband and wife. He hoped to be able to determine the fortunes of the poor girl in some not undesirable way. He listened, he allowed himself to seem convinced; he was discreet and unobtrusive, and conducted himself in his own way with sufficient prudence. There was but one occasion on which he uniformly forgot himself — when he found an opportunity for giving his opinion upon subjects to which he attached a great importance. He lived much within himself, and when he was with others, his only relation to them generally was in active employment on their behalf; but if once, when among friends, his tongue broke fairly loose, as on more than one occasion we have already seen, he rolled out his words in utter recklessness, whether they wounded or whether they pleased, whether they did evil or whether they did good.

The evening before the birthday, the Major and Charlotte were sitting together expecting Edward, who had gone out for a ride; Mittler was walking up and down the saloon; Ottilie was in her own room, laying out the dress which she was to wear on the morrow, and making signs to her maid about a number of things, which the girl, who perfectly understood her silent language, arranged as she was ordered.

Mittler had fallen exactly on his favorite subject. One of the points on which he used most to insist was, that in the education of children, as well as in the conduct of nations, there was nothing more worthless and barbarous than laws and commandments forbidding this and that action. "Man is naturally active," he said, "wherever he is; and if you know how to tell him what to do, he will do it immediately, and keep straight in the direction in which you set him. I myself, in my own circle, am far better pleased to endure faults and mistakes, till I know what the opposite virtue is that I am to enjoin, than to be rid of the faults and to have nothing good to put in their place. A man is really glad to do what is right and sensible, if he only knows how to get at it. It is no such great matter with him; he does it because he must have something to do, and he thinks no more about it afterwards than he does of the silliest freaks which he engaged in out of the purest idleness. I cannot tell you how it annoys me to hear people going over and over those Ten Commandments in teaching children. The fifth is a thoroughly beautiful, rational, preceptive precept. 'Thou shalt honor thy father and thy mother.' If the children will inscribe that well upon their hearts, they have the whole day before them to put it in practice. But the sixth now? What can we say to that? 'Thou shalt do no murder;' as if any man ever felt the slightest general inclination to strike another man dead. Men will hate sometimes; they will fly into passions and forget themselves; and as a consequence of this or other

14

feelings, it may easily come now and then to a murder; but what a barbarous precaution it is to tell children that they are not to kill or murder! If the commandment ran, 'Have a regard for the life of another — put away whatever can do him hurt — save him though with peril to yourself — if you injure him, consider that you are injuring yourself;' — that is the form which should be in use among educated, reasonable people. And in our Catechism teaching we have only an awkward clumsy way of sliding into it, through a ' what do you mean by that ?'

"And as for the seventh; that is utterly detestable. What! to stimulate the precocious curiosity of children to pry into dangerous mysteries; to obtrude violently upon their imaginations, ideas and notions, which beyond all things you should wish to keep from them! It were far better if such actions as that commandment speaks of were dealt with arbitrarily by some secret tribunal, than prated openly of before church and congregation ——"

At this moment Ottilie entered the room.

"'Thou shalt not commit adultery,'" — Mittler went on — "How coarse! how brutal! What a different sound it has, if you let it run, 'Thou shalt hold in reverence the bond of marriage. When thou seest a husband and a wife between whom there is true love, thou shalt rejoice in it, and their happiness shall gladden thee like the cheerful light of a beautiful day. If there arise anything to make division between them, thou shalt use thy best endeavor to clear it away. Thou shalt labor to pacify them, and to soothe them; to show each of them the excellencies of the other. Thou shalt not think of thyself, but purely and disinterestedly thou shalt seek to further the well-being of others, and make them feel what a happiness is that which arises out of all duty done; and especially out of that duty which holds man and wife indissolubly bound together.'"

Charlotte felt as if she was sitting on hot coals. The situation was the more distressing, as she was convinced that Mittler was not thinking the least where he was or what he was saying: and before she was able to interrupt him, she saw Ottilie, after changing color painfully for a few seconds, rise and leave the room.

Charlotte constrained herself to seem unembarrassed: "You will leave us the eighth commandment," she said, with a faint smile.

"All the rest," replied Mittler, "if I may only insist first on the foundation of the whole of them."

At this moment Nanny rushed in, screaming and crying: "She is dying: the young lady is dying; come to her, come."

Ottilie had found her way back with extreme difficulty to her own room. The beautiful things which she was to wear the next day were laid out on a number of chairs; and the girl, who had been running from one to the other, staring at them and admiring them, called out in her ecstasy, "Look, dearest madam, only look! There is a bridal dress worthy of you."

Ottilie heard the word, and sank upon the sofa. Nanny saw her mistress turn pale, fall back, and faint. She ran for Charlotte, who came. The medical friend was on the spot in a moment. He thought it was nothing but exhaustion. He ordered some strong soup to be brought. Ottilie refused it with an expression of loathing: it almost threw her into convulsions, when they put the cup to her lips. A light seemed to break on the physician; he asked hastily and anxiously what Ottilie had taken that day. The little girl hesitated. He repeated his question, and she then acknowledged that Ottilie had taken nothing.

There was a nervousness of manner about Nanny which made him suspicious. He carried her with him into the adjoining room; Charlotte followed; and the girl threw herself on her knees, and confessed that for a long time past Ottilie had taken as good as nothing; at her mistress' urgent request, she had herself eaten the food which had been brought for her; she had said nothing about it, because Ottilie had by signs alternately begged her not to tell any one, and threatened her if she did; and, as she innocently added " because it was so nice."

The Major and Mittler now came up as well. They found Charlotte busy with the physician. The pale, beautiful girl was sitting, apparently conscious, in the corner of the sofa. They had begged her to lie down: she had declined to do this; but she made signs to have her box brought, and resting her feet upon it, placed herself in an easy, half recumbent position. She seemed to be wishing to take leave; and by her gestures, was expressing to all about her the tenderest affection, love, gratitude, entreaties for forgiveness, and the most heart-felt farewell.

Edward, on alighting from his horse, was informed of what had happened; he rushed to the room; threw himself down at her side; and seizing her hand, deluged it with silent tears. In this position he remained a long time. At last he called out: " And am I never more to hear your voice? Will you not turn back toward life, to give me one single word? Well, then, very well. I will follow you yonder, and there we will speak in another language."

She pressed his hand with all the strength she had; she gazed at him with a glance full of life and full of love; and drawing a long breath, and for a little while moving her lips inarticulately, with a tender effort of affection she called out, "Promise me to live;" and then fell back immediately.

"I promise, I promise!" he cried to her: but he cried only after her; she was already gone.

After a miserable night, the care of providing for the loved remains fell upon Charlotte. The Major and Mittler assisted her. Edward's condition was utterly pitiable. His first thought, when he was in any degree recovered from his despair, and able to collect himself, was, that Ottilie should not be carried out of the castle; she should be kept there, and attended upon as if she were alive: for she was not dead; it was impossible that she should be dead. They did what he desired; at least, so far as that they did not do what he had forbidden. He did not ask to see her.

There was now a second alarm, and a further cause for anxiety. Nanny, who had been spoken to sharply by the physician, had been compelled by threats to confess, and after her confession had been overwhelmed with reproaches, had now disappeared. After a long search she was found; but she appeared to be out of her mind. Her parents took her home; but the gentlest treatment had no effect upon her, and she had to be locked up for fear she should run away again.

They succeeded by degrees in recovering Edward from the extreme agony of despair; but only to make him more really wretched. He now saw clearly, he could not doubt now, that the happiness of his life was gone from him for ever. It was suggested to him that if Ottilie was placed in the chapel, she would still remain among the living, and it would be a calm, quiet, peaceful home for her. There was much difficulty in obtaining his consent; he would only give it under condition that she should be taken there in an open coffin; that the vault in which she was laid, if covered at all, should be only covered with glass, and a lamp should be kept always burning there. It was arranged that this should be done, and then he seemed resigned.

They clothed the delicate body in the festal dress, which she had herself prepared. A garland of asters was wreathed about her head, which shone sadly there like melancholy stars. To decorate the bier and the church and chapel, the gardens were robbed of their beauty; they lay desolate as if a premature winter had blighted all their loveliness. In the earliest morning she was borne in an open coffin out of the castle, and the heavenly features were once more reddened with the rising sun. The mourners crowded about her as she was being taken along. None would go before; none would follow; every one would be where she was, every one would enjoy her presence for the last time. Men and women, and little boys, there was not one unmoved; least of all to be consoled were the girls, who felt most immediately what they had lost.

Nanny was not present; it had been thought better not to allow it, and they had kept secret from her the day and the hour of the funeral. She was at her parents' house, closely watched, in a room looking towards the garden. But when she heard the bells tolling, she knew too well what they meant; and her attendant having left her out of curiosity to see the funeral, she escaped out of the window into a passage, and from thence, finding all the doors locked, into an upper open loft. At this moment the funeral was passing through the village, which had been all freshly strewed with leaves. Nanny saw her mistress plainly close below her, more plainly, more entirely, than any one in the procession underneath; she appeared to be lifted above the earth, borne as it were on clouds or waves, and the girl fancied she was making signs to her; her senses swam, she tottered, swayed herself for a moment on the edge and fell to the ground. The crowd fell asunder on all sides with a cry of horror. In the tumult and confusion, the bearers were obliged to set down the coffin; the girl lay close by it, it seemed as if every limb was broken. They lifted her up, and by accident or providentially she was allowed to lean over the body; she appeared, indeed, to be endeavoring with what remained to her of life to reach her beloved mistress. Scarcely, however, had the loosely hanging limbs touched Ottilie's robe, and the powerless finger rested on the folded hands, than the girl started up, and first raising her arms and eyes towards heaven, flung herself down upon her knees before the coffin, and gazed with passionate devotion at her mistress.

At last she sprang, as if inspired, from off the ground, and cried with a voice of ecstasy: "Yes, she has forgiven me; what no man, what I myself could never have forgiven. God forgives me through her look, her motion, her lips. Now she is lying again so still and quiet, but you saw how she raised herself up, and unfolded her hands and blessed me, and how kindly she looked at me. You all heard, you can witness that she said to me: 'You are forgiven.' I am not a murderess any more. She has forgiven me. God has forgiven me, and no one may now say anything more against me."

The people stood crowding around her. They were amazed; they listened and looked this way and that, and no one knew what should next be done. " Bear her on to her rest," said the girl. " She has done her part; she has suffered, and cannot now remain any more among us." The bier moved on, Nanny now following it; and thus they reached the church and the chapel.

So now stood the coffin of Ottilie, with the child's coffin at her head, and her box at her feet, inclosed in a resting-place of massive oak. A woman had been provided to watch the body for the first part of the time, as it lay there so beautifully beneath its glass covering. But Nanny would not permit this duty to be taken from herself. She would remain alone without a companion, and attend to the lamp which was now kindled for the first time; and she begged to be allowed to do it with so much eagerness and perseverance, that they let her have her way, to prevent any greater evil that might ensue.

But she did not long remain alone. As night was falling, and the hanging lamp began to exercise its full right and shed abroad a larger lustre, the door opened and the Architect entered the chapel. The chastely ornamented walls in the mild light looked more strange, more awful, more antique, than he was prepared to see them. Nanny was sitting on one side of the coffin. She recognized him immediately; but she pointed in silence to the pale form of her mistress. And there stood he on the other side, in the vigor of youth and of grace, with his arms drooping, and his hands clasped piteously together, motionless, with head and eye inclined over the inanimate body.

Once already he had stood thus before in the Belisarius; he had now involuntarily fallen into the same attitude.

And this time how naturally! Here, too, was something
of inestimable worth thrown down from its high estate.
There were courage, prudence, power, rank, and wealth
in one single man, lost irrevocably; *there* were qualities
which, in decisive moments, had been of indispensable
service to the nation and the prince; but which, when
the moment was passed, were no more valued, but flung
aside and neglected, and cared for no longer. And *here*
were many other silent virtues, which had been summoned but a little time before by nature out of the depths
of her treasures, and now swept rapidly away again by
her careless hand — rare, sweet, lovely virtues, whose
peaceful workings the thirsty world had welcomed, while
it had them, with gladness and joy; and now was sorrowing for them in unavailing desire.

Both the youth and the girl were silent for a long time.
But when she saw the tears streaming fast down his
cheeks, and he appeared to be sinking under the burden
of his sorrow, she spoke to him with so much truthfulness
and power, with such kindness and such confidence, that,
astonished at the flow of her words, he was able to
recover himself, and he saw his beautiful friend floating
before him in the new life of a higher world. His tears
ceased flowing; his sorrow grew lighter; on his knees he
took leave of Ottilie, and with a warm pressure of the
hand of Nanny, he rode away from the spot into the
night without having seen a single other person.

The surgeon had, without the girl being aware of it,
remained all night in the church; and when he went in
the morning to see her, he found her cheerful and tranquil. He was prepared for wild aberrations. He thought
that she would be sure to speak to him of conversations
which she had held in the night with Ottilie, and of

14*

other such apparitions. But she was natural, quiet, and
perfectly self-possessed. She remembered accurately
what had happened in her previous life; she could
describe the circumstances of it with the greatest exactness, and never in anything which she said stepped out
of the course of what was real and natural, except in her
account of what had passed with the body, which she
delighted to repeat again and again, how Ottilie had
raised herself up, had blessed her, had forgiven her, and
thereby set her at rest for ever.

Ottilie remained so long in her beautiful state, which
more resembled sleep than death, that a number of persons were attracted there to look at her. The neighbors
and the villagers wished to see her again, and every one
desired to hear Nanny's incredible story from her own
mouth. Many laughed at it, most doubted, and some
few were found who were able to believe.

Difficulties, for which no real satisfaction is attainable,
compel us to faith. Before the eyes of all the world,
Nanny's limbs had been broken, and by touching the
sacred body she had been restored to strength again.
Why should not others find similar good fortune? Delicate mothers first privately brought their children who
were suffering from obstinate disorders, and they believed
that they could trace an immediate improvement. The
confidence of the people increased, and at last there was
no one so old or so weak as not to have come to seek
fresh life and health and strength at this place. The
concourse became so great, that they were obliged, except at the hours of divine service, to keep the church
and chapel closed.

Edward did not venture to look at her again; he lived
on mechanically; he seemed to have no tears left, and

to be incapable of any further suffering; his power of taking interest in what was going on diminished every day; his appetite gradually failed. The only refreshment which did him any good was what he drank out of the glass which to him, indeed, had been but an untrue prophet. He continued to gaze at the intertwining initials, and the earnest cheerfulness of his expression seemed to signify that he still hoped to be united with her at last. And as every little circumstance combines to favor the unfortunate, and every accident contributes to elate him; so do the most trifling occurrences love to unite to crush and overwhelm the unhappy. One day as Edward raised the beloved glass to his lips, he put it down and thrust it from him with a shudder. It was the same and not the same. He missed a little private mark upon it. The valet was questioned, and had to confess that the real glass had not long since been broken, and that one like it belonging to the same set had been substituted in its place.

Edward could not be angry. His destiny had spoken out with sufficient clearness in the fact, and how should he be affected by the shadow? and yet it touched him deeply. He seemed now to dislike drinking, and thenceforward purposely to abstain from food and from speaking.

But from time to time a sort of restlessness came over him; he would desire to eat and drink something, and would begin again to speak. "Ah!" he said, one day to the Major, who now seldom left his side, "how unhappy I am that all my efforts are but imitations ever, and false and fruitless. What was blessedness to her, is pain to me; and yet for the sake of this blessedness I am forced to take this pain upon myself. I must go after

her; follow her by the same road. But my nature and
my promise hold me back. It is a terrible difficulty,
indeed, to imitate the inimitable. I feel clearly, my dear
friend, that genius is required for everything; for mar-
tyrdom as well as the rest."

What shall we say of the endeavors which in this
hopeless condition were made for him? his wife, his
friends, his physician, incessantly labored to do something for him. But it was all in vain : at last they found
him dead. Mittler was the first to make the melancholy
discovery; he called the physician, and examined closely
with his usual presence of mind, the circumstances under
which he had been found. Charlotte rushed in to them;
she was afraid that he had committed suicide, and accused
herself and accused others of unpardonable carelessness.

But the physician on natural, and Mittler on moral
grounds, were soon able to satisfy her of the contrary. It
was quite clear that Edward's end had taken him by
surprise. In a quiet moment he had taken out of his
pocket-book and out of a casket everything which
remained to him as memorials of Ottilie, and had spread
them out before him; a lock of hair; flowers which had
been gathered in some happy hour, and every letter
which she had written to him from the first, which his
wife had ominously happened to give him. It was impossible that he would intentionally have exposed these
to the danger of being seen, by the first person who
might happen to discover him.

But so lay the heart, which but a short time before
had been so swift and eager, at rest now, where it could
never be disturbed ; and falling asleep, as he did, with
his thoughts on one so saintly, he might well be called
blessed. Charlotte gave him his place at Ottilie's side,

and arranged that henceforth no other person should be placed with them in the same vault.

In order to secure this, she made it a condition under which she settled considerable sums of money on the church and the school.

So lie the lovers, sleeping side by side. Peace hovers above their resting-place. Fair angel faces gaze down upon them from the vaulted ceiling, and what a happy moment that will be when one day they wake again together!

Printed in the USA
CPSIA information can be obtained
at www.ICGtesting.com
LVHW090925030224
770855LV00001B/14